71.95
AM

The "New Negro" in the Old World: Culture and Performance in
James Weldon Johnson, Jessie Fauset, and Nella Larsen

LUND STUDIES IN ENGLISH 111

Editors

Marianne Thormählen and *Beatrice Warren*

LUND STUDIES IN ENGLISH was founded by Eilert
Ekwall in 1933. Published by the Department of English at Lund
University, the series consists of books on the English language
and on literature in English.

The "New Negro" in the Old World:
Culture and Performance in James Weldon
Johnson, Jessie Fauset, and Nella Larsen

Lena Ahlin

LUND UNIVERSITY

LUND STUDIES IN ENGLISH

The "New Negro" in the Old World: Culture and Performance in
James Weldon Johnson, Jessie Fauset, and Nella Larsen

Lena Ahlin

LUND STUDIES IN ENGLISH III
ISBN 91-975158-0-9
ISSN 0076-1451

Publisher
Department of English, Centre for Languages and Literature, Lund University
P.O. Box 201
SE-221 00 LUND, Sweden

Distribution and sales
Almqvist & Wiksell International
P.O. Box 7634
SE-103 94 STOCKHOLM, Sweden

Contents

Acknowledgements

It is said that thesis writing is a lonely task, but this is only partly true. There are a number of people who have worked together with me on this project and for whose efforts I feel deeply grateful. My supervisor Professor Gunilla Florby has been my most ardent reader, providing unfailing support and encouragement. I also wish to thank my assistant supervisor Professor Vera M. Kutzinski, whose input during my time as an affiliate graduate student at Yale University provided great inspiration, and who has kept giving me valuable advice and constructive criticism. In the context of the public defense of my dissertation, Professor Carolyn Wedin, who was the Faculty Opponent, offered pertinent comments for which I am very grateful. Many thanks to Professor Marianne Thormählen for helpful comments on my final draft. Thanks are also due to Ric Fisher for stylistic and linguistic advice.

Financial support has been gratefully received from Svenska Institutet, Knut & Alice Wallenberg Stipendiefond, Hjalmar Gullberg & Greta Thotts Stipendiefond, Crafoordska stiftelsen, Syskonen Anna Cecilia och Otto Sigfrid Granmarks stipendiefond, Fil. Dr. Uno Otterstedts fond.

Sincere thanks to my friends and colleagues at the English Department, Lund University, particularly Sara Bjärstorp, Lena Christensen, Berndt Clavier, Stefan Holander, Annelie Hultén, Petra Ragnerstam, Björn Sundmark, and Cecilia Wadsö-Lecaros. In your company, thesis writing was both fun and challenging.

I warmly thank my family and friends for always believing in me and being there for me. Finally, special thanks to Henrik for making it all worthwhile.

Introduction

> Someone, someday, should do a study in depth of the role of
> the American Negro in the mind and life of Europe, and the
> extraordinary perils, different from those of America but not less
> grave, which the American Negro encounters in the Old World.
>
> *James Baldwin*

The inter-war years were turbulent times in American society. The country was struggling to come to terms with the great blow that World War I had dealt Western civilization and its mythos of rationality and progress. The New World of America was coming of age and sought to (re-)define its national identity. African-American culture now became an important part of the debate about what this "modern" life meant:

> In a society that had recently suffered a war of tremendous proportions,
> and was increasingly changing into an urban, impersonal, and
> industry-driven machine, black culture was viewed, interchangeably,
> as life-affirming, a libidinal fix, an antidote for ennui, a sanctuary
> for the spiritually bereft, a call back to nature, and a subway ticket
> to modernity. The "New Negro" was the perfect metaphor for this
> moment of great social rupture because, like a medicine-show elixir, it
> was perceived as the cure for everything. (Powell 42)

Richard J. Powell speaks of a tension between the valorization of black culture and its association with vitality and a hope for re-generation of a Western culture threatened with de-generation. This view rested on the perception of black culture as anti-modern, or pre-modern—the "call back to nature" of primitivism. On the other hand, the African-American jazz music that had become the hallmark of the era—the period is sometimes called the Jazz Age—seemed remarkably well suited to the fast pace of modern urban life. The concept of the "New Negro" that was at the center of this cultural flowering was of importance not only to black Americans, providing as it did a vision of what they could become and helping them replace old derogatory images of themselves. For white Americans (and Europeans) it was a way to re-imagine one's self. For example, white New Yorkers flocked to the jazz clubs in Harlem to have a good time and to experiment with a new identity: "The uninhibited, carefree Negro was, curiously, a hidden role model for white New Yorkers in their attempts to reinvent themselves. Constructing a black alter ego was a means by which to free themselves from Puritan attitudes and a preliminary step in taking on a modern identity" (Lemke 86). This was undoubtedly the time when "the Negro was in vogue," as Langston Hughes would put it in his autobiography *The Big Sea* (1940), although that vogue clearly represented different things to different people.

The aim of this dissertation is to analyze how "the Old World" of Europe relates to the cultural moment of the "New Negro." Thus, it is centered on the interchanges between black and white (European and American) cultures, which were just beginning to be recognized in the early twentieth century and have continued to shape the century. It has, for instance, been established that the French appreciation of jazz created an audience for this kind of music, which paved the way for its subsequent success in the home country. Likewise, it is well known that it was in Paris that artists such as Picasso and Braque developed a "primitivist modernism" inspired by African art. But what is the obverse side of the picture? How is Europe figured in African-American art, in this case literature, at the time? Following a general tendency to assert a national identity, many African-American authors made use of significant settings, such as Harlem or the American South, in their works. James Weldon Johnson, Jessie Fauset, and Nella Larsen, however, were among the handful of authors who turn outward, to Europe, to articulate their idea of "the New Negro" and her/his relationship to "Western" culture and civilization. They accomplished this by depicting geographical journeys that are also psychological journeys undertaken on the way to reconciliation with life in segregated America. As they did this, they all made use of the trope of performance, through which we can interpret the complexities of cultural identity and belonging.

The novels I study are James Weldon Johnson's *The Autobiography of an Ex-Colored Man* (first published anonymously in 1912, republished under the author's name in 1927), Jessie Fauset's *There Is Confusion* (1924), and Nella Larsen's *Quicksand* (1928).[1] Included are also a number of articles written by Fauset for the NAACP magazine *The Crisis*, which deal with her encounters

---

[1] Other works from this period dealing with Europe are Gwendolyn Bennett's short story "Wedding Day," Claude McKay's *Banjo*, and some of Hughes's poetry (and later his autobiography The Big Sea, 1940).

with European culture. As I see it, these articles and those sections of the novels that are set in Europe, and/or deal with Europe as the originator of culture, provide us with a key to the authors' understandings of "race" and "culture." A reconceptualization of these terms is produced by the trope of space as Europe becomes a lens through which to interpret the role of the African-American in Western civilization.

The novels of Fauset, Johnson, and Larsen have been analyzed as accounts of passing and of the particular situation of the middle-class, well-educated mulatto, or as renditions of the new urban experience. However, there is room for intensifying the focus on the meaning of Europe as an important symbol of issues of cultural belonging and representation. In addition, the field of performance studies opens significant ways of interpreting issues of selfhood, as well as visions of social change, as presented in the novels.

In their novels, Fauset, Johnson, and Larsen all depict a similar type of character – a character who had not before then been extensively treated in fiction. This was the light-skinned, middle-class, educated, urban Northern African American – what appears to be a fictional version of the "New Negro." Furthermore, in the works I study, these characters have a significant relationship to African-American art. In this respect, and others, Johnson's *The Autobiography of an Ex-Colored Man* is an important predecessor to Larsen's novel. One important parallel between *The Autobiography* and Larsen's *Quicksand* is the theme of African American musical contributions to Western culture and the artist as a creator and reflector of culture. Larsen's protagonist Helga Crane is, however, not a stage performer herself, but a social performer who, more than any of the other main characters, is engaged in a performance of self. Jessie Fauset also uses the trope of performance as a means of discussing culture, race, and historical agency. Through their focus on performance, these authors indicated a vital feature of contemporary culture since performers had important functions to fill at this time, both as entertainers and literary figures:

> Although in 1912 James Weldon Johnson had already drawn attention to the importance of black dancers, singers and musicians in the construction of a modern American cultural identity, it was the writers and visual artists of the "New Negro" arts movement who placed these black performers at the theoretical center of the culture. In a profusion of art forms, they cast the entertainers as cultural intermediaries who articulated in their acts the problems, hopes, desires, and aspirations of the "New Negro." (Powell 55)

Like Johnson, Fauset and Larsen also cast artists as cultural intermediaries in their novels, and in this study, I examine why and how they do this. The intermediary position of their protagonists is highlighted through the motif of traveling which emphasizes that the characters are part of more than one culture (the African-American and the Euro-American). Artists appear in all of these novels and function as keys to the most important questions of my study. In the novels I have chosen, music and the performing arts can be seen as metaphors for cultural identity. Black artists could imagine and perform new images of themselves in an act that provided relief from, and resistance to, social oppression. The move between geographical places is coterminous with the search for a cultural space of freedom and resistance—a sought-after space that is interrogated through the trope of performance. Through the symbolical geography of Europe, this study examines the extent to which Europe functions as a space where performances related to African-American culture and identity could be re-imagined and re-enacted.

Introduction to the authors

James Weldon Johnson (1871–1938)

James Weldon Johnson's long and varied career included working as a writer, musician, songwriter, and U.S. Consul to Nicaragua (1906–1909). He was also the first black leader of the NAACP, the editor of a landmark work of African-American poetry, *The Book of American Negro Poetry* (1922), and a poet in his own right through the publication of the poems collected in *Fifty years* (1917), and *God's Trombones* (1927), a set of sermons in free verse. He also edited two collections of American Negro spirituals (published in 1925 and 1926) and a book on the history of black Americans and black American artistic life in New York entitled *Black Manhattan* (1930).

When *The Autobiography of an Ex-Colored Man* first appeared in print in 1912, it was published anonymously by a small publishing firm called Sherman, French and Co, and there was much speculation about its authorship. It was taken to be an authentic autobiography by most readers and reviewers, until it was republished in Johnson's name in 1927 (by Alfred A. Knopf, with an introduction by Carl Van Vechten), at the height of the Harlem Renaissance. In 1933, Johnson was to publish his own autobiography under the title *Along*

This Way. Before 1923, when Jean Toomer's *Cane* was published by Boni & Liveright, Johnson's *The Autobiography* and w.e.b. Du Bois's *The Quest of the Silver Fleece* (1911) "were possibly the only novels by Negroes that gained country-wide recognition by readers of both races," according to Hugh Gloster (111). After World War I, there was increasing interest in novels about or by blacks, accompanied by a growing African-American reading public (Carl Van Vechten's *Nigger Heaven* of 1926 contributed to this increased interest). Almost all novels by African-Americans were published in New York City, many of them with the greatest publishing firms, such Alfred A. Knopf; Harcourt, Brace and Company; and the aforementioned Boni & Liveright (among them Fauset's *There Is Confusion*).

Criticism of Johnson's novel has generally been favorable. Reviewers and critics have particularly noted not only that the narrator is near-white and middle-class but also the fact that Johnson with this book explores a cosmopolitan, artistic and European milieu not previously explored in African-American fiction. In this respect, the book offers a variation on the Jamesian theme of a young American's meeting with the old culture of Europe. In terms of the detailed use of setting, especially of New York and of night life scenes there, *The Autobiography* can be considered a forerunner of the Harlem Renaissance (Collier 372-73). Another such link to authors of the 1920s is the issue of dual heritage: to be neither African nor American, yet both. Eugenia Collier observes that "[in] literature (as in life) the near-white Negro is often romanticized or vilified but seldom treated with anything like realism and compassion. Johnson's novel fills this gap. Probably nowhere in the entire range of black literature is the dilemma of the light-skinned Negro treated so exhaustively" (373). Collier also notes that Fauset and Larsen were to continue in the vein of Johnson, describing similar milieus and characters.

Robert Bone also sees Johnson as a forerunner of the Harlem Renaissance, claiming that "Johnson indisputably anticipates the Harlem school by subordinating racial protest to artistic consideration" (48). From the 1970s onwards, several critics, such as Robert Fleming, Marvin Garrett, and Roxanna Pisiak, have addressed the importance of irony to *The Autobiography*. While other recent critics, such as Samira Kawash and Elaine K. Ginsberg, do not analyze the novel in terms of its irony *per se*, they often discuss the text in terms of instability, unreliability, or even the complete breakdown of the certainties of the categories that structure social life. All these terms suggest the prominence of an inconsistency between appearance and reality in the text, concurrently forming the basis of verbal irony and drawing attention to the text as performance.

Other aspects of *The Autobiography* that critics have dealt with include comparisons between Johnson's book and Richard Wright's *Black Boy* (Lucinda MacKethan) and Ralph Ellison's *Invisible Man* (Houston A. Baker). Over the past few years, a couple of interesting studies of the significance of music in *The Autobiography*, have appeared. These articles by Cristina Ruotolo (2000), Alessandro Portelli (2001), and Salim Washington (2002) have inspired my study of the meaning of music in Johnson's work.

The unnamed narrator of *The Autobiography*, who is the offspring of a union between a wealthy white man and a "colored" woman, frequently engages in traveling, and his travels follow a route roughly similar to that of Larsen's protagonist in *Quicksand*. The reader first encounters Johnson's narrator in his early childhood home in Georgia, in the American South. A few years later, he moves with his mother to Connecticut. After an incident in school when he is made to understand that he is considered a "Negro," he starts dreaming of becoming "a great colored man" and decides to go back South, to Atlanta University, to realize this ambition. However, he ends up in Jacksonville, Florida, working at a cigar factory instead. When the factory closes after three years, he goes north to New York City and lives a bohemian life in the Tenderloin district. Johnson's descriptions of "The Club," where the narrator gambles all night, prefigure those found in Harlem Renaissance literature. To avoid suspicions of involvement in a shooting at the Club that he becomes witness to, he takes the opportunity to accompany his wealthy friend – known only as "the Millionaire" – to Europe. Together with the Millionaire, the narrator takes rooms in Paris, playing the piano for his patron and traveling all over Europe: to London, Berlin, Spain, Belgium, etc. Having reached the conclusion that he wants to develop the folk music of the African Americans, he eventually decides to go back home. In order to reach his goal, he needs to travel into the American South to immerse himself in the culture of the Black Belt. However, this attempt is aborted when he becomes witness to the lynching of a black man – an event that brutally makes him realize how people of his color "could with impunity be treated worse than animals" (139). Once again, he feels obliged to leave the South to go to New York, where he ends up passing as a white man.

Jessie Redmon Fauset (1882–1961)

Jessie Redmon Fauset's novel *There Is Confusion*, published in 1924, was the first of its genre to come out of the period of literary activity known as the Harlem Renaissance.[2] *There Is Confusion* was the first of four novels written by Fauset between 1924 and 1933, making her the most prolific of the Harlem Renaissance novelists. In addition to the novels *Plum Bun* (1929), *The Chinaberry Tree* (1931), and *Comedy: American Style* (1933), she wrote poetry and essays for *The Crisis* and functioned as the magazine's literary editor from 1919 to 1926. At this time she moved from Philadelphia to New York, sharing an apartment with her sister Helen Lanning in Harlem, where she used to hold a kind of literary salon that was a meeting place for African-American intellectuals. As a literary editor she discovered, or published early in their career, the works of Nella Larsen, Jean Toomer, Langston Hughes and others. Hughes was to give her the epithet "midwife" of the Harlem Renaissance, and it is clear that she was an important intellectual and literary figure during this period (Hughes *The Big Sea* 218). Fauset was the first black woman novelist to be a college graduate, holding a Phi Beta Kappa B. A. from Cornell and an M. A. from the University of Pennsylvania. In addition, she studied for a time at the Sorbonne in Paris, and worked as a teacher of French at the famous college preparatory M. Street High School in Washington D. C. and New York's De Witt Clinton High School for many years. She was also active in the work of such organizations as the Pan-African Congress and the National Association for Colored Women.

Jessie Fauset's novels were widely read and reviewed at the time, but like many of the Harlem Renaissance authors, both Fauset and Larsen were neglected after the 1930s. Their works fell into oblivion and did not receive much critical attention before the upsurge of interest in women's literature in the 1970s. Since then, the number of studies of their works has increased decade by decade. However, unlike Nella Larsen, who by now is considered a canonical African-American author, Fauset's position is more contested. Late twentieth-century critics have often claimed that Fauset's fiction was not representative of the life of the mass of African Americans, that she was creating an ideal that was not sensitive to the experiences of the working classes or the complexity of women's issues, and that the aim of creating role models often came at the expense of complexity and depth of character and plot. As Thadious Davis puts it

---

[2] Claude McKay's collection of poems *Harlem Shadows* was published in 1922. The poetry of Hughes, Cullen, and others was published in *The Crisis* and other New York magazines after WWI.

in the foreword to *There Is Confusion*: "her writings [...] mainly functioned as a corrective to misconceptions about people of color, especially women" (xiii). At the time that her novels appeared, many African-American reviewers were relieved at their "anti-primitivism." Fauset's decision to become a novel writer is connected to the publication of T. S. Stribling's novel *Birthright* (1922), which she reviewed in the June 1922 issue of *The Crisis* and which included derogatory representations of American blacks. As Fauset later explained: "A number of us started writing at that time [...] Nella Larsen and Walter White, for instance, were affected just as I was. We reasoned, 'Here is an audience waiting to hear the truth about us. Let us, who are better qualified to present that truth than any white writer, try to do so'" (Starkey 218-19).

Fauset's books and articles are clearly formed by the historical moment in which she was working, as is seen in her depictions of black people, which were designed to counter common cultural stereotypes. Her effort to get African-American authors published was one way to instill a sense of pride in African-American achievement and create role-models for generations to come. Her own essays in *The Crisis* often dealt with the achievements of men of African descent around the world.[3] In the 1932 interview by Marion Starkey quoted above, Fauset also stated that there was a lack of writing about great African-American historical personalities, and so she felt that biography was a genre that she would have liked to engage in (Starkey 220). Fauset herself was one of the "Talented Tenth," whom W. E. B. Du Bois had designated as the leaders of the race, and her motivation was to create art that could serve the purpose of "uplift." In June 1922, Fauset wrote a review of James Weldon Johnson's anthology *The Book of Negro Poetry*. In the introduction to the collection Johnson writes:

> The final measure of greatness of all peoples is the amount and standard of the literature and art they have produced...The status of the Negro in the United States is more a question of mental attitude toward the race than of actual conditions. And nothing will do more to change that mental attitude and raise his status than a demonstration of intellectual parity by the Negro through the production of literature and art. (9)

This reads like the credo of "New Negro" ideology, and is an attitude that

---

[3] See e. g. "The Emancipator of Brazil," *The Crisis*, (March 1921): 208-09; "Saint-George, Chevalier of France," *The Crisis*, (May 1921): 9-12; "Looking Backward," *The Crisis* (January 1922): 125-26.

has found its way into Fauset's fictional world. In each of her four novels, we encounter middle-class, educated African Americans and the specific kinds of racial struggles pertaining to this class. Important themes in her works are the role of women and the particular possibilities and limitations faced by black women with respect to career, family life, etc. Like Nella Larsen, Fauset discusses passing in several of her novels. All these themes appear in *There Is Confusion* along with a range of others, such as the influence of history, of heredity, and of environment and the possibility of free will (Wedin Sylvander 142). Furthermore, as Davis points out in the foreword to *There Is Confusion*: "At a time when racial identity and heritage were becoming major topics of discussion and when artistic control over the portrayal of African Americans was imperative, the novel addressed those concerns" (vi).

In the Starkey interview, Fauset also talks about her problems in having *There Is Confusion* published: "Like all of her books, it is a story of hard-working, self-respecting Negroes, who forge steadily forward in their chosen work. It contains no descriptions of Harlem dives, no race riots, no picturesquely abject poverty. For that reason it found a publisher with some difficulty. 'White readers just don't expect Negroes to be like this' explained the first publisher to see the manuscript as he rejected it" (Starkey 219). Declining to offer another portrayal of night life in Harlem clubs, Fauset offered an alternative to the primitivist novels currently in demand, and was therefore described, for example by her contemporary Claude McKay, as a "prim" author.

One of the first literary historians of the Harlem Renaissance, Robert Bone, fails to see any quality in Fauset's novels, finding them "uniformly sophomoric, trivial, and dull" (Bone 101). In the late 1970s and 1980s, critics have become aware of more complexity in Fauset's work. However, feminist critics have been unhappy with what they see as Fauset's endorsement of a patriarchal ideology, since her heroines often end up giving priority to the domestic rather than the public (see, for example, Barbara Christian and Cheryl Wall). In *There Is Confusion*, for example, Joanna Marshall gives up her ambition of becoming a successful dancer and singer and devotes herself to being a good wife and mother. In general, critics have thought little of Fauset's literary artistry, particularly criticizing her disregard for the black vernacular and her tendency toward the sentimental. Her novels generally follow the Victorian pattern of the "marriage plot" in that romantic relationships, and eventually marriage, occupy a central place in them (Levinson 838). She was thus dubbed "the potential Jane Austen of Negro literature" by William Stanley Braithwaite, an early, celebratory critic of her works (Braithwaite 26). Her works have also been compared to those of Edith Wharton because Fauset, like Wharton, deals with the marriage market as a means of financial opportunity for women.[4]

Carolyn Wedin Sylvander's book *Jessie Redmon Fauset: Black American Writer*, 1981, was one of the first positive revaluations of Fauset's fiction. Finding that Fauset has been brushed aside by critics such as Robert Bone and Hugh Gloster, Wedin suggests that their poor estimate of her is a misunderstanding due to the shortcomings of the critics rather than of the author: "Understanding the double discrimination suffered by the Black woman as well as her particular strengths and particular longings lends a helpful insight into some of Fauset's plots and themes" (Wedin Sylvander 7). Wedin's own work importantly provides this kind of information, anchoring Fauset firmly within her historical, literary, and critical context.

More recently, there have been some further interesting revaluations and revisions of Fauset's work. In her 1993 book *The Coupling Convention: Sex, Text, and Tradition in Black Women's Fiction,* Ann duCille takes note of—and issue with—"how the current moment's deification of certain black women writers (such as Zora Neale Hurston) and the elision of others (such as Jessie Fauset) discursively construct both texts and tradition" (10). DuCille's reply to the current "Hurstonism" which privileges the "folk" literature of Zora Neale Hurston is to read the literature of Fauset and Larsen, as "bourgeois blues," thus redefining the meaning of the blues singers and blues aesthetics as more "authentic" or true to the black experience. The questions she raises concerning authenticity, the black experience, and the blues have inspired much of my understanding of how Fauset's literary works are positioned vis-à-vis these issues.

Nella Larsen (1891–1964)

Because of the similarities in background between Nella Larsen and *Quicksand's* heroine, Helga Crane, critics have often read Larsen's novel as semi-autobiographical. Thadious Davis's biography of Nella Larsen, appearing in 1994, lent credence to this connection. Larsen was born in Chicago, in 1891, as the daughter of a Danish woman and a "colored" man (from the West Indies, Larsen would later state). Her father either disappeared a few years after Nella was born or, as Davis suggests, decided to pass as white (Davis 27). It is clear, however, that Nella Larsen grew up as the only visibly "colored" child in a "white" fam-

---

[4] See Elizabeth Ammons, "New Literary History: Edith Wharton and Jessie Fauset," 1987.

ily, living in a white neighborhood. She gradually lost touch with her family and Davis concludes that the essential homelessness of *Quicksand's* protagonist Helga Crane reflects that of her creator. Davis argues that Larsen's absent mother plays a particularly important role in the daughter's search for self. This she sees reflected in *Quicksand*, together with the physical correspondence between author and protagonist, and the similar trajectories of traveling.

Before she started a career in writing, Larsen worked as a nurse at the Tuskegee Institute, apparently finding the atmosphere there as oppressive as Helga Crane finds the school Naxos in *Quicksand* (Davis 97-110). According to George Hutchinson Nella Larsen stayed in Copenhagen between 1908 and 1912. She had also accompanied her mother to Denmark as a little girl in the 1890s (Hutchinson, *In Search of Nella Larsen* 2-5). On her return to America, Larsen worked for a while as a public health nurse in New York city, but she soon started working at the Harlem branch of the New York Public Library. It is during this time that she becomes involved with the writers of the Harlem Renaissance.

Among Nella Larsen's first published works—produced under the supervision of Jessie Fauset in her capacity as editor of *The Brownies' Book*—were the articles "Three Scandinavian Games" and "Danish Fun," in which she describes games played by Danish children. In the introduction to these games, Larsen situates herself as someone who has spent her "childish days" in Denmark. Her biographer Thadious Davis notes that it was important for Larsen to start her public career, as an author, with a reference to her mixed heritage. Davis finds that Nella Larsen would emphasize her Danish background to gain social prestige among her peers (Davis 140-41). Linking herself with Danish traditions in this way was a strategy for increasing her own social and cultural capital. The issues of miscegenation and racial passing were to become important themes in Larsen's literary work. Nella Larsen's works have been appreciated, not only by feminist critics, for their portrayal of the search for identity and the particular pressures of race, gender, and sexuality that beset the African-American woman.

The two novels on which Nella Larsen's reputation as a major Harlem Renaissance author rests were published within a year of each other, *Quicksand* in 1928 and *Passing* in 1929. Both books received favorable reviews, and in 1928 Larsen won the Harmon Bronze Award for Distinguished Achievement in Literature. However, Larsen ceased to publish after accusations of having plagiarized Sheila Kaye-Smith's "Mrs. Adis" (1922) in her short story "Sanctuary"

(1930). Her works soon fell into oblivion and were only rediscovered during the "second renaissance" of African American literature in the 1960's. In 1930, Larsen won a Guggenheim fellowship, which enabled her to go to Spain and France to do research for a novel. The Guggenheim fellowship testifies to Larsen's interest in comparing America and Europe. In her fellowship application she describes the theme of the planned, but never finished, book as "the difference in intellectual and physical freedom for the Negro, and the effect on him—between Europe" and the United States (Davis 363). This theme was initiated in her novel *Quicksand*, which is the story of the young woman Helga Crane's search for self, which takes her from the southern school of Naxos, north to Chicago and New York, where she tries different jobs and gets acquainted with (night) life in Harlem. From there she goes on to Copenhagen to stay with her mother's Danish relatives. After two years in Denmark, Helga returns to New York, where she marries a preacher and moves with him to a rural, black community in Alabama. Thus, her journey follows a kind of circular pattern beginning and ending in the American South, including the ascent North as well as an unsuccessful attempt to heal her sense of loneliness through immersion into the Black Belt of the South. But how does the eastward move across the Atlantic fit into this schema? Of particular interest to my study is the fairly lengthy part of *Quicksand* that takes place in Copenhagen, Denmark. In the subsequent chapters I will show how Larsen uses this European interlude to discuss issues like stereotyping and performance in relation to culture and "race." Larsen's second novel *Passing* (1929) is mainly concerned with the lives of light-skinned African-Americans in the US. The theme of Europe as originator of culture and provider of education occurs here as well, but not in a positive way. As noted by Lindberg-Seyersted, "the middle-class heroine reveals her conventional and materialistic values when she proposes to send her son to school in Europe, while her husband, the more 'authentic' of the two, is against the idea: America is good enough for him" (119).

Larsen's use of the American as well as the European urban setting was remarkable and of importance to the African-American literary tradition as a whole: "It is important that Larsen returned her readership to the urban landscape and refused a romantic evocation of the folk, for in this movement she stands as a precursor not only to Richard Wright and Ralph Ellison but to a neglected strand of Afro-American women's fiction" (Carby 175). Critics were always more positive to Nella Larsen's works than to those of Jessie Fauset, not only when they first appeared. The initial reviews and early criticism of

Larsen's novels tended to focus on the problems of mixed-race existence in America. They were often read as early twentieth-century versions of the theme of the "tragic mulatta," who is torn between the white and the black world and unable to feel at home in either of them. Hugh Gloster, for example, reads *Quicksand* and *Passing* as "studies of the warped lives of two attractive young women of biracial parentage" (146). From the mid-1980s onwards, feminist critics began to note other complexities in Larsen's fiction. In the introduction to *Quicksand* (1986), Deborah McDowell suggests that in reading Helga Crane's story as that of the "tragic mulatta," we miss the more urgent problem of female sexual identity, which Larsen tried to explore. This concern is also related to the structure of Larsen's novels, particularly the endings, which were often conceived of as too abrupt and contradictory (Helga's religious experience and precipitate marriage in *Quicksand*, Clare Kendry's leap, or fall, to a sudden death in *Passing*). Studying her novels "through the prism of black female sexuality," McDowell argues,

> not only do [the endings] make more sense, they also illuminate the peculiar pressures on Larsen as a woman writer during the male-dominated Harlem Renaissance. They show her grappling with the conflicting demands of her racial and sexual identities and the contradictions of a black and feminine aesthetic. Moreover, while these endings appear to be concessions to the dominant ideology of romance—marriage and motherhood—viewed from a feminist perspective, they become much more radical and original efforts to acknowledge a female sexual experience, most often repressed in both literary and social realms. (xii)

In *Reconstructing Womanhood: The Emergence of the Afro-American Woman Novelist* (1987), Hazel V. Carby also focuses on the sexual politics of *Quicksand*. She argues that, through the description of Helga's repressed sexual desire, Larsen criticizes the burgeoning black middle-class morality and the ideology of racial uplift. In fact, Carby claims that *Quicksand* embodies the "crisis of representation" of the period (169). Failing to find an acceptable mode of existence either among the middle classes of the urban North, or among the rural "folk" on the South, Helga Crane gives in to a slow death by childbirth. My reading of *Quicksand* is informed by these, and other, critics' consideration of how a combination of racial and sexual oppression conditioned black female existence in the 1920s.

Methodological starting-points

Many of the issues that were addressed by the Harlem Renaissance authors, such as migration, cultural belonging, the process of racialization, and performance are still topical today. Theories associated with the latter part of the twentieth century, such as post-colonialism and post-structuralism, have helped shed new light on the authors' treatment of these complex issues. For example, post-colonialism has been instrumental in uncovering the Eurocentric perspective inherent in the grand narratives of Enlightenment and emancipation, and emphasized the importance of looking for alternative versions of historiography. Moreover, post-structuralism describes an approach to meaning and to human identity that agrees very well with the narratives of Johnson, Fauset, and Larsen, and which also ties in with the connection between performance and identity in their novels. In their different and complex ways of conceiving culture and race, Johnson, Fauset, and Larsen speak to the present moment and to how the intersections of race, class and gender affect African-American identity.

Shelley Fisher Fishkin calls the early 1990s "a defining moment in the study of American literature" (Wonham 251). She goes on to explain that "[t]he essentialist paradigms that accompanied the move to recover and value black writers and black texts in the 70s and 80s began to give way in the early 1990s to a more complex view of African-American culture. Scholars increasingly analyzed the interpenetration of black and white culture in African-American letters and life" (Wonham 269). This is the critical field that has inspired my study, which deals with the mingling of African-American, European and Euro-American cultural forms and identity formations. However, the study of the interpenetration of black and white American culture is not entirely new to the 1990s. For example, in his 1964 review of "Blues People" by LeRoi Jones/Amiri Baraka, Ralph Ellison warned against "the very natural defensive impulse to treat black culture as an ethnocentrically closed field, hermetically closed off from the dominant culture" (Wonham 4). As Eric Sundquist points out, Ellison's essay "suggests that the mainstream of American culture, whether the fact was widely recognized or not, had always been significantly black and southern, bearing the clear inflections of African American language and creativity in popular as well as high culture" (Sundquist 3). In the 1980s, the works of Toni Morrison were particularly effective in raising public awareness of the fact that a separation of white from black American culture was possible only as a result of a blindness to "the Negro's presence" in American life (Wonham 2).

Along the same lines, Ann duCille in *The Coupling Convention: Sex, Text, and Tradition in Black Women's Fiction* (1993) argues that black literary critics should stop short of "claim[ing] an African American literature as an island, entire unto itself, separate from and uninfluenced by so-called white cultural constructs and Western literary conventions" (9). Intertextual references, she goes on, should thence not only be sought for in other black American authors. Instead, "such resonances must be viewed as cutting across racial identities, cultural spaces, and historical moments" (9). And yet, the 1990s is a decade in which a lot of work has been done to establish a distinctly African-American literary tradition. For example, 1997 saw the publication of both the first *Norton Anthology of African-American Literature* and the *Oxford Companion to African-American Literature*. The Harlem Renaissance authors of the 1920s were only beginning the work of defining what was to be considered part of their heritage—work that has continued throughout the twentieth century. The literature of the 1990s raises the same kinds of questions about what it means to be an American and how to claim a place in American society and history, and suggests that similar contradictions and complexities have to be navigated today as in the 1920s.

Often, studies of African-American literature in relation to Europe have been concentrated on the post-World War II political expatriates in Paris. A community of African Americans comparable to that of the Lost Generation of the 1920s was formed only after World War II, centered on Richard Wright. However, the foundations of this community were laid during the inter-war years. The most extensive survey of the presence of African American writers in Europe and their works is Michel Fabre's *From Harlem to Paris: Black American Writers in France 1840-1980* (1991). But Fabre deals only with France, and thus a novel like Nella Larsen's Quicksand, on which I will focus here, is not included in his study. He provides thorough biographical information concerning the authors, but his treatment of the works of Fauset and Johnson is brief and descriptive rather than interpretative. Works such as Fabre's, Tyler Stovall's *Paris Noir: African Americans in the City of Light* (1996), and Farah J. Griffin and Cheryl J. Fish's anthology, *A Stranger in the Village: Two Centuries of African American Travel Writing* (1998), testify to a contemporary interest in the transatlantic connection, but also make clear that the fictional representation of Europe in the works of the Harlem Renaissance authors is an as yet largely unexamined issue.[6] However, there are a couple of articles on the subject that deserve to be mentioned. In "Coloring Books: Black Writing on Europe"

(1993), Charles Martin links the writings of Harlem Renaissance authors like Langston Hughes, Claude McKay, and Nella Larsen to "the concern to find a place for self expression" (59). He concludes, however, that "the spongy terrain of rhetoric" complicates this search (60). By this he means the rhetoric concerning (skin) color, according to which "color" pertains only to non-whites. White is regarded as "colorless" (what Martin calls the "degree zero" of rhetoric), and other colors, seen in relation to it, are found to be "different" or even "defective." This particular use of language, Martin argues, becomes evident when considering the role of Europe in these authors' writing. A similar idea concerning the meaning of whiteness is developed by Richard Dyer, and I will expand on this concern in relation to Larsen's Quicksand in chapter 2.

A chapter of Birgitta Lindberg-Seyersted's book *Black and Female: Essays on Writings by Black Women in the Diaspora* (1994) is devoted to the study of "The Image of Europe in Writings by African-American Women." Lindberg-Seyersted here provides a useful study of African-American fiction on Europe, from the nineteenth-century slave narratives to Toni Morrison's *Tar Baby* of 1981. She notes that while European settings were quite common in this early fiction, Europe rarely figures as a significant setting in African American women's literature after World War II. However, both Richard Wright and James Baldwin lived in Paris after the war and wrote about the relationship between the New World and the Old. The 1960s and 1970s inaugurated a turn to settings and subject matters directly related to black life in America. Lindberg-Seyersted concludes that

> [a]lthough such rigorous demands are less heard today, the substance and sound of black writing will surely continue to render their own specific segment of the American turf, and the role of Europe in setting, plot and characterization will remain minimal. If African-American writers turn to other cultural regions for literary material, it may be Africa or the Caribbean, rather than Europe, that will be their choice. (127)

---

[6] Works dealing with the Harlem Renaissance without paying specific attention to international connections are Amritjit Singh, *The Novels of the Harlem Renaissance: Twelve Black Writers 1923-1933* (1976) and Singh, Shiver and Brodwin, eds., *The Harlem Renaissance: Revaluations* (1989); Nathan Huggins, *The Harlem Renaissance* (1971); David Levering Lewis, *When Harlem Was in Vogue* (1979); Houston A. Baker, *Modernism and the Harlem Renaissance* (1987); Arna Bontemps, *The Harlem Renaissance Remembered* (1972).

It is beyond the scope of this study to validate this prediction, but what is important to note at this stage is that Lindberg-Seyersted's article confirms the idea that the Harlem Renaissance authors were building on a long tradition of African-American writing about Europe. The Harlem Renaissance in fact reached far beyond the borders of New York.

In the article "Europe in the novels of Jessie Redmon Fauset and Nella Larsen" (1994), Mary Condé notes that a recurrent idea in American fiction—found for example in Huck Finn's idea of "lighting out for the territory"—is that "happiness is a place" (15). Observing that neither Fauset nor Larsen displayed any interest in Africa, she goes on to question whether Europe is figured as a place of happiness in their fiction. The conclusion Condé reaches is that while Europe could not be a permanent stopping-place for Fauset's characters, she still believed that "the encounter with Europe would make America a better place" (25). This idea applies to my own reading of *There Is Confusion* as well. Condé's interpretation of Helga Crane's meeting with Europe in *Quicksand* is more depressing, since she concludes that "Larsen felt that the African-American woman's complex legacy of oppression had compromised her too deeply for any happiness" (25). In my analysis of Helga Crane's experiences in Europe, I have exchanged this idea of a search for happiness into a search for freedom, another metaphor with spatial connotations in American fiction.

Responding to Condé's discussion of happiness as a place, Zoltan Simon examines *There Is Confusion, Quicksand* and Claude McKay's *Home to Harlem* in the article "From Lenox Avenue to the Charlottenborg Palace: the Construction of the Image of Europe by Harlem Renaissance Authors" (1999). Here, Simon demonstrates how the images of Europe presented in these works "usually fall between two extremes, both mistaken, of an uncritical, even utopian reading of Europe and a largely generalizing and hostile depiction of the continent as the cradle of evil Nordic colonizers" (106). Being in basic agreement with this observation, I aim to add a further dimension by considering the specific role of the African-American artist in relation to the geo-cultural symbolism of Europe.

Some of the more recent critical works about African American literature have been dedicated to looking at black Americans as historical agents in a global perspective, thus forming an integral part of the Western cultural tradition. All these works also relate to the modernism of the early twentieth century. An example of this approach is Paul Gilroy's *The Black Atlantic: Modernity and Double Consciousness* (1993), in which he argues that the project of modernity rests on an equivocation. Constant progress and human emancipation are key words of the

Enlightenment, but history has shown that racial slavery, including life in bondage for millions of peoples of African descent, was also integral to the development of Western civilization. Gilroy's influential theory of "the black Atlantic" culture links the experiences of black people on both sides of the Atlantic, and is an argument for a black diasporic culture not limited by national borders. Shared characteristics of such a culture would, for example, be an African heritage, the colonial experience, and oppression because of race (195). "The black Atlantic" is also characterized by a stream of cultural exchanges across the Atlantic. Gilroy suggests that "cultural historians could take the Atlantic as one single, complex unit of analysis in their discussions of the modern world and use it to produce an explicitly transnational and intercultural perspective" (15). Racial categories would then gain precedence over national categories when it comes to articulating the shared experiences of black people. Although it is a contentious concept, I submit that "the black Atlantic" and the theorization of "creolisation, métissage, mestizaje, and hybridity" (Gilroy 2), suggested by Gilroy, provides the possibility of a better understanding of ethnic and national identity as depicted in the works of Larsen, Fauset and Johnson.

The novels I have chosen to deal with all address issues of ethnic and national identity, but provide no simple, absolute interpretations of these concepts. In locating part of their novels in Europe, these authors open the way to an extended discussion of African American identity and nationality. The "black Atlantic" perspective forms a framework for analyzing how Europe played a part in the formation of the "New Negro." A narrow focus on African American identity or American nationality leads to reductive or, in Paul Gilroy's words, "overintegrated" conceptions of culture, and does not suffice for an analysis of the complexity of the identity issues that are raised in the novels. For example, Gilroy suggests that the Atlantic and the cultural exchanges taking place across the waters should replace the sign "Africa" when appealing to black commonality: "Africa" is not enough to cover "the irreducible plurality of new world black styles" (120). Furthermore, he claims that the metaphor of the journey has a central place in the black cultural tradition. The motifs of exile and homelessness that are part of the Black Atlantic culture form

> the basis of a privileged standpoint from which certain useful and critical perceptions about the modern world become more likely. It should be obvious that this unusual perspective has been forged out of the experiences of racial subordination. I want to suggest that it also represents a response to the successive displacements, migrations, and

journeys (forced and otherwise) which have come to constitute these
black cultures' special conditions of existence. (Gilroy 111)

Apart from the theme of the possibly emancipative effect of traveling, I am
interested in investigating what "useful and critical perceptions of the modern
world" emerge in the narratives of Johnson, Fauset, and Larsen. The phrase
suggests self-reflection, a situated interpretation of the world and a conscious,
historical positioning of oneself in it.

Sieglinde Lemke's *Primitivist Modernism: Black Culture and the Origins of
Transatlantic Modernism* (1998) focuses on aesthetic collaboration and formal
connections between "white" and "black" cultures in early twentieth-century
art and literature. Lemke is not interested in separating "white modernism"
from a "black counter-modernism" (as is Houston Baker in *Modernism and the
Harlem Renaissance*, for example) but instead concentrates on how the two are
interrelated. Rather like Toni Morrison, who in *Playing in the Dark* points to
the presence of blackness in American culture, Lemke aims to highlight the
presence of blackness, or "Africanism," in modernism in general. Thus Lemke
claims that our understanding of this historical moment should begin with
a recognition of the interrelatedness of African cultures on the one hand and
American and European cultures on the other. This claim provides support for
the challenge that Johnson, Fauset and Larsen make in their novels as I read
them, namely, that African-Americans are an integral part of, or indeed at the
center of, modern American culture.

Ann Douglas's *Terrible Honesty: Mongrel Manhattan in the 1920's* (1995) explores the increased social and cultural interchange between blacks and whites
in the New York of the 1920s. Douglas's work shows the influence of black
American culture on white American culture during the inter-war years, but
does not include a trans-Atlantic perspective. Significantly, Ann Douglas suggests that the 1920s be seen as "[w]hat one might call the 'post-colonial' phase
of African-American culture, the self-conscious emergence of black culture
from white" (303). She goes on to describe this process of emancipation as twofold: it meant looking inward and drawing on the resources of the black community, but in doing so the African American "adopted global interests and
aims. For blacks as well as whites, the war produced a new sense of culture as
an international activity, and in its wake the Negro found for the first time
a worldwide audience and arena, one that might aid him in his fight against
injustice at home" (Douglas 303). Here we see that the international scope of

African American culture was an important part of the Harlem Renaissance. Furthermore, the connection Douglas makes between artistic success abroad and expectations of increased social equality at home is crucial for my argument about the importance of Europe as a fictional space with emancipative connotations. In her analysis of the American modernism of the 1920s, Douglas finds that the standard Freudian diagnosis (which was gaining ground at the time) of the modern psyche is inadequate when it comes to accounting for a black experience or psyche at this time. She writes:

> It is not yet clear what psychology can best produce fruitful and inclusive paradigms of black consciousness. Perhaps the complexities of performance, the dialectic of individual and group, the art of masking, both political and aesthetic, in which all black Americans have been to one degree or another, willy-nilly, trained, offers the best starting-point for such a paradigm, and it suggests the nature of black psychic pain in the dark aftermath of the 1920s. (Douglas 473)

All three psychological parameters proposed by Douglas – performance, the interplay between individual and group, and masking – are relevant to my readings of Fauset, Johnson and Larsen. My analysis of the performances in the novels deals specifically with the use of performance both as self-definition and social critique. That is to say, performance supplies an approach to personal identity as well as to the social/cultural situation in which the staging of the performance takes place.

Performance as self-definition

Artists have significant roles to play in the novels I have chosen to study. The narrator of *The Autobiography* is a piano player who passes, Joanna Marshall of *There Is Confusion* is a dancer and singer, and even *Quicksand*'s Helga Crane may be considered an artist "without an art form" (Wall 109). That is to say, her art is not performed on the stage but consists of a self-fashioning that is enacted through the use of clothes, speech and behavior that help categorize her in terms of group identity and class status. Approaching identity through the perspective of performance means that just like the stage performer, any individual can play different social roles according to expectation and need.

The performance perspective on identity counters the notion of an essence, a stable core on which personal identity is based. The idea of performance as related to personal identity is found in post-structuralist psychology, which takes issue with the notion of a subject that is autonomous, integrated, and in control. Another idea that is questioned is the possibility of a pre-discursive and pre-social subject, that is, a subject that exists independently of its discursive and social context. In the post-structuralist view, the subject is seen as constituted through linguistic signs. This means that it is context-dependent and sometimes contradictory. It is also dynamic and open to change. The (pre-Freudian) view of the autonomous subject can then be analyzed as a form of discourse in itself, through which subjects construct different versions of themselves. In other words, "the self is a form of narration," meaning that language not only describes, but also produces, the self (Blackman & Walkerdine 112).

Judith Butler has analyzed how gender is a position that is assumed and confirmed every time it is being performed. Butler's analysis of gender acknowledges the constitutive role of discourse in the materialization of the body. Matter and discourse never appear without each other: it is discourse that makes matter intelligible (Butler, *Bodies* 33). From this starting-point Butler goes on to question the distinction between sex (as biologically grounded) and gender (the cultural construction of "woman"). In her analysis, the two concepts become inseparable: all is gender. This means that there can be no body without its cultural construction, since the body is given meaning through its cultural interpretations. The process whereby gender is created she calls performativity. Since there is no essential identity in place in the body that can be given a more or less truthful expression, Butler sees identity as produced through performance. Identity is not fixed as immutable essence but created through repeated acts and therefore multiple and open to change. It also means that acting is creating, not merely reflecting what is already in place.

The performance of the artists in the novels can be analyzed as moments of imagining and enacting a new personal identity for the performer (and by extension, the social groups that are given embodiment by the performance). However, the idea that the individual can take on different social roles does not mean that the individual can freely choose which identity to assume. The choices are still being made within set categories, from which we cannot get away. For example, Butler observes that the performance of gender is a repetition of certain rigidly defined norms. In fact, to Butler, the individual is "subjectivated by gender," that is, one cannot be a subject without being gendered. The process of becoming a subject takes place within the "matrix of gender relations," by which she refers to conventional categorizations of what it means to be a man or woman. However, gender is not the only category that sets up norms for the subjects: it is possible to see racial relations as another such matrix that subjectivates the individual. One parallel between the discourses of race and gender is the conflation of nature and culture that Butler has clarified. In a relationship similar to that between sex and gender, the biological referent to difference because of "race" has become increasingly spurious, and instead it is more fruitful to analyze how bodies are "racialized" through a set of social and cultural acts. Further, Butler urges the study of how to analyze not only the convergence of race, sexuality and sexual difference, but "the sites at which the one cannot be constituted save through the other" (Butler, *Bodies* 168). The tragic mulatta and the other black female literary figures, in the light of which Fauset's and Larsen's works must be seen, can be read as such sites. As we will see, this site is quite differently figured in the case of the male narrator of Johnson's *The Autobiography*.

Performance as cultural critique

As was suggested in the introduction, performers – particularly entertainers – acted as cultural intermediaries during the Harlem Renaissance. In their acts, they articulated "the problems, hopes, desires, and aspirations of 'the New Negro'" (Powell 55). This intermediary position was also one from which they could bridge the white and the black worlds, as well as mediate between different positions within the black American culture, such as between the Talented Tenth and the mass of working-class people who were part of their audience. They contributed to formulating a new concept of African-American culture, in which their cultural heritage was seen as a source of pride. In this sense, the performers functioned as mediators between past and present as well. The search for a "usable past" that the Harlem Renaissance artists were engaged in leads us to the question of how performance relates to cultural memory.

In *Cities of the Dead. Circum-Atlantic Performance* (1996), Joseph Roach discusses a range of performances as "restored behaviors that function as vehicles of cultural transmission." He sees performance as a continuing process of substitution, or "surrogation," as he calls it. The process of "surrogation" involves a reenactment of the past, which is simultaneously an affirmation and a transformation of this past. Thus, his view of performance differs from Butler's, which is more pessimistic concerning aspects of affirmation, transformation, and choice. Roach's approach addresses performance on a partly different level than Butler's. Whereas Butler discusses performance as constitutive of subject and body, Roach's scope is cultural (historical) performance in a broad sense, including ritual, attitudes, and beliefs that give rise to certain behaviors. His analyses couple a cultural belief to its enactment through performance, for example, "death and burials, violence and sacrifices, laws and (dis)obedience, commodification and auctions, origins and segregation" (13). To Roach, the kinesthetic imagination that flourishes on the stage also operates in the performance of everyday life, and is "reinforced by paradigmatic systems of behavioral memory such as law and custom" (27). However, it is worth pointing out that Roach and Butler share the belief that performance is productive of culture and identity at the same time as it is reflective of norms and attitudes already in place. Just as human identity is constructed through cultural acts and interpretations, the cultural field is also the result of repeated creative acts. That is, cultural production is not merely reflective of social ideas already in place, but is capable of shaping them. During the Harlem Renaissance we see the linking of cultural production and social action as a clearly formulated goal, for example in the influential collection *The New Negro*.

Of particular interest for my own analysis is Roach's discussion of places of performances. He observes that "[t]echnological invention (architectural innovation particularly) and social organization create […] vortices of behavior. Their function is to canalize specified needs, desires, and habits in order to reproduce them […] The vortex is a kind of spatially induced carnival, a center of cultural self-invention through the restoration of behavior" (27-28). Vortices of behavior are typically found in the city, in areas where people congregate and where "fictions of identity, difference, and community come into play (28)." Examples of such places are the grand boulevards of the cities, marketplaces, theater districts, squares, cafés, and burial grounds. Again, this type of site forms a significant part of the (European) setting in the novels of Fauset, Johnson and Larsen. However, what they describe are not the same kinds of scenes of mass action that Roach describes (such as pageants) – but key passages are set in public places. For example, important encounters between Helga and the Danes occur as she is walking the streets of Copenhagen, or visiting the Circus hall to watch a vaudeville show. Similarly, pivotal events in *The Autobiography* take place when the ex-colored man visits the Paris Opera, or when Joanna in *There is Confusion* meets with a group of colored children playing ring games in the street.

The vortices of behavior also relate to what Roach describes as performances functioning as "counter-memories" to history as it is discursively transmitted. This means that performances make room for possible alternative versions of cultural memory: alongside officially documented history other influential but silenced versions may be transmitted through, for example, gestures, dance, storytelling, and proverbs. Here, then, is a chance to find what is left out of the official picture – and here is also the possibility for imagination and change. Indeed, change and making new is the very core of what performance is all about: no two performances are ever exactly alike and something new appears with every enactment. To talk of performance as "restored behavior" suggests that it is fundamentally a repetitive as well as an imitative practice, apparently putting something in the place of something else. Roach sees this restored behavior as involved in a continuing process of surrogation or substitution. Performance is, fundamentally, repetition with a difference.

Along the same lines Peggy Phelan, critic and author of several books in the field of performance studies, suggests that performance "is precisely the site in which concealed or dissimulated conventions might be investigated" (Diamond 5). In this sense, a performance is always what she calls "a doing and a thing done," in that it "embeds features of other, previous performances: gender conventions, racial histories, aesthetic traditions—political and cultural pressures that are consciously and unconsciously acknowledged" (Diamond 1). Phelan's observation points once more to the tension between the notion of performance as a possibly liberating activity and the "inescapable framework" pertaining to Butler's notion of performance as determining of all human behavior. This tension is explored in the fiction of Fauset, Johnson, and Larsen.

Literature and performance

My concern with the literary performances in Johnson, Fauset and Larsen should be seen in the context of the more general question of how performance relates to literature. As regards literary language, there are two parameters that are relevant for this study, and that have been examined by theorists of language and performance: the idea of speech (or the utterance) as an *act*, and the consideration of the *context* of the utterance (which includes attention to repetition/citation and to the audience). John L. Austin (followed by John R. Searle) was the first to talk about a linguistic utterance as "performative." The performative statement, according to Austin, performs an action, such as christening a ship. The performative statement, in Austin's sense, is one which the phrase "I hereby" can be added before the verb, for example, "I hereby baptize/promise/ order." The distinction between performative and "constative" utterances was later questioned. Constative utterances are events of stating, describing, or affirming—actions which can also be seen as performative depending on how we conceive of the relationship between language and the world. The possibility of this kind of division between performative and constative utterances has continued to be a topic of debate, and to recount the various turns this debate has taken falls outside the scope of this study. What I will focus on here is rather how the notion of the performative relates to literary language. [7]

Seeing literature as a performance means to be attentive not only to what the work of literature *says* but to what it *does*. Jonathan Culler likens the literary utterance to the performative in that it "does not refer to a prior state of affairs and is not true or false. The literary utterance too *creates* the state of affairs to which it refers" (Culler 96). There are several ways in which the literary utterance accomplishes this. The first, Culler suggests, is that it creates characters and their actions. Second, ideas and concepts are brought into being and developed by the work. In the context of this study, race (or performance) is one such example. Thus, relating literature to the performative brings to the fore "an active, world-making use of language" and helps us see literature as an "act" or "event" (Culler 96). With this perspective, the novels of Johnson, Fauset, and Larsen are acts through which new concepts of race are formed.

Another aspect of the performative, which has been developed by Jacques Derrida, is its dependence on repetition and convention. A performative statement has to be recognized as repeating a certain norm or convention in order to be successful, Derrida argues. That is, language performs acts in that it repeats established discursive practices (Culler 98). For example, at a baptism or wedding there are certain formulas that have to be followed in order for the act to be performed. Relating the idea of repetition of norms or conventions to literature, we find that literary language has to follow conventions of genre, for example, so as to be recognized as literature. In addition, the literary work is dependent on its social context, and is likely to reiterate social norms (be it in affirmative or negative terms) that are recognizable as characteristic of its time and place. Performance is a repetitive and imitative practice, in which making new is determined by what has come before (previous acts or pre-existing models). There is thus a temporal aspect involved here, in that the past is always-already a part of the performance in the present.[8] Thus the separation between the linguistic performance as dependent on more or less stable abstract struc-

---

[7] I refer the interested reader to, for example, John L. Austin, *How To Do Things with Words* (Cambridge, Mass.: Harvard U P, 1975) and John R. Searle, *Speech Acts: An Essay in the Philosophy of Language* (Cambridge: Cambridge U P, 1969).

tures and the physical presence of the oral (and kinetic) performance is called into question. The presence of the literary work, which is linked to its ability to make new, relates crucially to its context. A repetition is always a repetition with a difference, a difference that is context-dependent—that is, determined by the context of other utterances in which it is embedded. And while the context of the oral performance includes a physical audience, the textual performance has a reader, providing new interpretations of the literary act.[9] The analysis of textual performances in this study thus concerns the text as a whole studied as a performance or act, alongside the analysis of the literary depictions of performances that are a part of this act.

Minstrelsy and the roots of African-American stage performance

The figure of the minstrel performer epitomizes the issues that are probed in this study. With the minstrel show the first steps onto the national stage were taken by African Americans. This type of performance traces its origins to antebellum America (1830s), a time when blacks were forbidden to appear on stage. It originated as a performance by white men imitating black men (and women) by blackening their faces with burnt cork. The usual minstrel performance had a tripartite structure. The first part was led by an interlocutor and mainly consisted in singing. The second part was called the olio and was an interlude featuring acrobats and dancers. The third and last part included both singing and dancing. After the Civil War, freed slaves could form their own minstrel companies but, just like the white minstrels, they darkened their faces. The same tradition was upheld in vaudeville and carried on into the twentieth century. These later vaudeville shows would build on the basic minstrel structure of burlesque humor, singing, and dancing. Although highly compromised, the minstrel show offered a way onto the stage for black talent, and in the early twentieth century "Negro" revues were to become very popular. For example, in 1921, the musical comedy *Shuffle Along* was the first all-black production to be a great success on Broadway.

---

[8] Jacques Derrida has developed the notion of "citation" to show how the performative is dependent on being recognizable as part of an iterable convention or model. Hereby, the notion of "presence" is destabilized, as the presence can only be effective if it relates meaningfully to a past. For more on the notion of citation, see Derrida's "Signature Event Context" in *Limited Inc.* (Evanston, Ill: Northwestern U P, 1988).

[9] Reader-response theorists have also taken an interest in language as performance, See, for example, Stanley Fish, *Is There a Text in This Class* (Cambridge, Mass.: Harvard U P, 1980) and Richard Ohmann, "Literature as Act" in Seymour Chatman (ed), *Approaches to Poetics* (New York: Columbia U P, 1973).

There are several ways in which the minstrel performer relates to the literature of Johnson, Fauset, and Larsen. To begin with, this character, with his blackface mask, wide grin, and happy-go-lucky attitude is the stereotype of the "Old Negro" of plantation slavery that the Harlem Renaissance authors were seeking to replace with their version of a well-bred, urban "New Negro." Furthermore, issues of cultural and racial authenticity are embodied by the minstrel. In *Blacking Up. The Minstrel Show in Nineteenth-Century America* (1974) Robert C. Toll, one of the first historians of minstrel performance, emphasizes "the reciprocal relationship between white and black cultures" that was part of this genre (Toll 43). The first minstrel performers were white men who had picked up African-American folklore and had drawn inspiration from African-American dancing and music. Combining this acquisition—and often distortion—of African-American culture with the characteristic burnt-cork mask, the minstrel performers highlight the questions of cultural and racial authenticity.

As late-twentieth-century studies of this phenomenon, such as Eric Lott's *Love and Theft: Blackface Minstrelsy and the American Working Class* (1995), have shown, minstrel performance is characterized by a play with racial images, drawing attention to the fluidity of racial categories. The white performers assumed the markers of blackness, including facial mimicry and bodily gestures, creating a counterfeit blackness. Appearing as blacks on the stage, the white minstrels were actually involved in a complex play of reinforcing and yet unsettling of images, not only of blackness, but of whiteness. As Toll suggests: "Although it offered its audiences no heroic white characters, it provided even more certain assurances of white common people's identity by emphasizing Negroes' 'peculiarities' and inferiority. Even sympathetic black characters were cast as inferiors" (67). While the denigrating, stereotypical images of blacks of the minstrel performance served to maintain American racial hierarchies and keep the black subject in an inferior social position, the ambivalence of the racial images in minstrelsy can be read as destabilizers of the certainty of racial categories. Ideas of racial essentialism are questioned by this credible assumption, on the stage, of markers of racial difference. While based on the rigid separation of black and white, minstrel performance also unsettles these categories, highlighting the performative nature of human identity. The minstrel performer embodies an uneasy play between "original" and "copy" that has implications for the issue of racial essentialism. The race performances of minstrelsy (and although differently framed, the practice of race passing) refer to an assumed original, but this original is lost sight of in the presence of the new version that the imitation presents. This temporary dislocation of the original has the further consequence of throwing the status of the original permanently into doubt, and risks opening an endless search for origins. The performative aspect of human identity, and by extension the performativity of culture, is thus brought to light.

Black minstrel performers, who began to appear in large numbers on the vaudeville circuit after the Civil War, were also involved in these constructions of racial authenticity. Toll writes: "Because the notion that blacks were inherently musical was already deeply embedded in the public's images of Negroes and because these performers stressed their authenticity, they were thought of as natural, spontaneous people on exhibit rather than as professional entertainers" (201). The black minstrels thus used their musical or dancing skills to fit the pattern of the "darky" that was already established in the genre. Why did black performers enter into such a compromised field of racial representation? According to Toll, minstrelsy served as an outlet for black stage talent. It was often the only chance African Americans had of making a livelihood as entertainers, musicians, actors, or composers (Toll 216). The minstrel entertainment circuit brought several African-American musical talents to light, for example W.C. Handy, one of America's first recognized blues artists, and the "Queens of the Blues," Gertrude "Ma" Rainey and Bessie Smith.

In addition, Toll notes that "[g]iven the circumstances, participation at least gave blacks a chance to modify these caricatures" (228). This observation raises important questions concerning the possibility of resistant performance. Examples of how the black performers could make modifications within the framework of the minstrel show include concentrating the lyrics of their songs on topics that concerned them. There were lyrics expressing strong antislavery sentiment, for example, and songs about the threatened black family. They invented ways to meet their double audience in a way that is echoed by the Harlem Renaissance authors, as I will show. Often, they would express themselves on two levels, both directly and indirectly, by making covert jibes that the black audience would understand but the white audience was not likely to recognize. The black audience flocked to the entertainment halls where minstrel shows were put on. At times, they could even cause a temporary moment of desegregation as they became so numerous that they had to be let into seating areas otherwise reserved for white people.

There is yet another aspect of the minstrel performance that is relevant for my study of Johnson, Fauset, and Larsen. In accounting for the rise of this genre of entertainment, Toll places minstrelsy in the context of early-nineteenth-century America seeking to see its egalitarian and democratic ideals reflected in a "common man's culture." In the early nineteenth century there was a need for "cultural forms that reflected the average man's nationalism and egalitarianism, glorified 'plain people,' were aggressively antiaristocratic and anti-European, and could replace rural folk culture with symbols that white 'common men' could all unite around" (5). This explanation of minstrelsy's success sets up a dichotomy between American, folk, or popular entertainment for the worker and common man on the one hand and, on the other, European aristocratic or "high" culture, which runs as an undercurrent in the literature of Johnson, Fauset, and Larsen. They were all navigating the often conflicting demands of producing an art that would be for the common African American while still appealing to the European-American, that would be popular but yet not simple. They wanted to create an art that affirmed a modern African-American self-concept formulated in positive terms, while still having universal appeal. Putting the works these authors created in the context of African-American stage performance is as useful for their interpretation as tracing their literary antecedents. Does the fact that Johnson, Fauset, and Larsen chose literature as their medium of performance align them with their European predecessors and so make them less authentic representatives of the African-American culture, with its oral roots? Or can their works instead be seen as acts of resistance to this common contemporary definition?

The minstrel performer, then, evokes questions of authenticity in relation to both race and culture: just what *is* African-American culture and who represents it? Are bodies truthful markers of racial difference, and is it possible to talk of characteristics that typically belong to a group of people that is racially marked? Is personal identity a reflection of an inner essence or can it be seen as a performance that varies with the context? In the following, we will see how the works of Johnson, Fauset, and Larsen provide answers to these questions by means of the trope of performance in relation to the symbolic use of Europe and European culture.

The vexed issue of whiteness performed in distinction to blackness, and the anti-European, low-brow culture evoked by minstrel performance, indicates that the notion of Europe is a symbolically important part of the cultural backdrop against which nineteenth-century and early-twentieth-century African-American performances took place. Extending the analysis from the minstrel performer to the textual performances of Johnson, Fauset, and Larsen, I propose that Europe is a kind of symbolic geography through which ideas of high culture as opposed to the popular or folk culture of the African-American performance tradition can be charted. Europe's association with whiteness plays into the discussion of racial essentialism as opposed to the performative nature of racial identity. Actual depictions of being in the contact zone that is Europe bring various conceptions of racial identity to light, but the symbol of Europe has a similar effect as well. Finally, there is the question of whether the literary performances of Johnson, Fauset, and Larsen are a means of resistance in their function as counter-narratives to the dominant racial ideology—a discussion in which I propose that the notion of Europe functions as a sounding board.

The Harlem Renaissance: depicting the "New Negro"

If previous research on Johnson, Fauset, and Larsen long lacked critical focus on the fictional European episodes and the interdependence of black and white artistic life, the question remains to be asked: why? One way of interpreting this lack is to see it as an effect of the establishment of what Paul Gilroy calls "the great ethnocentric canon of African American literature" (186). The focus has been on experiences of African cultural retention or on the struggle for recognition in American society. Arguably, this "ethnocentricity" has historically been a response to being denied literacy and "history," or a cultural heritage. The aesthetics of writing was from the outset coupled with social and political aims. In the introduction to the *Norton Anthology of African American Literature*, Henry Louis Gates and Nellie McKay claim that:

> African American slaves, remarkably, sought to write themselves out of slavery by mastering the Anglo-American bellettristic tradition [...] In a very real sense, the Anglo-African literary tradition was created two centuries ago in order to demonstrate that persons of African descent possessed the requisite degrees of reason and wit to create literature, that they were, indeed, full and equal members of the community of rational, sentient beings, that they could, indeed, write. (xxvii-xxviii)

Through their writing, the ex-slaves sought to prove their humanity, and at the beginning of the twentieth century the Harlem Renaissance writers sought to prove through their art that they were worthy of full citizenship as Americans. African-American artistic production was thus from the start seen as a means of gaining social rights. To claim "a literature of one's own" formed part of an attempt to gain acceptance as artists and citizens. Behind this work is a belief in literary language as a performative speech act, that is, through their literary works early African-American authors established themselves as intellectual and creative subjects with a story to tell. In addition, this has implications for the writer's responsibility as a representative of the race. McKay and Gates go on to describe the author and her/his works as a "synecdoche, a part standing for the ethnic whole" (xxxiv). This indicates the relationship between race and historical representation and documentation, that is, the responsibilities, limits, and possibilities of representing a history of oppression.

In this chapter, the cultural event usually referred to as the Harlem Renaissance is probed. Some of the vital questions that concerned artists and intellectuals of this time are addressed in order to situate Johnson, Fauset, and Larsen in the historical context in which they were writing and to discuss what was at stake for the artists in representing the "New Negro" on the stage or in literature. These questions primarily concern the subject matter and form of African-American literature, debates in which the notion of cultural authenticity and the representation of primitivism and particularly female sexuality figure importantly. The notion of place is also of moment here, as the trans-Atlantic interchanges between Harlem and Paris are explored. A discussion of how the symbolism of Europe is related to the idea of cultural authenticity is initiated here.

It should perhaps be added as a preliminary that, having two publication dates (1912 and 1927), Johnson's *The Autobiography of an Ex-Colored Man* in its original, anonymous version preceded the literary (re)naissance of the inter-war years. The second publication took place during the heyday of this creative historical period, and Johnson was indeed, in his novel as well as his critical and poetic work, very much a writer and personage of the moment.

The "Old Negro"

African-American writers of the early twentieth century took issue with the images of African Americans that were circulated in popular culture and that formed the way black Americans came to be perceived by white Americans. They were the first to claim that common ideas of "black folk" had come into being out of a specific historical context and were not to be seen as objective reflections of actual circumstances. What is more, as they could be identified and analyzed, these largely negative images could be changed. These images can be read as semiotic signs, similar to the linguistic signs of the language. Like words, images are signs with certain meanings that can be understood by relating them to their context. For example, Roland Barthes's reading of images in advertisements has shown how messages are encoded in the signs

(114-16). These messages can be understood through cultural codes. Pictures belong to a signifying system analogous to that of language and, like the signs in the linguistic system, images can be read as "text." Like the literary text, images like that of the *tom* and the other stereotypes studied by Bogle—described below—are not merely descriptive but "world-making." Music and dressing are additional examples of signs that convey meaning and that are relevant to the particular context of this study.

In his history of early American film, Donald Bogle identifies five recurrent images through which a black cultural presence was registered. These five basic types were the tom, the black buck, the coon, the tragic mulatta and the mammy (Bogle 4-18). Early versions of these characters were stock characters of the nineteenth-century minstrel shows, such as the plantation rustic Jim Crow and the urban dandy Zip Coon (Lott 23).

The tom is of course named after the protagonist of Harriet Beecher Stowe's *Uncle Tom's Cabin* and refers to a subservient, docile character who, throughout any hardship, remains true to his white master and his Christian faith. The coon is a slow-witted, backward country type. Versions of this type could sometimes appear in the guise of a child, a "pickaninny," or an elderly, quaint "Uncle Remus." The buck is brutal, savage, over-sexed and especially desirous of white women. The tragic mulatta is a mixed-race character, always very beautiful and sexually attractive. Her balancing act between the two separated racial worlds of black and white leads to her inevitable downfall. Finally, the mammy is typically a very black, obese domestic who is more loyal to the white family she works for than to her own biological family. About these types Bogle writes:

> Fun was poked at the American Negro by presenting him as either a nitwit or a childlike lackey. None of the types was meant to do great harm, although at various times individual ones did. All were merely filmic reproductions of black stereotypes that had existed since the days of slavery and were already popularised in American life and arts. The movies, which catered to public tastes, borrowed profusely from all the other popular art forms. Whenever dealing with black characters, they simply adapted the old familiar stereotypes, often further distorting them. (Bogle 4)

In addition to the mammy figure, two more female stereotypes were often used in literature by white southern writers of the slavery and Reconstruction era:

the concubine and the conjure woman (Christian 3-19). These representations were conceived in contrast to idealized representations of white womanhood. For example, the mammy is black, fat, nurturing, religious, kind, strong, and enduring, as opposed to the southern mistress who is white, beautiful, frail, and incapable of doing hard work. Most importantly, "all the functions of the mammy are magnificently physical. They involve the body as sensuous, as funky, the part of woman that white southern America was profoundly afraid of. Mammy, then, harmless in her position as a slave, unable because of her all-giving nature to do harm is needed as an image, a surrogate to contain all those fears of the physical female" (Christian 2). These images, then, were widely circulated in American popular culture, in literature as well as in early film and advertisement, and were part of the "Old Negro" images that the Harlem Renaissance authors sought to replace with new, more positive concepts of African-American identity. One response was to revise these figures, such as the tragic mulatta, in their own fiction (these revisions are probed in the following section).

These "Old Negro" stereotypes were also part of the inspiration for the anthology *The New Negro*, which was published in 1925 and marks the formal launching of the Harlem or New Negro Renaissance, as it was then often called. The editor, Alain Locke, identifies the most important points of the work in his introductory essay, also entitled *The New Negro*. Here, he analyzes the psychological effects of discrimination and stresses the importance of taking issue with the denigrating images of black people that were widely circulated and often caused an inferiority complex. The "Old Negro," says Locke, is "more of a myth than a man [...] more of a formula than a human being" (3). He calls for the replacement of this myth, which was often internalized by blacks themselves, with a positive, forward-looking attitude and the refusal to see oneself as "a social burden." Thus exhorting his fellow African-Americans not to accept these negative images Locke aims to instill in them "race pride." "The New Negro" that he visualizes is characterized by self-respect and self-dependence.

There were a number of factors that coincided to make the historical moment of the 1920s auspicious for the introduction of the "New Negro." To begin with, there had been a great migration from the segregated south to the north before and during World War I. In this process of transplantation, says Locke, the African-Americans have also been transformed (6). While they previously shared only "a condition" (of segregation and subjugation) the move north and the consequent gathering together in urban centers led to "a common consciousness." There was increased inter-racial contact: where previously only workers had met, on the farms or in factories, now other segments of the black community came together. This stronger, more unified community wanted their full share in the country's institutions and thus underscoring their previous marginalization they drew attention to the discrepancy between American social creed and social practice. Now, the "New Negro" aimed to be an active collaborator and participant in American civilization. In fact, Locke declared that this new man would be guided by a "sense of a mission of rehabilitating the race in world esteem from that loss of prestige for which the fate and conditions of slavery have so largely been responsible" (14). Art and other forms of cultural production were at the center of this work of restoration. By proving their artistic and intellectual capabilities Locke and his contemporaries hoped that they would qualify for full and equal social status.

In the eyes of white Americans this "New Negro" (so recently freed from slavery) seemed to have found a capacity for enjoyment of life that was largely lost to their own post-war generation. It is striking that the "New Negro" appears at a time when European Americans used images like a "waste land" and a "lost generation" to account for their situation and outlook on life. By contrast, *The New Negro* "exudes a quality suspiciously like joy" as Arnold Rampersad put it in his 1992 introduction to the anthology (xxiii). To the white American, then, the "New Negro" was both a threat—since he claimed increased social space—and a promise.[10]

The tragic mulatta
and the literature of passing

James Weldon Johnson, Jessie Fauset, and Nella Larsen all make specific use of mulatto characters, and passing, in their works. Of the novels included here, Johnson's *The Autobiography* is the only one to deal with passing in the traditional sense, while Larsen's *Quicksand* offers a reversal of the passing novel. Significantly, all three novels employ metaphors of masking.

---

[10]Locke was, however, very cautious in political terms saying that separatism must not be a goal, only full inclusion in American democracy, and calling the New Negro a "'forced radical,' a social protestant rather than a genuine radical" (11).

Literature featuring mulattoes light-skinned enough to pass as white questions the idea of the body as a truthful signifier of difference and destabilizes the polarized identities of "black" and "white." In addition, the mulatto calls into question the power of vision, by which bodies are ordered in racial categories. As a literary figure, the mulatto appears most frequently in the post-Reconstruction era, at a time when the segregation of blacks and whites was institutionalized. It was the least offensive of the black stereotypes and the one with the greatest potential for social critique. Today, the literature of race passing has gained significance as a part of post-modern investigations into the "grand narratives" of Enlightenment and emancipation. Through the concept of passing, categories and classifications such as "race" are deconstructed and the fictions behind them revealed. In the introduction to the anthology *Passing and the Fictions of Identity*, Elaine K. Ginsberg writes that "[i]n its interrogation of the essentialism that is the foundation of identity politics, passing has the potential to create a space for creative self-determination and agency: the opportunity to construct new identities, to experiment with multiple subject positions, and to cross social and economic boundaries that exclude or oppress" (16). Despite its origin in a deprivation of rights, passing can thus be interpreted positively, as a subversive strategy for eschewing a legally assigned social identity, involving a destabilization of the "colorline."

The result of a union between black and white, the mulatto character functions as a device for exploring the relationship between the races (Carby 89). His or her intermediary position between two separate worlds suggests the close but separate co-existence of black and white. The fictions of Nella Larsen and Jessie Fauset are modern revisions of the literature of the tragic mulatta, which was most often employed in works with a female protagonist. The genre was initiated in the nineteenth century by works such as William Wells Brown's *Clotel, or, the President's Daughter* (1853) and Frances E. W. Harper's *Iola LeRoy, Shadows Uplifted* (1892), the first published novel by a black woman. There were also white authors who made use of this literary figure, such as George Washington Cable and William Dean Howells.[11] In *The Politics of Color in the Fiction of Jessie Fauset and Nella Larsen* (1995), Jacquelyn Y. McLendon shows how Fauset and Larsen developed the nineteenth-century stereotype of the tragic mulatta as used by these, and other, white authors. In their fiction, the figure of the mulatta becomes a vehicle for exploring "the concept of double-

---

[11]See, for example, Cable's *Madame Delphine* (1881) and Howells' *Imperative Duty* (1891).

ness as it inheres in the experience of African Americans generally, and to satirize the bourgeois class" (11). As they do this, McLendon observerves, they are particularly concerned with how issues of identity and difference relate specifically to being female.

The works in which early African-American novelists made use of the figure of the tragic mulatta were written mainly for a white audience and sought to refute prevalent stereotypes of the black woman. Owing to the prevalent myth of the super-sexuality of the black woman and its severe historical consequences, the issue of sexuality was often submerged in early African-American women's literature. For example, in the works of Frances Harper and others, sexuality is submerged or denied. In *Quicksand*, Nella Larsen confronted the denial of sexuality, making Helga Crane "the first truly sexual black female protagonist in Afro-American fiction" (Carby 1987: 174).

The novels featuring the tragic mulatta raise fundamental questions about the institution of slavery. By their very existence, the mulatto figures are an indictment of the ideology that proclaimed them to be less than human beings since they are the product of a union between white and black. The tragedy of the literary mulatta is that she is caught between the black and white worlds. If she exhibited characteristics thought to derive from her white heritage, such as sensitivity or capacity for intellectual work, they could not be expressed in her daily existence within the black world. In fact, her situation was often perceived as so untenable that the novel's resolution demanded her death. In relation to plot, the mulatta as a literary figure allows for the movement between the black and the white world. Thus, she underscores the theme of traveling and identity of the novels dealt with here, drawing attention to the trope of border crossing.

Passing relates fundamentally both to the performance perspective on identity and to place as it connotes the (physical) passing from one side of the color line to the other. Passing was the topic of Fauset's second novel, *Plum Bun*, as well as of Nella Larsen's second novel, *Passing* (both published in 1929). In an analysis of *Plum Bun*, Sonja Kroell uses a spatial metaphor when she likens passing from one's own black world into the white world to being an expatriate (40). There were people who passed only on occasion, but the passer often had to leave her or his family and give up all ties with the black community. In *Plum Bun*, for example, Fauset depicts how the protagonist Angela denies her own sister before the white man she hopes to marry one day. The connection between space and race, which is a fundamental part of passing, is retained and queried throughout this study. The passage to Europe means entering into a white world, leaving all ties with the black community.

"The Negro in Art:" Race (wo)man or exotic primitive?

The issue of literary representation was a topic of lively debate among African-American intellectuals in the 1920s. The main points of the debate are worth recapitulating as they indicate that, regardless of their individual persuasions on these matters, the authors of the Harlem Renaissance shared a belief in the performative potential of language. They saw in literature a possible means of transcending or transforming their present untenable social situation.

In sum, the debate was centered on three questions. First, should the black author be emphatically a black author? That is, should the art s/he produced be "racial" or "universal"? Second, should the black author cater to the demands of the largely white-dominated reading public? What this audience expected (and therefore what sold best) were often descriptions of low-life, night-life scenes in Harlem spiced up with the characters' display of uninhibited sexuality. While depictions of this kind may have reflected one part of black life, they ran the obvious risk of reinforcing common stereotypes of African Americans. This led to the third issue of debate, which concerned what responsibility the black authors should take for portraying only the positive aspects of the African-American characters. Should the authors indeed defend, and even sometimes glorify, the race in order to counter all the negative images of African Americans that already circulated within American culture, or should they opt for a more honest art of portraying their people as they happened to find them, good or bad? These questions arise as the audience for black literature changes from being primarily white for earlier authors, such as Paul Lawrence Dunbar or Charles Chesnutt, to being mixed, black and white. They are contested issues that have continued to be of concern for African-American authors during the twentieth century. Alternatively, this can be formulated as a debate about the relationship between art and propaganda. The leading black intellectual of the time, W.E.B. Du Bois, wrote in the October, 1926, issue of *The Crisis* that "all art is propaganda and ever must be, despite the wailing of the purists" (296). However, the primitivist expectations were figured differently for men and women. The issue of gender and how it affects Fauset and Larsen on the one hand and Johnson on the other is addressed in connection with the analyses in chapter 3.

The two polarities of the contemporary debate are represented by Langston Hughes and George Schuyler. In 1926, the two authors both published articles discussing the question of whether the black artist was just another American, or if there really was a specific African-American art. In "The Negro Art-Hokum," Schuyler stressed the similarity between black and white Americans and argued that there was no genuinely black art. Hughes, on the other hand, in "The Negro Artist and the Racial Mountain" relates with sadness the story of a friend who expressed the wish to be "a poet—not a Negro poet." Hughes believed that this desire really stemmed from a wish to be white, as he denounces the "urge within the race toward whiteness" (Huggins, *Voices* 305). Having said this, Hughes goes on to expresses his regard for jazz and black folk art in order to claim that the black artist must above all be free to be himself. However, this notion of freedom seems somewhat paradoxical given the opening of the article, where any inclination towards what could be connected to whiteness or universalism was dismissed as deplorable. Most important perhaps, the often-quoted finishing lines of Hughes's article assert that, whatever the writer may choose to write about, s/he should not be governed by public opinion:

> We younger Negro artists who create now intend to express our individual dark-skinned selves without fear or shame. If white people are pleased we are glad. If they are not, it doesn't matter. We know we are beautiful. And ugly too. The tom-tom cries and the tom-tom laughs. If colored people are pleased we are glad. If they are not, their displeasure doesn't matter either. We build our temples for tomorrow, strong as we know how, and we stand on top of the mountain, free within ourselves. (Huggins, Voices 309)

The portrayal of African Americans was also debated in a series of articles published between March and November, 1926, in *The Crisis*, under the heading "The Negro in Art: How Shall He Be Portrayed?" Jessie Fauset was one of several authors who were asked to answer a number of questions on the topic. Others were Sinclair Lewis, Sherwood Anderson, and Countee Cullen. Here, Fauset expresses clear ideas on the roles of both audience and publishers. Publishers have a fixed idea of what topics and characters are appropriate to African-American literature. Therefore, it is right to criticize authors for refusing works that portray educated and accomplished African Americans in favor of those works that include "the sordid, foolish and criminal among Negroes convincing the world that this and this alone is really and essentially Negroid." The reading public also has an important role to play. Best sellers are made—not born, Fauset says, as she urges black readers to actually go out and buy the books they clamor for, that is "good novel[s] about colored people by a colored author" (71). In her own work, Fauset refused to comply with the demand for "primitivist" literature.

James Weldon Johnson and Nella Larsen also had to negotiate the demands of the white and the black audience. In the essay "Double Audience Makes Road Hard for Negro Authors," originally published in the *Philadelphia Tribune* on November 29, 1928, Johnson describes the predicament of the black author who had to face a double audience of black and white readers: "[M]ore than a double audience it is a divided audience, an audience made up of two elements with differing and often opposite and antagonistic points of view" (Wilson 409). While the African American audience expected him to deal only with "their best points," the Euro-American audience expected entertaining diversion in accordance with plantation stereotypes. The challenge, then, was to try to write "so as to fuse white and black America into one interested and approving audience" (412). In chapter 3, I discuss how Johnson's *The Autobiography* negotiates the balance between the mixed demands of his audience in greater detail. There are a few matters I want to bring up at this point, however. In *The Autobiography*, Johnson lets his characters state opinions that he was later to voice himself in other contexts. For example, a friend of the narrator (the doctor he meets on his passage back to America from Europe) declare a belief that sounds very much like the credo of the Harlem Renaissance: "Every race and every nation should be judged by the best it has been able to produce, not by the worst" (114). Johnson's own work certainly deals with a highly accomplished man, moving between jobs, countries and languages without any problem. While the book refers to Club life in NYC, and includes scenes of gambling, violence, and theft on the part of its black characters, the superior intellect and accomplishments of the narrator balance the negative aspects of these scenes. In addition, the artistic achievements of African Americans are continually referred to as a source of pride. In the novel, the narrator vents his theory on the matter of artistic achievement and its social consequences:

> It is my opinion that the coloured people of this country have done
> four things which refute the oft-advanced theory that they are an
> absolutely inferior race, which demonstrate that they have originality
> and artistic conception, and, what is more, the power of creating that
> which can influence and appeal universally. The first two of these
> are the Uncle Remus stories, collected by Joel Chandler Harris, and
> the Jubilee songs, to which the Fisk singers made the public and the
> skilled musicians of both America and Europe listen. The other two
> are ragtime music and the cake-walk. (63)

The same four examples are referred to by Johnson in the preface to *The Book of American Negro Poetry* (10). Johnson was an important promoter (as well as creator) of African-American arts. Like Fauset, he worked as both author and editor of works of contemporary poets. In his critical as well as his fictional work, Johnson chooses to celebrate African-American achievement. However, the main point for Johnson is not that they are *African*-American achievements, but that they are American. As Sondra Kathryn Wilson notes in the introduction to *Lift Every Voice and Sing* (vii), Johnson was always a universalist. Recognizing the distinctiveness of African Americans, he still emphasized their similarity with other Americans. To him, the cultural production of black and white Americans was differently figured as a result of social and material differences, rather than intellectual or moral differences. These differences could be overcome if the social and material conditions were altered. Johnson's own writings were acts designed to buttress this theory.

Nella Larsen's novel about Helga Crane reflects "the quicksands of representation," as Hazel Carby put it (163). At a time when the primitivist trend encouraged depictions of African-Americans as sexually uninhibited, it was a precarious task to try to give a complex presentation of a young black woman's sexuality. This was a charged topic, given the very recent history of slavery and the widespread stereotypes of the promiscuity of the African American woman that were used to legitimize sexual slavery. Carby writes: "Racist ideologies proclaimed the black woman to be a rampant sexual being, and in response black women writers either focused on defending their morality or displaced sexuality onto another terrain. Larsen confronted this denial directly in her fiction" (174). As we see in the novel, Helga Crane is positioned between the extremes of virtuous mother-woman and promiscuous black concubine. Ultimately, her alternatives come to depend on men through the ideology that dictates that female sexuality is only to be given outlet within marriage. The result of Helga's limited choices is tragic. The terrain of sexual independence turns out to be a quicksand for Helga, who at the end of the novel is nearly dying from too-frequent childbirths in her precipitate marriage with a Southern preacher.

The content of the art was not the only point of contention, however. The implications of the choice of form are further probed in chapter 4.

Josephine Baker—a primitivist icon

The most successful of all African American artists in Europe at this time was dancer and singer Josephine Baker. In 1925, she became an overnight success in Paris with her *danse sauvage* (the savage dance), in which she made the most of the contemporary primitivist fad. She would enter the stage half naked, dressed only in feathers, and start dancing with rolling eyes and angular body movements. While her stage persona owed more to French exotic fantasies than to African culture, Baker's performance was steeped in the traditions of African-American jazz and vaudeville. Contemporary African-American press was divided in its comments on Baker's overseas success. Some expressed pride in the fact that a black woman had made it in the white world and was able to mix with European aristocracy. Baker even married a French Count, Pepito de Abatino. Others considered her a sell-out to white values and felt disappointed that she had abandoned her home country (Lemke 103-104). The example of the world-famous dancer and revue artist Josephine Baker offers a vivid illustration of the stakes involved in primitivist representation, and of the role of Europe in this representation, for the African-American artist. Indeed, Baker emblematizes the significance of performance, in relation to both stage and social appearances, and of the role of Europe in African-American culture at this time. Baker's persona, both on and off-stage, was a conscious production, and thus, Sieglinde Lemke suggests, "prototypically modernist" (106). To Ann duCille, Baker is an icon of the eroticized black woman in Western civilization (73).

Baker's European experiences were to be partly fictionalized by African-American author Nella Larsen. In fact, Helga Crane adapts a kind of stage persona for Danish social circles much like Josephine Baker's in her Parisian revues. In fact she is made, both literally and figuratively, into an object of art, to be gazed and often gaped at. In *Quicksand*, Helga's Danish uncle Poul "detest[s] tears," and when he sees Helga weeping he finds her "insufficiently civilized." Such a comment might lead us to suspect that uncle Dahl himself is overly civilized, as it were. This was actually a real anxiety during the first decades of the 20th century. Freud's exposition of civilized man's repression of basic instincts had helped increase the interest for what was thought of as more "primitive" lifestyles. Furthermore, the Great War had dealt the ultimate blow to the belief in constant rational progress and led to a loss of faith in Western civilization. Now, the African, and the African American, who had long been dismissively ascribed an irrational, naïve, and spontaneous approach to life, were suddenly valued for these same qualities. Painters like Picasso and Braque were already looking to African art to find inspiration for a new aesthetic idiom. White Americans turned to Harlem clubs for black music and entertainment, hoping to gain some lost quality for enjoyment of life. The African American thus came to represent the hope for a reinvigoration of Western culture. For example, jazz music was one of the first cultural products that were exported from the USA to Europe. In Larsen's *Quicksand*, there is an ambivalence regarding primitivism and civilization, which can also be found in Josephine Baker's European experiences. On the one hand, primitivism was associated with anti-modernism, a longing for a return to a pre-rational life. On the other hand, the primitivism of the 1920s was a kind of ultra-modernism: it was in fact the primitivism of African cultures that would provide regeneration for a Western civilization threatened with degeneration.

DuCille notes a resurgence of interest in Josephine Baker in the 1990s, evidenced by the British documentary *Chasing a Rainbow* (1987) and the movie *The Josephine Baker Story* (1991). Furthermore, two films featuring Baker from the 1930s were re-released and shown in movie theaters as well as made into video cassettes (duCille 168). Many of her recordings were collected and produced as CD's in the 1990s as well. This leads duCille to draw parallels between the cultural moment of the late twentieth century and that of Baker in the 1920s and 30s, and prompts her to ask: "Are we, in our attempts at cultural criticism, modern-day primitivists? Are our Afrocentric interests and our vernacular theories and our feminist concerns for female agency colluding with primitivist proclivities like those that helped to bring the black 'other' into vogue in the 1920s? Are we, like the moment in which they lived and worked, inventing these artists as icons?" (duCille 85). This she asks apropos of her observation that the blues artists of the 1920s, like Ma Rainey and Bessie Smith, have been constructed by many feminist critics (for example Angela Y. Davis, Cheryl Wall and Hazel V. Carby) as sexual icons as well, but in more affirmative terms. The blues artists are conceived of as more grounded in the experiences of the majority of African Americans, and as being able to voice a more independent black female sexuality. Not only was the blues an art that had grown out of the folk and reached the folk. In addition, the blues singers were freer to express themselves in affirmative, sexual terms, claiming independence and status as sexual subjects in their own right. DuCille concludes that this privileging of the blues artists as superior representatives of black culture needs to be questioned, since it postulates that certain versions of blackness and the black experience are considered more authentic than others when dealing with the 1920s. This has led to the privileging of a "blues aesthetic" over literary works of arts, such as the novel, and a writer like Zora Neale Hurston. With this perspective, the art of Larsen and Fauset, although eschewing Baker's kind of primitivism and dealing with middle-class characters, using the novel as medium, is conceived of as less authentic. The discussion of the blues vis-à-vis written literature is revisited in the final chapter.

Harlem and Paris: centers of African-American culture on two sides of the Atlantic

Place and geographical movement were of central importance to the historical period in which Johnson, Fauset, and Larsen worked. In the 1920s, the ongoing African-American cultural flowering was usually referred to as "the New Negro Renaissance," suggesting that this was a formative moment in the history of a collective African-American identity. The period has subsequently become known as the Harlem Renaissance[12] in recognition of the fact that Harlem was a major cultural center attracting many of the best known artists of the time. The name change not only emphasizes the significance of place to this moment of cultural production, but points to a significant relationship between place and subjectivity. The name also refers back to the European Renaissance, which suggests a desire to be linked with the European tradition. An important part of that earlier Renaissance, as of the Harlem Renaissance, was the idea of a new

---

[12] There has been a lively debate concerning the period, for example, whether Harlem was in fact the only Northern urban center to function as an important creative center or if Washington DC could not be considered of equal importance. Other issues debated concern the duration of this "Renaissance" since different authors see different years as its starting-point and ending respectively; the "success" or "failure" to achieve the political aims of the art; the elitism inherent in the work of the Talented Tenth; and the alleged failure to represent the majority of African Americans.

man, a man of education and a strong sense of self-consciousness in the place of a concept of self that was associated with a less enlightened past.

Demographic shifts and the war experiences form the background for the cultural flourishing of the Harlem Renaissance. In the Great Migration of the first decades of the twentieth century, large numbers of African Americans who were disillusioned with the continued racial segregation in the post-Reconstruction South traveled north. Often, they gathered in urban centers, such as New York's Harlem, where a new racial consciousness and self-assertiveness were expressed. By the sheer force of numbers, African Americans now felt they could be a political force. The experiences of black Americans in France also played a part in this development. Black soldiers who were returning home from the war were faced with continued racial segregation, and the inconsistency between the values of freedom and democracy that the soldiers had been fighting for on foreign ground and the treatment they received on their return to their native country was glaring. During the "Red Summer" of 1919, race riots erupted all over the country and led to the lynching of eighty-three blacks. Another important event in 1919 was the publication of Claude McKay's sonnet "If We Must Die" in the New York socialist magazine *Liberator*. McKay's poem voiced a bold defiance of oppression and, perhaps even more significantly, showed what an important part literature could play in the communication of a new racial consciousness. The sonnet was featured in African-American newspapers and magazines throughout the country and led Jessie Fauset, who was made literary editor of the NAACP magazine *The Crisis* in November 1919, to announce that "[t]he portrayal of black people calls increasingly for black writers" (Davis 132).

The New Negro or Harlem Renaissance emerged out of this post-war tumult, with the aim of creating an image of the New Negro: "one who would not allow himself, his family, or his race to be victimized without fighting back" (Davis 131-32). The authors of the period thus sought to refute previous literary stereotypes and create a new, positive self-concept for African Americans. To talk of a "New Negro" was to claim a specific identity, a particular set of shared characteristics for African Americans—characteristics related to a shared history and a culture that could function as a source of pride and yield increased self-respect. It was felt that legitimacy and recognition as a people and a culture required a heritage. The search for self-definition that was part of the Harlem Renaissance thus often occasioned an interest in history and the folk tradition. The aim was twofold: formulating a positive image of a modern, urban, educated African American marked by her/his distance from the "Old Negro" of plantation slavery would not only inspire African Americans but also help motivate demands for equal rights in the eyes of white Americans. Art had a central position in this struggle, and in the introduction to *The New Negro* Alain Locke stresses the role of the artists and intellectuals as leaders and interpreters of their people. The engineers of the "New Negro" movement, such as Locke and Charles S. Johnson, conceived of a new, positive black identity that could be "taught" by an educated elite, the Talented Tenth. Although the purpose was positive, as they were trying to change derogatory images of black people, any new "prescription" of what an African-American identity could or should be also had to rely on very particular, exclusive ideas of what this identity was supposed to mean. Johnson, Fauset, and Larsen tackled this issue in various ways in their novels, as we will see in the following, and Europe figures as an important space affecting their renditions of "blackness."

The works of the Harlem Renaissance authors usually have a national, American perspective, dealing with American settings and specifically American experiences, such as life in Harlem. Alternatively, in their attempt to articulate an African-American cultural tradition, some Harlem Renaissance writers, such as Jean Toomer and Zora Neale Hurston, turned to the American South to trace the folk traditions established there since slavery. The project of "digging up one's past" also involved relating to African cultural forms in order to define what was distinctly African American in American culture. Whereas many of their contemporaries are concerned singularly with the American experience in the American setting, Johnson, Fauset, and Larsen are among the handful of authors who have attempted to relate African-American culture to European culture through fictionalized accounts of the meeting between "the New Negro" and Europe. They turn outward, to Europe, in order to comment on America. In doing so, they draw our attention to the international tendencies of the Harlem Renaissance, built on a long tradition of African-American writing about Europe.

As indicated above, France played a part in the self-consciousness of the "New Negro" as the black soldiers felt they received better treatment there than in their home country. Many chose to stay on, especially in Paris. Tyler Stovall, in *Paris Noir: African Americans in the City of Light* (1996), observes that the black GI's laid the foundations for the formation of a black community in Paris after the war. He writes: "The classical music of black America, jazz has always played a key role in the life of Paris's black community during the twentieth century, and it was the African American GI's of World War I who first introduced it to the French people" (Stovall 20). The community was a loose formation, centered mainly on jazz clubs, which also provided meeting places between black and white Americans. Paris was of course an artistic center that attracted many Americans at this time, be it aspiring writers or tourists come to have a good time. Some of the best-known writers that resided in Paris during the 1920s are Ernest Hemingway, F. Scott Fitzgerald, and Gertrude Stein, but many African-American artists went there as well. Paris has in fact been called the "second home" of the Harlem Renaissance, as most of the artists connected with the movement lived there at some point (Griffin & Fish 168). Jessie Fauset, Gwendolyn Bennett, Claude McKay, and Langston Hughes are a few of them. During this time the African-American expatriate literary community in Paris was neither as large nor as close as the one created by the white American authors of the Lost Generation. There does not seem to have been much artistic collaboration or interaction between the African-American authors and their Anglo-American counterparts in Paris. For example, Jessie Fauset sought contact with Sylvia Beach (the owner of the famous English book store Shakespeare and Company) but was rebuffed (Lewis 124). When *Quicksand* had just been published, Nella Larsen sent a copy to Gertrude Stein, together with a letter in which she praises Stein's portrayal of the African-American characters in "Melanctha" (Davis 251). Respectfully, Larsen asks for a meeting with Stein, but this was never to come about.

Travel is in itself a part of the modernity of the "New Negroes." There was a larger number of educated middle-class black Americans with the financial means to travel abroad than ever before. In the inter-war years, approximately as many black as white Americans came to Europe. According to Michel Fabre,

> [m]others of soldiers killed in France came on pilgrimages to the battlefields from Flanders to Alsace; tourists sought culture and freedom, trying to forget the "red summer" of 1919 and the increasing number of lynchings. Black and white alike were fleeing from Prohibition and Puritanism. They took advantage of the strong dollar to have a good time at little expense. The Europe they encountered was imbued with jazz and Negro art. (3)

Here, Fabre indicates that Europe played a part in the valorization of music and art of African origins. In the early twentieth century, traveling to Europe was, in fact, not only a way of getting in touch with a European heritage but also a means for African Americans to gain a better sense of themselves in relation to other blacks in the diaspora. Again, place and subjectivity are significantly connected. Paris, which has been called "the gateway to Africa," often served as a meeting place between blacks from America, the Caribbean, and Africa (Griffin & Fish xvi). Traveling to Europe could thus be a step on the way to gaining the self-consciousness that the "New Negroes" sought but that was so hard to attain on American soil. In this sense, Paris is—along with Harlem—at the center of modern black experience. During the interwar years, movements like Pan-Africanism and negritude brought blacks from America, Africa, and the Caribbean together in Paris. For example, in 1919 the Pan-African Congress, which w.e.b. DuBois and 15 other African Americans attended, was held there. So, while the New Negro Renaissance artists aimed to claim space for themselves in American society, much of their work sprung out of international connections, and their search for space was often rerouted via Europe, where new enactments of self could be staged.

"Home...What is home?"

Many of the central questions that these authors addressed, and that I examine in the present study, are dealt with by Jessie Fauset in an article titled "Nostalgia," which was published in *The Crisis* in August, 1921. Here, Fauset points to a crucial difference between the African Americans and the other immigrants that populate America, concerning the meaning of "home." The article describes Fauset's meeting with a young black soldier who has just returned from the war in France. On his return to America, he finds himself feeling not relieved but confused: "Home […] is it where mentally and spiritually he is recognized and taken for what he is? What is home?" Feeling that he has been "taken for what he is" in France, he is starting to doubt whether France is not more of a home than his native country, America. Fauset expands on his predicament:

> It is from the spiritual nostalgia that the American Negro suffers most. He has been away so long from that mysterious fatherland of his that like all the other descendants of voluntary and involuntary immigrants of the seventeenth century,—Puritan, pioneer, adventurer, indentured servant,—he feels himself American. The

> past is too far past for him to have memories. Very, very rarely does
> he have a backward reaching bond, be it never so tenuous. (157)

What Fauset is saying here is that Africa does not mean anything in terms of home to the African American of the 1920s.[13] He is American, and as such, linked to the descendants of Europe and a part of the culture of the "West." However, as long as America fails to live up to its constitutional ideals, the country will not be a home to its black population. "Nostalgia" ends with a wistful query: "the black American is something entirely new under the sun. Shall he ever realize the land where he would be?" (158). The artists of the Harlem Renaissance were seeking to attain their constitutional rights and, by extension, a home by means of their art. As they were not quite accepted in their new homeland America, and so many generations removed from Africa, Europe appeared as an alternative place to search for acceptance and a home. Fauset's essay hence offers part of a motivation for African-Americans to leave for Europe at this time.

As Gertrude Stein put it with regard to the stream of Americans who came to Paris in the 1920s: "It was not what France gave you but what it did not take away from you that was important" (Marks and Edkins 201). The statement seems to suggest that freedom—and restrictions of freedom—is spatially enacted. Concordantly, the reason why the protagonists of *There Is Confusion*, *The Autobiography of an Ex-Colored Man*, and *Quicksand* decide to leave the US for Europe is that they feel their possibilities are, in some way, limited at home. The connection Stein makes between space and freedom leads to the question of how place affects what kind of social and cultural roles the African Americans—as represented in the fiction of Johnson, Fauset, and Larsen— were allowed to play. In the following, I will examine what place Europe occupies in the African-American literary imagination.

---

[13]There were, of course, those who were of another opinion, notably Marcus Garvey, founder of the Universal Negro Improvement Association. Within this organization, Garvey worked for the repatriation of black Americans to Africa (Lewis 34-44).

Chapter 2

Between two worlds: on being an African American in Europe

If we don't know where we are, we have little chance of knowing who we are.

Ralph Ellison

African-American travelers and writers in Europe

In the nineteenth century, the number of African-American travelers who had the physical and financial means to go abroad was rather small, even after Emancipation. Most of those who could after all go abroad in the nineteenth and early twentieth centuries visited France and England. France, in particular, has occupied a special place in the American imagination since the French Revolution. The ideals of liberty and egalitarianism had been made a part of the American constitution, but for the African-American population of America they had so far proved to be unfulfilled promises. Many early travelers were attracted to the country where these ideas had originated, and they often found a more hospitable environment there than in their own home country. Frederick Douglass, for example, visited the country several times during the latter part of the nineteenth century, and to him France was "the embodiment of 'liberté, egalité, fraternité'" (Fabre 32). African Americans often went to France in search of an education not available at home. A major link between France and African America was New Orleans in the former French colony Louisiana, where French culture lived on and race laws were a little less strict (for more on the New Orleans connection, see Fabre 9-21).

However, for many Anglophone African-American travelers, England offered an advantage over France in that there was no language barrier to be overcome. Among the first African-American travelers to Europe were former slaves turned abolitionist workers, who went on lecture tours. At the beginning of the nineteenth century, there was a strong movement against slavery in England, which served as a model for the North American abolitionists. Many American workers for the abolitionist cause came to England to rally support; and as slavery was abolished in England in 1833, the country sometimes served as a haven for black Americans before the American Civil War. France, however, did not abolish slavery in her colonies until about a decade later. In the slave narratives written for the abolitionist cause in the late eighteenth and the nineteenth century, which were the first prose works by African Americans, Europe was often figured in positive terms as a place of refuge from racial discrimination. Harriet Jacobs, writing her story of life in bondage under the pseudonym Linda Brent, travels to England as the nursemaid of a northern American family after having escaped slavery. Later, she goes back to England to try to find help getting her book published by English abolitionists. Other early travelers were missionaries, such as the Methodists Zilpha Elaw and Amanda Berry Smith, and, as mentioned above, people who had come to get an education not available at home. [14]

William Wells Brown, a former slave, worked as an anti-slavery lecturer and was selected as a delegate to the International Peace Congress in Paris in 1849. The Peace Congress was a huge meeting with over 800 delegates from countries throughout the Western world, presided over by Victor Hugo. An account of Brown's experiences at the congress was published in 1855 under the title *The American Fugitive in Europe: Sketches of Places and People Abroad.* [15] When the Fugitive Slave Law was passed in the US in 1850, Brown could

---

[14] In their survey of two centuries of African-American travel writing, *A Stranger in the Village* (1998), Farah J. Griffin and Cheryl J. Fish identify a couple of main groups of travelers (not all of them went to Europe but to Africa, Russia, or the American West). There are adventurers, such as Matthew Henson who was part of Robert Peary's expedition to the North Pole in 1909, missionaries to Africa (missionary work being one of the few opportunities for women to travel in connection with work in the nineteenth century), other travelers to Africa, France, and Russia. From the 1930s and onwards the travelers are categorized as statesmen, scholars and journalists, as well as visitors and tourists. Among the former was Booker T. Washington whose account, "The Man Farthest Down," (1912), which compares the conditions of African Americans with those of the white European working class, was written after a visit to Italy.

[15] According to *The Oxford Companion to African-American Literature*, *The American Fugitive* is a revised edition of *Three Years in Europe, or Places I Have Seen and People I Have Met* (1852). This book is a first-person narrative that is considered the first travel book by an African American. It consists of more than twenty letters describing William Wells Brown's experiences from visits to a similar number of European countries.

not return to his home country. He stayed on in Europe until 1854, when he was able to purchase his freedom. William Wells Brown chose to set what is usually regarded as the first African-American novel, *Clotel, or, The President's Daughter: A Narrative of Slave Life in the United States* (1853), partly in Europe. The story of Clotel is loosely built upon Thomas Jefferson's relationship with his slave Sally Hemings, by whom it is assumed that he had at least one child (Fabre 10). The part of Brown's novel that is set in Europe concerns the slave George who, after a masked escape north to Canada, embarks for England (Liverpool) where he lives, passing as white. Within a few years, he rises from porter to clerk to businessman. On a trip to Dunkirk, France, George is re-united with his beloved Mary (the dead Clotel's daughter), and the two are finally happily married.

Representations of Europe are also found in the novels of Pauline Hopkins, who was active as editor, novelist, and leading proponent of activist black journalism during the post-Reconstruction era. In three of her novels; *Contending Forces: A Romance Illustrative of Negro Life North and South* (1900); *Winona: A Tale of Negro Life in the South and Southwest* (1902); and *Of One Blood; or, The Hidden Self* (1902-03), England, in contrast to the US, is depicted as a country where people are not judged on the basis of their skin color and a place of refuge from racist discrimination. Europe also figures as the source of high culture in all three novels (Lindberg-Seyersted 115-17).

All of the most important African American leaders and activists went to Europe at some point during their careers: Frederick Douglass, Booker T. Washington and W.E.B. DuBois. Among the women we find, for example, the educator Anna Julia Cooper, who was the first African American to obtain a Ph.D. from Sorbonne University in Paris in 1902, dealing with French attitudes and policies concerning the slave trade during the period of the French revolution. Mary Church Terrell, who was the president of the National Association for Colored Women (NACW), traveled to Europe on several occasions, for example to attend the International Congress of Women held in Berlin in 1904. She was also a delegate to the International Peace Congress of 1919, in Paris (Fabre 38-39).

Fabre suggests that the example of Terrell and other early visiting activists and educators was of great importance to the Renaissance of the 1920s, thereby pointing to the international scope of that movement: "the New Negro movement was far from being limited to the American scene and [...] the European, and specifically French, experiences of its forerunners at the turn of the century were probably instrumental in fostering this renaissance" (42). Again, Paris appears in a central position in African-American culture at this time. As Fabre sees it, the African-American cultural flowering of the inter-war years was from the outset an international phenomenon, stemming from intercultural exchanges across the Atlantic. African-American music, particularly jazz, was to be an important part of this. I have mentioned Josephine Baker and the musicians who stayed on in Paris after the war to create a vital jazz scene there, but they had predecessors in the entertainers who traveled to Europe in the late nineteenth century. A survey of this tradition of entertainment with African-American roots provides a context for interpreting the vaudeville performance in *Quicksand*, as well as a perspective on the discussion of the genuinely African-American art forms that James Weldon Johnson enumerates in *The Autobiography* and in his critical writings. The slippages between whiteness and blackness are a vital part of these performances, and in the contemporary debate about them anxieties of racial purity and difference surface.

Minstrelsy prepared the way for jazz by popularizing African-American music in the late nineteenth century. In *Impossible Purities: Blackness, Femininity and Victorian Culture* (1998), Jennifer DeVere Brody focuses on the British version of blackface minstrelsy. According to Brody, minstrel shows—with predominantly white male performers—in England have an almost equally long tradition as in America. After the publication of Harriet Beecher Stowe's *Uncle Tom's Cabin* in 1852, there was a spate of adaptations for the stage, more or less true to the book version: "In the six-month period between September 1852 and February 1853, the Lord Chamberlain, who censored plays, approved more than fifteen productions based on the novel" (Brody 75). Cultural events thus traveled quickly over the Atlantic, in this case probably with the help of British abolitionists who were interested in the fate of their darker brothers and sisters. Uncle Tom, of course, was a character who, with his Christian faith and submissiveness, found sympathy with many white people. He was also one of the first black characters to occupy a central role in literature and drama (Toll 28). However, the docile Uncle Tom was to become a stereotype of contested status within the African-American community, and the many minstrel-like stage versions of the novel contributed to this conception.

But there were other issues involved in British minstrelsy than creating stereotypical portraits of black people, most importantly fears of miscegenation and racial impurity. To Brody, what is really at stake in this genre of performance is whiteness: "Indeed, the entire practice of blackface minstrelsy as it was performed in England had everything to do with the construction of Englishness as white. Taking on the guise of another was a sure way to discover oneself or at least to attempt to define through negation of what one might be if not who one was" (85). In other words, the mask of burnt cork served to project an image of foolery, underneath which could be discerned a presence of whiteness functioning as point of reference. The opposition of white and black was embodied in the stage performer, the presence of the one being the guarantor of meaning of the other. But to Brody, the minstrel show's attempt thus to naturalize and essentialize characteristics as typically white or typically black actually served the opposite purpose: "By imitating black people, pretending to copy black forms, 'white' practitioners mixed up the difference between imitation and original and invented the blackness they copied" (85). By extension, if blackness was a fluid marker that could be improvised in this manner, whiteness, as its direct opposite, could too.

In his meticulous study *Black People: Entertainers of African Descent in Europe, and Germany* (1997), Rainer E. Lotz observes that, at the turn of the twentieth century, colored musical clowns known as "Negro Clowns, Negro Eccentrics or Negro Knockabouts" were very popular in Europe (Lotz 151). Apart from the use of instruments typical of the minstrel show, such as the tambourine, harmonica, banjo and bones, very few facts are actually known about the delivery and repertoire of these performances. Often, the instruments were home-made from such articles as brooms or chairs. What is also known is that these clowns, like the minstrels, were often black and nearly always blackened-up. One of the most popular African-American musical clowns in Europe at the turn of the century was Edgar H. Jones who, according to Lotz, was "an acrobat, a pantomimist, a dancer, and multi-instrumentalist" able to perform in three different languages (152). An 1894 German advertisement for Jones's show presents him as "Mr. Edgar Jones, Original Musical-Excentric (Wirklicher Schwarzer)," and the assertion that he was "really black" indicates that white people blackened up and performed in this genre too, and that blackness was an asset making for a greater authenticity of the performance (Lotz 153). The fact that these clowns were professional entertainers, and their performance not one of "natural blackness," was largely neglected. Jones toured Scandinavia—performing at the Copenhagen Circus (which is the locus of the vaudeville performance in Larsen's *Quicksand*) several times between 1893 and 1895—and extensively in Germany, the Netherlands, as well as other countries in Central Europe before he disappeared somewhere in Siberia in 1906.

Among the earliest groups to become famous in Europe were the Fisk Jubilee Singers, whose renditions of the spirituals were among the major African-American contributions to American culture in James Weldon Johnson's view. The singers went on several European tours, to raise funds for Fisk University in Nashville, Tennessee. Fisk was one of the first black American universities, opened after the Civil War in 1866. This group is interesting because it was quite different from the other African-American entertainers that could be seen and heard in Europe at this time. The presence of this serious group of college-educated singers on the stage, with a repertoire consisting of spirituals with a Biblical content, was a source of confusion to their European audiences. This act did not have the comic edge that the minstrel performance had, dealing rather with matters like slavery, injustice, faith and hope for a better world to come. Further, Lotz notes that a new and important aspect of the Fisk singers' performance was their choice of formal clothing: "Black tie and tails had replaced the plantation costumes, melons, coon song and banjo stereotypes of monstrous minstrelsy. In this, as in so many aspects of black entertainment, the original Fisk singers had led the way" (162). Avoiding dressing in the working clothes of plantation slavery or the comic, often over-sized garments of the musical clowns, the Jubilee singers fashioned an image of themselves as spiritual brethren and sisters, not unlike their European audiences.

Although they were eventually very successful and became very popular in Europe, not least in Germany where the group stayed more often than anywhere else, press reactions in Sweden and Denmark were initially mixed. By way of contextualizing Larsen's depictions of the Danes' susceptibility to the black presence on the stage, Erik Wiedemann's suggestion for an interpretation of the mixed Danish reception of the Fisk Jubilee Singers in 1895 is valid: "spirituals [...] præsenterer negeren for den hvide i en fulstændig 'sikker' sindsstemning. Her er negeren underdanig, religiøs, overtroisk, dybt troende og uden tilbøjelighed til at synge ord, som de hvide frygter at de ikke kan forstå" (Wiedemann 44).[16] That is to say, the singers seemed to conform to an image of African Americans as former slaves that the white Danes could understand, having adopted the Christian faith of their masters and comporting themselves with humility. In this seeming assimilation, they were not a threat or challenge to their white audience. The Fisk Jubilee Singers left the audience

---

[16] "the spirituals [...] present the Negro to the white person in a completely "safe" frame of mind. Here, the Negro is meek, religious, superstitious, faithful and not likely to sing words that white people fear they will not understand."

feeling "safe," notes Wiedemann, in that they did not call into question the order of things in the way that the jazz musicians of the twentieth century would.

In *The Autobiography,* James Weldon Johnson referred to the cakewalk as an original form of African-American art. This was actually a highly contested form of art. The dance had its roots in the dance competitions held among the slaves on southern plantations, where the winning couple were awarded the prize of a cake. The cakewalk actually originated as a form of parody of the movements occurring in the dances the slaves had seen their white owners perform. This created the incongruous situation that the fashionable Paris couples who took to the dance were in fact engaged in a parody of themselves (Wiedemann 48). Wiedemann further notes that Danish critics were worried about what effect this "barbaric" dance would have on European civilization (this is a kind of criticism that will recur with reference to jazz).

We have seen how nineteenth-century African-American travelers sought out Europe as a place of freedom from racial discrimination, a place to get a better education than at home, or a place where one could find an appreciative audience for one's art. In the literature about Europe, we find that these are recurrent themes. Freedom, education and art were also important parts of the early twentieth-century "New Negro" ideal. In her survey of the depictions of Europe in African-American fiction, Brita Lindberg-Seyersted writes:

> In nineteenth-century literature Europe appears as a potential refuge for escaped slaves and as support for abolitionists; as a place for acquiring education and culture; and in post-Reconstruction years for providing a certain breathing space at a distance from the demeaning restrictions of Jim Crowism. In our century the image of Europe has been more ambiguous, expressing both attraction and distrust. (126)

The tension between "attraction and distrust" will be further explored and discussed below. This ambiguity can be related to the historical moment of the "New Negro" and to the issues of freedom, education, and art.

The travel motif in African-American literature[17]

In the African-American cultural tradition, marked as it is by bondage and restricted mobility, traveling assumes a particularly symbolic role. The original, or archetypal, journey is the forced movement of more than 60 million Africans to life in bondage in the Americas. Literary descriptions of this often horrific voyage across the Atlantic, known as "the Middle Passage," are found in the eighteenth- and nineteenth-century slave narratives, Charles Johnson's *Middle Passage* from 1990 forming a recent example. Another such archetypal journey describes the flight from slavery in the American South to freedom in the North. This is one of the central motifs of the slave narratives. In *From Behind the Veil: A Study of Afro-American Narrative* (1979), Robert B. Stepto links this symbolical journey to the very roots of African-American literature: "[I]f an Afro-American literary tradition exists, it does so not because there is a sizeable chronology of authors and texts, but because those authors and texts collectively seek their own literary forms—their own admixtures—bound historically and linguistically to a shared pregeneric myth" (ix-x). This pregeneric myth is the quest for literacy and freedom, symbolized by the ascent from South to North. The motif of the journey, then, is a constitutive element of African-American literature. Before the publication of w. e. b. Du Bois's seminal work *The Souls of Black Folk* (1903), the most important journey in the African-American literary tradition was the journey north, to freedom, as typically represented in the slave narratives. In Stepto's terminology, *The Souls* is the prime example of a "narrative of immersion," in which the narrator travels into the Black Belt of the South to immerse himself in, and learn more about, life there. This is a move undertaken to counteract loneliness or alienation from one's people and one's roots experienced by the protagonist after the ascent North (167). Both kinds of ritualized journey can be found in the works of Johnson and Larsen.

In the post-Reconstruction era, the fictionalized journey from South to North is primarily figured as a journey from country to city. In *"Who set you*

---

[17] In their anthology of African-American travel writing, Griffin and Fish list the genres included in their definition of travel narrative: "autobiographical materials and selections from books, pamphlets, personal letters, notes, diaries, dispatches, travel guides, official reports, lectures, and ethnographies. The genre of travel writing is blessed with a hybridity that incorporates and employs many other sources, including polemics, manifestos, oratory, anthropology, poetry, letter writing, maps, and fiction"(xiv). My focus is only on fictional accounts.

flowin'?" The African-American Migration Narrative (1995), Farah Jasmine Griffin discusses migration as a major theme in a wide range of genres in twentieth-century African-American cultural production, such as literature, painting, music, etc. At the center of her concept of African-American migration is the move from the traditional, rural lifestyle of the South to the fast-paced, industrialized urban North, retaining the associations of a "freer North" from the slave narratives. The demographic shifts of the Great Migration of the early twentieth century were instrumental in the formation of the Harlem Renaissance. The northward journey of the Great Migration assumes importance as a way of claiming space in American society and forms part of the self-definition as Americans. Thus, the ascent from South to North, characteristic of the Great Migration, is an essential part of the symbolism of modern African American life, indicating the link between freedom and geographical space (Griffin 3).

Another significant trajectory of African-American traveling—literary as well as historical—is the journey eastwards across the Atlantic. To leave America for Africa is to embark on a symbolically charged journey; a reversal of the Middle Passage. Traveling to Europe amounts to meeting a continent with a different set of connotations. It is significant that the protagonists of the novels I study are all mulattoes. That is, for them the notion of a homeland or place of origin is dual—in both a literal and a figurative sense. The "Old World" of Europe is associated with progress and modernity, together with a highly developed culture, whereas Africa denotes a different kind of "Old World." Rather than being associated with enlightenment, Africa was often described as the Dark Continent in reference to its vast and largely unknown interior, its inhabitants, as well as a cultural darkness.[18] According to Paul Gilroy, "Africa emerged [...] as a mythic counterpart to modernity in the Americas" (113). While none of the novels of my study makes explicit reference to Africa or to European encounters with Africans, Europe functions metaphorically as a link to Africa. As we will see in the following analyses of the novels, being in Europe leads the protagonists to face and question their African heritage.[19]

In this charting of the meaning of traveling in African-American literature, it is useful to consider what Ulla Rahbek writes concerning Afro-British travel

---

[18] For a discussion of the myth of Africa as the Dark Continent see Patrick Brantlinger, "Victorians and Africans: The Genealogy of the Myth of the Dark Continent" in Gates, *Race, Writing and Difference* 185-222.

[19] For more on early African-American travelers to Africa, see Griffin and Fish 97-149.

writing, which she suggests that we see as a "portmanteau genre, capable of embodying several qualities at the same time, such as socio-political reflection, ideological analysis, personal growth, narrative experimentation and the sentimental manipulation of willing readers" (22). To the black British writers, travel writing is not merely a question of relating adventure stories. There are a host of other concerns of and motives for writing about traveling, such as education or instruction of the reader along the lines suggested in the quotation. It is "a literature set out to delight and teach: teach the reader about history and particularly about the history of slavery; about economics and geography; about ontology and semantics (where does the diasporic writer belong and what does 'home' really mean?); and, of course, about travel as such" (Rahbek 22). As I aim to show in the following analyses of the novels of Johnson, Fauset, and Larsen, the journeys of their protagonists become a device for initiating discussions on topics such as race, culture, history, home, and belonging.

How, then, can the travel motif be related to the construction of race? Travel writing is a genre whose origins are closely linked to European imperialism and exploration outside of Europe, offering a Eurocentric viewpoint on other cultures. M. L. Pratt notes that the genre of travel writing in itself implies a colonial situation: to relate "them" and "theirs" to "us" and "ours" involves passing judgment on another according to a limited perspective which is seldom, if ever, acknowledged by the writer. In a similar vein, Stuart Hall observes that, thanks to the European's dominant means of representation, such as the colonial discourse, books of adventure and exploration, exotic novels, ethnographic studies and travel narratives, and so on, the image of the black subject has been fixed in the mind of the European. In this sense, the European has narrated "blackness" and given it a certain meaning (Eriksson 239). Moreover, to Hall "blackness" is just this narration: it is not something natural or fixed, but it is something that is continually constructed, expressed, and represented. We can thus see how African-American novels depicting travels to Europe, such as those of Johnson, Fauset, and Larsen, can function as re-writings of this kind of narrative. The European journeys of their protagonists reverse the pattern of colonialism, as the subaltern enters the sphere of the dominant, Western cultural tradition. In the process, new representations of African-American identity can be written.

Double Consciousness

Traveling activates a double consciousness, one of the central metaphors of the African-American cultural imagination, formulated by W.E.B. DuBois in *The Souls of Black Folk* (1903):

> ...the Negro is sort of seventh son, born with a veil, and gifted with second-sight in this American world,—a world which yields him no true self-consciousness, but only lets him see himself through the revelation of the other world. It is a peculiar sensation, this double-consciousness, this sense of always looking at one's self through the eyes of others, of measuring one's soul by the tape of a world that looks on in amused contempt and pity. One ever feels this two-ness,—an American, a Negro; two souls, two thoughts, two unreconciled strivings, two warring ideals in one dark body, whose dogged strength alone keeps it from being torn asunder. (Writings 364-365)

Du Bois thus considers African-American identity as essentially split, dual. In spite of having been a part of American society for centuries, the African American is not fully integrated into it (granted basic civil rights, for instance) and occupies the position of an outsider looking in. As a result, s/he will experience a sense of alienation from American society. According to DuBois, this situation also affects one's sense of self: instead of gaining "true self-consciousness" one's self-concept is dependent on the reflection of the look of the other. Being black in early twentieth-century America often meant encountering degrading stereotypes, for example about one's intellectual capacity, appearance, and personal habits. "Double consciousness" also refers to being both African and American and to the striving to recognize—and reconcile—these two aspects of one's personality. The double consciousness that DuBois identified as characteristic of the African American's existence rests on an awareness of the Other's powers of interpretation of the Self. DuBois's metaphor recognizes the centrality of the visual, as one is put in one's place by the other's look. But it also describes a condition that allows a certain vantage point from which to observe the world around one and one's own place in it. "Double consciousness" as a condition of existence is embodied by the mulatto, who is sometimes able to lead separate lives in the white and the black worlds. Just as the mulatto traveler moves between continents, s/he is able to move between black and white communities.

The metaphor of double consciousness is made literal in the texts of Johnson, Fauset, and Larsen. As it rests on the notion that one's existence depends on being recognized by another, double consciousness is fundamentally concerned with sight and perspective. The notion of visibility—and its counterpart invisibility—is of vital importance in the discussion of African-American identity. Vision and visibility are crucial to the process of racialization that the authors depict in their novels. They explore the tension between vision, connoting powers of definition, and visibility, as in being the object of definition. Double consciousness gives the protagonists a keen awareness of perspective and right of interpretation. In these texts, double consciousness relates significantly to performance and/or place, and, of course, to the character of the mulatto. The concept of double consciousness constitutes another important link between traveling and performance, since both concepts depend to a great extent on visual impressions and require an act of interpretation by the involved parties, and relate to place. Both traveling and performance imply interaction, between traveler and 'travelee' (to borrow Marie Louise Pratt's term for the people encountered on one's journey) and between performer and spectator. As the notion of double consciousness indicates, there is yet another convolution involved here in the slippage between visibility and invisibility. Invisibility is a recurring metaphor for the situation of the African-American in American society, belonging to a group that is visible, that is, clearly marked "different," and yet invisible with respect to civil rights. Thus, the visible difference of blackness from the white norm paradoxically makes black people *invis*ible as subjects. In fiction, Ralph Ellison's novel *Invisible Man*, 1952, epitomizes this position that is at the same time one of extreme visibility and invisibility.

In their survey of African-American travel writing during the past two centuries, Griffin and Fish connect subjectivity and space by means of a reference to Du Bois's metaphor of double consciousness. They claim that going abroad often makes the African-American travelers realize the extent to which they are, in fact, American:

> [...] these travellers often find that in spite of their critiques of the land of their birth, they are made to feel their sense of being American on foreign soil. With classical educations and a fairly elite status within African-American communities, many of the travellers/observers included here tend to reproduce at least some values of Western superiority despite a desire to challenge white supremacy and classist, nationalist, or gendered barriers. This

contradiction reminds us that when African-American travellers
enter into the "contact zone" and confront otherness, they take
their values and sense of being American with them wherever they
go. As Eddy L. Harris writes, illustrating his sense of what W.E.B.
Du Bois called "double consciousness:" "I am an American. And
I am black. I live and travel with two cultural passports, the one
very much stamped with European culture and sensibilities...the
other was issued from the uniquely black experience...we are an
American people, products of a new culture and defined by it."
(xiv)

"Double consciousness" is thus useful in accounting for the African American's
intermediary position between cultures. The reference to Eddy L. Harris adds
another aspect to the duality of African-American identity. Here, Harris contrasts black culture with European/American culture—and the synthesis
is "African American." Not only is the American new in relation to the old
culture of Europe but, in the case of the African American, race is an additional dimension playing into her/his modernity. The "newness" of the African
American is an important imaginary concept during the inter-war years, as
the aspiration for a definition of a "New Negro" indicates. This new African
American is a cultural hybrid, and the trope of space highlights this aspect
of her/his identity. The New World Africanity of the mulatto protagonists of
Johnson, Fauset, and Larsen is thrown into relief in the European episodes, as
we see how they are received in Europe.

The symbolic geography of Europe

What kind of fictional space is the contact zone of Europe in the works of
Johnson, Fauset, and Larsen? What is the purpose of including the European
episodes at all? How are we to understand "Europe" as a geographical and
cultural entity? In my analyses of the novels, I often find that rather than, or
perhaps in addition to, considering the specific history and culture of each
country the protagonists visit, the notion of "Europe" is important as the antithesis of America. This can be seen, for example, in how the older history and
culture of the Old World is often contrasted to that of the New World. One
motivation for the inclusion of these episodes is that Europe is a space without
the imaginary limitations that pertain to America, and that this has a bearing

on the question of race. Reading these representations of Europe as symbolic geographies makes it possible to see that they are constructed so as to allow for the criticism of social and historical conditions in America. The meaning of "Europe" here is quite a reversal of what it has meant to generations of emigrants, who instead have fled the restrictions and hardships they experienced in Europe. The European setting represents a white world accessible to the black American. It is a fictional space where encounters that could not take place in the US can be staged, and onto which visions of the future are projected. As my introductory survey of African-American writing on Europe has shown, Europe was a place where African Americans went during the nineteenth century in search of freedom from slavery, or to find educational opportunities not available at home. Throughout history liberty, classical humanist educational ideals and civilization are, together with Christianity, the principles around which the idea of Europe has revolved (Wilson 13).

Although Benedict Anderson's concept of an "imagined community" was developed in relation to nation formation, it helps account for the sense of unity behind the idea of Europe in the novels I discuss. Just like the members of a nation, the members of the European community "will never know most of their fellow-members, meet them, or even hear of them, yet in the minds of each lives the image of their communion" (Anderson 6). [20] A sense of a shared past is a significant part of a European "imagined community." The construction of Europe centers on a notion of "a fantasy homeland that goes hand in hand with a retrospective invention of history as well as a moralisation of geography" (Delanty 8). Behind this "fantasy homeland" lie unifying narratives of origin and destiny. This is similar to the construction of the "nation" but in the case of Europe "the mystique of civilisation…is cultivated and reinforced by myths of high culture" (Delanty 8). Delanty argues that the notion of a unified European past is a construct of Romanticism. Thus, "given the politically divisive nature of the European polity, the idea of Europe as a culturally homogenizing notion made sense only on the level of culture. In this sense, then, the European cultural tradition has been invented retrospectively. Europe became identified with its cultural artefacts: the great cathedrals, opera houses, cafés

---

[20] Already in the 18th century, the French philosopher Voltaire would refer to Europe as a "république litteraire;" an expression that indicates his perception of the existence of shared, particularly European, customs and manners relating to education and worldview (Wilson and Dusser 60). The idea of a similar kind of European community is no less potent today, as is evident from the formation and ongoing enlargement of the EU.

and royal houses" (Delanty 80-81). This idea is echoed in the fictional settings of Johnson and Larsen, which are often urban, and centered on cultural venues, such as theaters or cafés.

Following in the tradition of Henry James, the American is featured as culturally "raw" in comparison with the sophisticated, often aristocratic European. The situation of the African American in a European setting of "high" culture is well described by James Baldwin. In the essay "Stranger in the Village," the African American remains a "stranger" to Europe and to the cultural artifacts of European civilization:

> ...this village, even were it incomparably more remote and incredibly more primitive, is the West, the West onto which I have been so strangely grafted. These people cannot be, from the point of view of power, strangers anywhere in the world; they have made the modern world, in effect, even if they do not know it. The most illiterate among them is related, in a way that I am not, to Dante, Shakespeare, Michelangelo, Aeschylus, Da Vinci, Rembrandt, and Racine; the cathedral at Chartres says something to them which it cannot say to me, as indeed would New York's Empire State Building, should anyone here ever see it. Out of their hymns and dances come Beethoven and Bach. Go back a few centuries and they are in their full glory – but I am in Africa, watching the conquerors arrive. (121)

The passage shows how Baldwin's stay in the Swiss village gives him a sense of his designated place in Western history. While recognizing that this place is the product of material historical circumstances, he still interprets his own subject position as an ahistorical phenomenon, that is, a position that can never be transcended or altered. Any achievements of his in the cultural sphere would not change his position, since true belonging to European culture is only to be had by birthright. "Culture" and race are thus conflated, as culture is seen not as something you acquire but as something you are born into. In *The Meaning of Race* (1996), Kenan Malik argues for the similarities of cultural and racial formalism when "[c]ulture becomes particularist and exclusive, delineating a common past to which some can belong and some cannot. And that past becomes determinist and teleological, holding power over the present through tradition and rootedness" (186). Baldwin's cathedral is a striking spatial expression of such European ideals as Christianity and "high" culture. The fictional

African-American protagonists of Fauset and Larsen share with Baldwin the outsider's perspective on the construction of European culture, spatialized in various material forms. The fictional encounters with Europe provide us with a lens through which we can see "Western civilization" and the role of the African American in the construction of this civilization. Implicit in the move to the European continent is the discussion of "the problem and meaning of Western civilization as a whole and the relation of Negroes and other minority groups to it" as Richard Wright put it about his own journey to France (Gilroy 165).

The inquiry into the importance of race, along with culture, in the construction of a European identity was initiated with the academic field we call post-colonial studies. For example, Edward Said observes in *Orientalism* (1978), which along with the works of Frantz Fanon is considered to have inaugurated post-colonial studies, that the European identity that grew out of imperial expansion and colonization centered on the dichotomy between Self and Other.[21] In the Middle Ages, European identity was first and foremost a Christian identity, marking the difference from the Muslim East. After the Reformation this antithesis was replaced by one of civilization versus nature, of 'civilized Europeans' versus 'uncivilized barbarians.' Thus, the European identity is largely a negative identity based on upholding a "difference" that would legitimize the conquest and subjugation of non-Europeans. As Europe became more secularized, the scientific discourse of race replaced religion as the constituent of essential "difference." As a result of the colonial expansion of the nineteenth century, European identity was partly formed in negation of the "dark continent" of Africa as well (Brantlinger 185). In other words, part of the European identity was the notion of being non-African (or non-black). Another aspect of the linking of geography and human difference is found in the work of philosophers such as Kant and Hegel, who saw differences between human beings as caused by environmental factors.

In *Orientalism*, Said looks into the symbolic aspects of material space as he analyzes the relation between the West and the "Orient." That is, by applying discourse theory to geography he studies what is beyond the physical geography and shows how ideology affects our perception of the world. From his analysis of the Orient as an "imagined geography" we see that any physical space can be historically contextualized and studied as reflective of a certain worldview. Furthermore, Said makes us see how space has played an important part in European self-defi-

---

[21]See e. g .Said's *Orientalism*, Miles'*Racism* and Delanty's *Inventing Europe*.

nition. The Eastern part of Europe and beyond, which is usually referred to by the term Orient, is in Said's analysis not so much a physical place as an ideological construct created to reinforce a sense of a shared European identity. It served the function of "negative identification," that is, onto the vague concept "orient" were projected ideas of difference that ultimately served the purpose of reinforcing a sense of "us" that could be set against "them." Together with a sense of a shared history, this "imagined geography" serves to increase, in this case European, self-respect through the dramatization of the distance and difference between what is close at hand and what is far away.

The parameters that form a place are not only geographical but also social. We can, for example, see the contiguity of geometrical space and social space as we begin to analyze how social order is spatialized in terms of proximity and distance, private and public, high and low. One striking example of this is the social order of American post-Reconstruction and early twentieth-century segregationist policies, according to which public space was divided into separate spheres for white and black Americans. The doctrine of "separate but equal," formalized in the case of *Plessy v Ferguson* in 1896, held that transportation, seating in theaters, drinking fountains and so on, were to be separated on the basis of skin color. This case confirmed the "one-drop rule," namely that "a person with one-eighth Negro ancestry could be legally defined as Negro under Louisiana law, even though, as in the case of *Plessy*, that ancestry was not physically visible" (Ginsberg 7). This paradox of "invisible blackness" made for the practice of race passing. In response to the physical and geographical circumscription of segregation many light-skinned black Americans chose to pass for white, as a means of gaining access to otherwise restricted space. It is this kind of spatialization of race that Du Bois's concept "the color line" addresses, stemming from this historical context and suggesting as it does a barrier (the famous metaphor of the "veil") between the black and the white worlds. A similar type of division is seen in more figurative terms in the discussion of high culture versus low culture, how the salons of high culture, and activities such as ballet, are closed to Joanna Marshall, the heroine of Jessie Fauset's *There Is Confusion*. This linkage between space and race through the color line will be further investigated in the following section on performance.

These examples also suggest the connection between space and power. According to Michel Foucault, "[n]othing is more material, physical, corporal, than the exercise of power" (Gordon 57-58). In several of his writings (for instance, *Discipline and Punish* and *The Birth of the Clinic*) Foucault shows how space is used to mark and separate out those who are considered differ-ent, and therefore do not belong in the social order, be it those who are defined as mentally ill, sexually aberrant, or criminal and dangerous. An example of the link between space and power in the African-American context is that, at the beginning of the 1920s, Chicago—and presumably other northern cities as well—was flooded by black people from the South within two weeks of a lynching (Griffin 16-17). And, of course, the demographic shifts of the Great Migration itself were in part the result of frustration with continued segrega-tion in the post-Reconstruction South coupled to the hope of finding greater freedom and room for social advancement in the North.

Griffin and Fish claim that, in the nineteenth century, travel was a "sur-vival tactic" when faced with lynching and restrictions on account of race, as well as a means to gain the possibility of social mobility through education and increased job opportunities. Getting away from the US was linked to a search for freedom, in terms of race, gender, and class (xv-xvi). Traveling to a new place meant not only a geographical transition, but a transition between different cognitive spheres as well. In the novels in question here, the protago-nists journey from the New World to the Old, which involves the navigation of a very different cultural landscape. A whole social and ideological spectrum is involved in this crossing to another continent. In order to discuss these im-material aspects of material space, the term "symbolic geography" will be used in the sense suggested by Robert Stepto in *From Behind the Veil*. Dealing with the topic of geo-cultural symbolism in African-American narrative, Stepto uses the term "symbolic geography" to account for how certain regions in time and space offer "spatial expressions of social structures and ritual grounds" (67). He goes on to define the social structure that confronts the early African-American literary hero-narrator as slavery, suggesting that "'institutionalized racism' may better describe the more subtle structures besetting the modern pilgrims" (ibid.). The concept "symbolic geography" forms a basis for my anal-ysis of the meaning of the European episodes in the novels of Johnson, Fauset, and Larsen. As we chart the journeys of the protagonists we will see what "spa-tial expressions of social structures" they encounter, as well as to what extent 'institutionalized racism' merely provides a point of departure and/or whether they can escape its effects through the journey. The analyses relate to the three themes associated with African-American traveling: freedom; education (here understood as *Bildung* and cultural 'literacy'); art and performance as related to African-American identity.

Essential to Griffin's previously mentioned study of migration narratives, *Who set you flowin'?*, is the question of how the migrants confront and learn to navigate the new urban landscape. As they move from the familiar southern rural surroundings to the unknown northern city they need to learn the codes of urban life, to make the city topography legible. In a similar manner, the topography of the continent of Europe needs to be decoded by the visitors. As I see it, Europe is a "text" for the travelers to "read;" a text rife with signifiers concerning African-American identity. As they become increasingly literate they gain insight into the processes of racialization and stereotyping, and the limits and possibilities of life for the "New Negro" in Europe. Although the European places are comparatively free spheres in the novels, each has restrictions that need to be followed in accordance with race, gender, and class.

An ex-colored man in Europe

The nineteenth-century themes of freedom, education, and art in relation to Europe all appear in James Weldon Johnson's *The Autobiography of an Ex-Colored Man*. The search for freedom is the actual motive for the ex-colored man's journey to Europe, since he travels to escape from possible suspicion of involvement in a murder at "the Club" in New York.

Although the narrator's primary reason for leaving the US is related to suspicions of involvement in a *crime passionel* and not primarily to education, his stay in Europe actually leads to a development of his career plans. It is here he decides to dedicate his life to making African-American music "classic." What the ex-colored man means by this is, as Salim Washington has pointed out, to give African-American music "the stature and some of the characteristics of European art music" (246). The significance of this choice is further discussed in the following chapter.

The milieus described by James Weldon Johnson in *The Autobiography* are similar to those found in Larsen's *Quicksand*. Both novels are centered on urban settings and cultural venues, such as concert halls, museums, or city cafés. In "Restaging the Racial Contract: James Weldon Johnson's Signatory Strategies" (2002), Jennifer L. Schultz finds New York with its fluid social and geographic parameters "a physical (and metaphorical) stage upon which he can rehearse his cosmopolitan identity." One example of such New York milieus is the nightclub, known simply as the "Club" in the Tenderloin district that he frequents (the ten blocks between 23rd and 33rd Streets, one block to the west of Sixth Avenue). In the early twentieth century, such New York places of entertainment often served to connect black and white performers and inspired artistic collaboration, which led to increased racial integration of the stage as well as increased social mobility for black performers. Schultz also suggests that New York will later become a "point of orientation for him while he navigates other social landscapes" (Schultz 38). For example, he compares the life he and the millionaire set up for themselves in Paris to that in New York, entertaining guests at parties where the narrator acts as musician (83). In Europe, the narrator performs the part of the cosmopolitan, perfecting his French by engaging in conversations with Parisians in the outdoor cafés and traveling freely across the continent.

As in Baldwin's description of the cathedral at Chartres, the idea of Europe is in this way given spatial expression through architecture. The narrator of *The Autobiography* moves between several European cities, among which Paris and London are given pride of place. The narrator connects physical space with social structures when comparing the French and the British capitals:

> How these two cities typify the two peoples who built them! Even
> the sound of their names expresses a certain racial difference. Paris is
> the concrete expression of the gaiety, regard for symmetry, love of art,
> and, I might well add, of the morality of the French people. London
> stands for the conservatism, the solidarity, the utilitarianism, and, I
> might well add, the hypocrisy of the Anglo-Saxon. (100)

Marvin Garrett reads the ex-colored man's reflections (or "digressions" as he calls them) on London and Paris—and the hypocrisy of the French—while he is in Europe as projections onto others of his own dishonesty and guilt. This Garrett sees as one of the "major elements in the novel's artistic design" (Garrett 8). For example, the kind of generalizing comments that the narrator makes on the characteristics of the English and the French are not discerning on an individual level. Instead, the comments are ironic evidence that the narrator is guilty of the same generalizations that he personally suffers from in his own life. On the whole his comments on Paris especially express the particular fondness for France that is also found, for example, in Douglass' writings. The narrator notes that the fascination appears to be mutual and that Americans are very popular in Paris.

According to Robert Stepto, *The Autobiography* "binds multiple expressions of mobility to multiple expressions of confinement," and he sees in this a link to tropes and conventions of the slave narrative (Stepto 97). For example, throughout the book the narrator travels widely over both the American and the European continents. He is endowed with attributes that facilitate his mobility between different physical and social environments, such as the fairness of his skin which makes it difficult to place him in a racial schema, the ease with which he acquires new languages and jobs. But there are certain restrictions to his mobility. Stepto notes that, despite all of the ex-colored man's traveling, he still shows distrust in open spaces, particularly in America (101). In Paris, however, he moves freely, apart from two encounters with racial overtones. These are significant events that propel the action in a new direction and have a bearing on the outcome of the novel. One of the events takes place at the Paris Opéra, where the narrator has gone to see *Faust*. Seated in front of him, he suddenly discovers, is his white father and a young girl who must be his half-sister, but he cannot approach them since he feels the matter of his color would be an embarrassment to his family. As Stepto suggests, this is an American dilemma being played out in Europe (102). Although they are in the imagined free space of Europe, the effects of American segregationist policies are still felt. This scene, which he calls "a real-life tragedy here in your midst" as opposed to that on the stage, relates to Gounod's opera in another way as well. It is against the background of this European work of art that the narrator's own situation at the end of the story is to be understood. Having given up his black heritage, represented particularly by music, in order to become "an ordinarily successful white man" he feels as if he has "sold [his] birthright for a mess of pottage" (154). Like Faust, the ex-colored man transgresses his present social position only to lose his soul.[22]

The other instance is described by the narrator as the only time he was embarrassed to be an American in Europe. A recently acquired friend from one of the many outdoor cafés of Paris asks him if it is true that a man was burned alive in the US, eliciting the following reaction from the narrator: "I never knew what I stammered out to him as an answer. I should have felt relieved if I could even have said to him: 'Well, only one' " (100). This is an example of how the European setting is used to highlight the specific American problem of racial terror. By lifting an action or attitude out of the social context where it has become naturalized, the authors point to the historical and cultural construc-

---

[22] His fate, of course, also bears resemblance to that of Esau, Isaac's son, in Genesis 25:19-34

tion behind it. Staging an American problem in a European context makes it possible to see what is taken for granted in a different light.

Apart from these instances, his freedom is only compromised by his relationship to his millionaire travel companion through whom the journey was made possible at all. This man, with whom he has a close relationship, also functions as a sort of patron of the arts as he provides the means and motivation for the ex-colored man to practice and develop his musical skills. Their relationship is also indicative of the patronage system, common during the Harlem Renaissance, a situation echoed by Helga and Axel in Copenhagen. The bond between the millionaire and the narrator has been variously understood as that of father—son, or master—slave, and several critics also read homoeroticism into it (e. g. Cheryl Clarke). Going to Europe, the narrator is something like a kept man to the millionaire, who provides him with clothes and lodgings, and takes him along on several journeys on the European continent. Other indices of this type of relationship would be the possessive terms in which the ex-colored man refers to his employer, variously as "my millionaire friend" and "my millionaire." But at the same time as he expects greater success as a "black" musician, Johnson's narrator gives up his position as the white millionaire's paid performer. Leaving Europe is yet another reversal, it is a journey in search of artistic freedom and a return to the black world.

During his sojourn in the American South, where he has gone to dig up traditional African-American music, the narrator becomes the witness of a lynching of a black man. The fear he feels at having to hide from discovery by the lynch mob (and perhaps meeting with a similar fate) is coupled to shame at belonging to a people who is so badly treated:

> A great wave of humiliation and shame swept over me. Shame that
> I belonged to a race that could be so dealt with; and shame for
> my country, that it, the great example of democracy to the world,
> should be the only civilized, if not the only state on earth, where a
> human being would be burned alive. (137)

And again, when he finally decides to "pass," it is a decision motivated by shame: "I knew that it was shame, unbearable shame. Shame at being identified with a people that could with impunity be treated worse than animals. For certainly the law would restrain and punish the malicious burning alive of animals" (139). The narrator's shame here turns into self-hatred, which results in a disavowal of his blackness (the internalization of the other's malevolent look as discussed by Frantz Fanon is further explicated below, in relation to Larsen's *Quicksand*). This lynching scene foreshadows, with a kind of brutal irony, the outcome of the novel. The lynching of black men in the South was related to a deeply ingrained fear of miscegenation. For the stated purpose of protecting white women, black men were often lynched on mere suspicion, without proper legal trials. The black man's body is thus differently encoded than the black woman's: he is made out to be the perpetrator of (particularly) sexual violence, while she is the victim of similar abuse by white men. Thus, the soon-to-be ex-colored man hides from the mob in fear of being caught on sight. After this terrifying experience, he decides to live as a white man: "I finally made up my mind that I would neither disclaim the black race nor claim the white race; but that I would change my name, raise a mustache, and let the world take me for what it would; that it was not necessary for me to go about with a label of inferiority pasted across my forehead" (139). As an "ex-colored man" he will, in fact, marry a white woman and have children by her, thus living to incarnate the lynch mob's worst fear.

The double consciousness of a traveling writer: Jessie Fauset and the *Crisis* essays

Jessie Fauset's extended traveling on the European continent is reflected in much of her writing. She visited Paris on no less than three occasions: once before World War I, when she was still very young; again in 1924-1925 when she also went to the Midi—that is, Carcassonne, Avignon, Nîmes, Arles, Marseilles; and a third time in 1934 (Fabre 115-20). Each stay lasted a couple of months, and some of her time was spent on studies at the Sorbonne and Alliance Française. In 1925, she also took a tour of several other countries, such as England, Scotland, Belgium, Austria, Switzerland, and Italy, and even ventured into the French colony of Algeria (Fabre 117). During her travels, Fauset kept writing essays for *The Crisis* with reflections on her experiences in the "contact zone." Among these is "Yarrow Revisited" (Jan. 1925). The Wordsworth reference in the title signals the speaker's development from innocence to maturity, in addition to indicating Fauset's predilection for nineteenth-century literature. This time, Fauset has come to experience everyday "life as it is" in Paris, visiting during the winter months and finding the city cold and rainy indeed. Her longing for the comfort of a modern American gas heater is employed to set France off as charming, but hopelessly old-fashioned and quaint. Despite Fauset's widespread European traveling and obvious liking for France, taking up permanent residence in Paris is never an option. Instead, staying in Paris only makes her identification with America clearer:

> In Paris I find myself more American than I ever feel in America. I am more conscious of national characteristics than I have ever been in New York. When I say: 'We do that differently in America,' I do not mean that we do that differently in Harlem, or on 'You' Street in Washington, or on Christian Street in Philadelphia. I mean that Americans white and black do not act that way. And I recall now that practically all the buildings here bear on them the legend: 'Liberté, Egalité, Fraternité.'" (109)

Here, Fauset expresses an acute sense of double consciousness. The national identity she refers to has two distinctly separate aspects that are highlighted by being in Paris. While recognizing her familiarity with life in Harlem and in other places typically inhabited by African-Americans, she also makes a claim for identification with Americans of any origin. Arguably, the unity she perceives between white and black Americans is expressed in the last sentence of the quotation, which is a reminder of the French revolutionary ideals that were made part of the American Constitution. The country's black population serves as a constant reminder that America has failed to honor these ideals. Yet, they are bound together with other Americans by these very ideals, by the myth of what America could be—if not what it is. Fauset ends her essay by celebrating the freedom from restrictions of movement in the French capital: "I shall go out presently and have tea and *I shall have it at the first tea room which takes my fancy.* This is also something to be considered in reviewing French 'life as she is'" (109). The freedom that Fauset experiences in France is a freedom she expresses in spatial terms (not in moral or artistic terms). Many are the African-American authors who bear witness to the integral relationship between spatial freedom and psychological freedom. Fauset herself writes in a letter to Langston Hughes from Paris on Jan. 6, 1925, that "[i]t is lovely just being oneself and not bothering about color or prejudice. I think strangely enough that's why my book progresses so slowly because I'm away from the pressure." In other words, her writing is prompted and sustained by the particular social circumstances she is living under. Addressing "the problem of the color line," her double consciousness is a creative source to her.

Highly educated herself and active as a teacher for many years, Fauset would also write about matters of education and pedagogy in *The Crisis*. In "The Enigma of the Sorbonne" (March 1925), Fauset traces the history of the educational system in France, comparing it with the American system and finally reaching the conclusion that the "specialty of the modern Sorbonne is its cosmopolitanism" (219). She describes how she enjoys watching and listening to the students as they meet in the courtyard of the university, and on this particular occasion she takes note of the appearance of two Haitian girls of African descent. She is struck by the fact that the girls appear to feel perfectly at ease in this setting: their conversation is confident, their movements unrestrained. Unlike James Baldwin at the cathedral of Chartres (referred to in the above section "The symbolic geography of Europe"), these girls are not in the least estranged by their meeting with Western culture. Fauset evokes the image of the benign and unruffled countenances of the statues of Victor Hugo and Louis Pasteur, representatives of the peak of French learning and culture, in the courtyard to suggest the acceptance of the self-evident place of the black women in the multitude of students. Rejoicing in how thoroughly at home the girls feel in this milieu—a center of Western culture—Fauset concludes: "In this atmosphere so completely are they themselves that tolerance is a quality which they recognize only when they are exercising it toward others" (219). Brief as this example may be, it brings home to us Fauset's belief in education as a way to establish rapport and equality between black and white; a belief that was central to "New Negro ideology." There is also an echo of the ideas of Franz Boas, a German-American anthropologist whose view of culture was highly influential in Fauset's circles. For example, both Larsen's and Fauset's conceptualizations of culture and "race" are indebted to the theories of Boas, as were those of w.e.b. Du Bois, the leading black intellectual at the beginning of the twentieth century. Boas was among the first to see "race" not as biologically determined, but rather as a sociological phenomenon. He saw race and culture as independent of each other, that is, cultural differences could not be explained by genetic racial differences. Instead, material conditions and other historical circumstances were determining factors. An early cultural relativist, he argued that cultures should be understood on their own terms, and opposed the common contemporary idea that cultures could be rated on an evolutionary scale, according to level of "civilization." White European, or what we call "Western," civilization was usually placed at the top of the hierarchy. Boas

and his followers were among the first to talk of "cultures" in the plural, as opposed to the monistic view of "Culture," according to which different groups
had achieved different "stages" of it. In addition, they believed that all cultures
are in the final analysis mixed, as interchanges between cultures are both un-
avoidable and beneficial. Most of these ideas can be traced in the novels of
Johnson, Fauset, and Larsen, as well as in the works of their contemporaries
(Hutchinson, *Harlem Renaissance* 65-66). For example, Boas's notion of the
mixture of cultures permeates all Fauset's work. The self-evident place of the
Haitian girls at the Sorbonne is only one instance of this idea.

That Fauset herself advocated the recognition of the inseparableness of
European-American culture (of the kind associated with the Sorbonne) and
African-American culture is evidenced in all her writing, from the world view
that emerges in her novels to the formal patterns of her verse. Her own position
in relation to her dual background is described in her essay "Dark Algiers the
White" (April and May 1925). The essay describes Fauset's visit to the capital of
Algeria, making her one of few African-Americans to actually visit Africa—a
continent that fascinated many black American intellectuals at this time.[23] Here,
it becomes clear that Fauset's own identification is with the French colonial
power rather than with the natives of the African continent. In this culture she
herself feels estranged, her frame of reference for comprehending what she sees
consisting of American movies and British literature. The people she meets and
the sights she sees are described in the same type of orientalizing discourse that
Said deconstructed. The title sets an interesting tone concerning the meaning of
contrasts, however. Merely by considering the juxtaposition in the title we get a
sense of Fauset's receptivity to how color links geographical and ethnic terms.
The title suggests the inherent cultural hybridity represented by this city at the
Mediterranean coast serving as an entrance into the continent of Africa. The
city is as much white—not only its buildings, but also in terms of its relation
to colonial French culture—as it is part of "dark" Africa. In this article, Fauset
chooses to describe her own adventures in a foreign land refraining completely
from commenting on colonialism. However, awareness of the pressures of colonialism emerges in "Impressions of the PAC," Fauset's account of the 1921 Pan-
African Congress, in which she was one of the few women to take part.

---

[23] Other contemporary visitors to Africa were W.E.B. Du Bois, who together with Fauset was involved in
the work of the Pan-African Congress, Langston Hughes, and Claude McKay (Wall 33-34). Marcus
Garvey's "Back-to Africa" helped fuel thoughts of Africa as an alternative homeland and unity with
African peoples. Similar ideas were later reflected by the *négritude* movement in France.

Jessie Fauset was also dedicated to disseminating a similar idea of the benefits of cultural hybridity in her publishing work. Between 1920 and 1921, when publication ceased, Jessie Fauset edited a magazine for children called *The Brownies' Book*. In both *The Crisis* and *The Brownies' Book*, Fauset did much to publish the work of women writers (Wall 54). In addition, she always kept an international perspective, writing about events among blacks in Brazil or translating the work of Francophone blacks for the benefit of her American readers. As the editor of *The Brownies' Book*, Jessie Fauset also encouraged contributions dealing with customs and traditions of other countries, for example from Langston Hughes during his stay in Mexico. These journalistic choices can be interpreted as a gesture of resistance to a narrow, ethnocentric definition of what African-American culture should include. At the same time they point to a contradiction inherent in "New Negro" ideology, that is, whether to emphasize difference or similarity in the struggle for equal rights. At the root of this question is the view not only of race, but of culture: should culture be seen as something innate or as something that could be acquired? This complex surfaces in the simultaneous, contradictory claims to a specific African-American culture and a firm rootedness in American culture. It follows that if the "New Negroes" were as much American as they were African, this would ultimately suggest a possible dissolution of what was thought of as distinctively African-American: if other cultures were open to appropriation and transformation, their own would be as well.

Fauset's essays in *The Crisis* clearly indicate her own constant pushing of boundaries—intellectual as well as geographical ones—her promotion of an internationalist perspective on African-American affairs and her belief in the importance of recognizing "the internality of blacks to the West," as Gilroy put it. Several of the questions raised by Fauset in her essays, concerning freedom, education, cultural hybridity and African-American identity, appear again in her novels.

There Is Confusion

The title of Fauset's first novel is taken from a British nineteenth-century poet: the source is Tennyson's poem "The Lotos-Eaters," which in turn is based on an episode in the *Odyssey* (9.82-97). By this reference to a classic Greek and a Victorian English writer, Fauset indicates the literary tradition in which she aspires to inscribe herself and to intervene with her own works. While formally resembling a Victorian novel, the subject of *There Is Confusion* is the turbulent postwar times of the Harlem Renaissance, in which and of which she was writing. Depicting a generation trying to find its direction at a time when they were still only two generations removed from slavery, Fauset is concerned with the confusion that racial relations in America have created. With this choice of title, Fauset anticipates James Baldwin who, a couple of decades later, would find that a "rich confusion" was characteristic of American society. In contrast to European society which rests on fixed class positions that allow for less social mobility, American society is one "in which nothing is fixed and in which the individual must fight for his identity," writes James Baldwin in "The discovery of what it means to be an American" (Baldwin 142).

One of Fauset's harshest critics, Robert Bone, has maliciously linked the title of *There Is Confusion* to the novel's multiple subplots and characters (Bone 101). Ann duCille, on the other hand, remarks that most of Fauset's novels display "a fundamental confusion of genre, being neither romance nor realism" (100). This, duCille argues, is perhaps Fauset's greatest strength: "She is interrogating old forms and inventing something new. This rewriting, re-creating, this confusion of genre, is indeed fundamental; it is precisely what African American writers have done historically, from William Wells Brown to Alice Walker. In this instance this 'confusion' is Fauset's particular, though unacknowledged, gift to modernism" (100). The juxtaposition of Bone and duCille is interesting, and marks the shift in Fauset criticism that has taken place in the three decades from 1965 to 1993—and which is still going on. Whereas Fauset was previously often considered a conventional and even boring narrator, her style is now appreciated as a special brand of modernism, finely attuned to the limitations and possibilities of African-American women—both as authors and as the subject of literature—of the 1920s.

The novel is centered on the Marshall and Bye families of Philadelphia. On the very first page of the book, we encounter the young girl Joanna Marshall and learn of her desire to be "somebody great." She finds inspiration in her father's stories of African-American achievement, about Frederick Douglass and Nat Turner and women like Harriet Tubman and Sojourner Truth. Firmly resolved not to let color keep her from becoming "great," Joanna grows up to pursue a career as a dancer and singer, and her struggles in this respect form a large part of the book. The other plot line has as its main character Maggie Ellersley, a girl of working-class origins, who befriends Joanna's sister Sylvia and becomes a part of the Marshalls' middle-class household. Weaving in and out of these two characters' lives are the romantic complications between Joanna and Peter Bye, and Maggie and Phillip Marshall.

Notably, *There Is Confusion* is a novel that deals with World War I, where the war experiences are told mainly from the perspective of a woman—Maggie—who goes to France to work as a nurse. The depictions of the black soldiers who went to war for America in France also demonstrate that Fauset was a writer of her times. In *There Is Confusion*, Fauset uses the war scenes for the exaltation of the valor of the colored soldiers who participated in the war. This marks the novel as an important Harlem Renaissance work, as these soldiers' participation in the war led to the claims for better treatment upon their return to America, and this in turn helped initiate the period of cultural achievement. The treatment that the colored soldiers received in France was invoked to support the claims for American revision of segregationist legislation.[24] There was no African-American war novel comparable to, for example, Ernest Hemingway's *The Sun Also Rises* (1926), in which Hemingway speaks for the "lost generation" of young people who were part of World War I. On the contrary, the African-American authors were beginning to think of themselves as a generation "found." As Ann Douglas observes, "the black writers and performers faced a national culture in which the Negro artist had always been 'lost'—until, the members of the Harlem Renaissance believed, the present. Now, they proclaimed, was the first hour of hope for the Negro in America" (88). This feeling of hopefulness and change can be traced in Fauset's work as an editor, journalist, novelist, translator, and poet.

Far from being a place of artistic and political freedom of the kind we see in Johnson, Fauset's France—being the scene of war—is compared to Dante's *Inferno*: a place where black men become slaves once more (248). Fauset uses the European interlude to comment on the treatment of African-American men in the armed forces, a much-debated issue at the time. The concrete descriptions of France in *There Is Confusion* are of course affected by the fact that the country is the site of war: Peter Bye and the other soldiers land at Brest, a town which Fauset calls "a horrible prelude to a most horrible war" characterized by "the deepest, slimiest, stickiest mud that the world has known" (247). The other European setting of *There Is Confusion* is Chambéry, in Southeastern

---

[24]See, for example, DuBois's articles in *The Crisis*: "The Black Man in the Revolution of 1914-1918" and "The Colored American in France."

France, the location of a rest center for colored soldiers where Maggie Ellersley goes to work. Throughout this part of the novel, a grand cross on a hillside functions as a symbol of hope and faith. Other than that, France is rather briefly described and functions, above all, as a symbolic geography onto which dreams for the future are projected and where important events occur that lead to the resolution of the plot. It seems to be both a dystopian setting, being the site of war, and a kind of utopia where distorted relations are sorted out, and the white and black members of the Bye family are reunited.

Maggie's decision to go overseas follows upon the death of her first husband, for which she feels guilty, and her growing doubts concerning her planned marriage to Peter Bye. At the beginning of the chapter telling us of her decision and her subsequent journey (chapter 31), Maggie's fate is linked to that of Alice Du Laurens, the heroine of Henri Bourdeaux's novel *La Peur de Vivre*, described as "the story of a young girl who, afraid to face the perils of life, forfeited therefore its pleasures" (254). By means of this reference to French literature, the reader is prepared for the lesson in store for Maggie during her time in France. Indeed, this perilous (or at least not very pleasurable) setting is to bring about a positive change in Maggie's life. The new surroundings, the appreciation she meets with in return for her work and her mere presence at the rest center, as well as the physical and mental struggles of the many wounded soldiers, all contribute to work a change in her. With their bravery in the face of physical pain and social injustice, the soldiers seem to be saying to her "life *is* worth living, and we mean to live it to the full" (260). Fauset describes how "a new sense of values came to Maggie" (259) as evidenced primarily by her new plans for the future. As soon as she gets a chance to talk to Peter Bye, she tells him she wishes to set him free from his engagement to marry her, as she wants to try life on her own (261). More precisely, what she has in mind is to go back to America and set up a chain of beauty shops, thus making use of her good business sense and skills at hair work: "She would stand on her own two feet, Maggie Ellersley, serene, independent, self-reliant" (ibid.).

The war, then, has had an unexpectedly positive effect on Maggie Ellersley, as this scene seems to constitute the climax of her journey of development. Maggie's decision renders Peter Bye free to retrieve his childhood love, Joanna Marshall, and the two are later united in a happy marriage. Shortly after Maggie's and Peter's encounter, Maggie meets *her* first love, Phillip Marshall. Phillip has been badly wounded in the war—he is described as a "gas case"— and is therefore reluctant to resume his courtship of Maggie. Odd as it may sound, it is a measure of her development that Maggie at last offers to become his mistress if he will not marry her: "'Then,' she said, and the last tatters of her old obsession, that oldest desire of all for sheer decency—fell from her, 'then I'll be your mistress Phillip'" (268). Until this point, her desire for respectability has governed all of Maggie's actions, as seen for example by her precipitate marriage to Henderson Neal, who rather ironically turned out to be a gambler. The longing for respectability was also what persuaded her to think she wanted to marry Peter Bye although she did not love him. Europe turns out to be the place of resolution of these entangled relationships. At the end of the novel, we see Maggie as the happy and successful owner of a chain of beauty shops—happy that although Phillip is dead, they had the chance to be reunited in spite of previous misunderstandings and mistakes.

While the idea of individual freedom as related to Europe is retained—as is made evident through the characters Maggie Ellersley, Phillip Marshall, and Peter Bye, on whose lives the sojourn in Europe is to have a profound influence—it is very clear that Fauset does not offer life in Europe as an alternative to be seriously considered for her main characters. Those who do consider this option, Tom Mason and Harvey Alexander, are alternatively scorned or pitied by the other characters. We get a sense of what is at stake here by the following conversation between Tom Mason and Peter Bye, who for a time work together as musicians:

> "…When I've made my pile, if I can't spend it here the way I please, Annie and me can pick up and go to South America or France. I hear they treat colored people all right there."

> "'Treat colored people all right,'" Peter mimicked. "What business has anyone 'treating' us, anyway? The world's ours as much as it is theirs. And I don't want to leave America. It's mine, my people helped make it." (182)

Peter's reaction indicates that, to him, leaving the country is merely a means of escape and a denial of one's right to the claim of full American citizenship. Tom and Annie eventually drop out of the story, and we are left uncertain as to whether Tom's intention to leave the country is ever realized. Harley Alexander, who went over to fight in France together with Peter Bye, is the only character we know who actually moves to France. His decision to remain there is presented to us less as a voluntary act in search of a good life than as a result of bitterness and resignation. It is clear enough that Harley Alexander, now described as "bitter and cynical," has lost his chance of happiness. His example indicates that the price to be paid for life in Europe is a loss of love and community with one's own people (272-73). Fauset returns to this outcome in her last novel, *Comedy: American Style,* in which the color-struck Olivia chooses a lonely life in Paris rather than joining the black community in America.

Peter plays the piano in bars and for private entertainment together with Tom as a means of earning money to get through medical school. However, Fauset's approach to this kind of musician is quite different from how Johnson depicts the similar position of the ex-colored man in *The Autobiography.* Rather than echoing Johnson's pride in the folk origins of rag-time, Fauset has a more critical approach to this type of entertainment music. However, her attitude may be less related to any musical qualities—or lack thereof—than to the terms of its performance. A revealing scene takes place when Peter Bye, in his capacity as a musician, meets Mrs. Lea, who has engaged him to play at a party later that night. As it happens, this Mrs. Lea is Meriwether's beloved, and when she comprehends the relationship between Peter and Meriwether her response discloses her view of the black musical performer: "It's so in keeping with things that the grandson of the man who was slave to his [white Meriwether Bye] grandfather should be his entertainer to-night" (184). Referring back to the shared history of the black and the white Bye families, which comprises the poisoned issue of miscegenation, she thus equals the entertainer with the slave. The shared family history of the Byes—symbolic of the history of America—has to be recognized and dealt with before Peter, and by implication the nation, can move on. The novel offers such reconciliation, but it was apparently so hard to give a credible literary expression that an alternative to the American setting was needed.

Jessie Fauset makes use of the European setting in a manner similar to Johnson's when she describes how American prejudice is brought over to France, this time with the armed forces in the war. For example, when Peter has just arrived in France to join the American troops, he agrees to go to a band concert with his newly found friend, Harley Alexander. The concert is never held, however, for when the white Americans see their black countrymen getting friendly with French women a violent fight erupts:

> Between the two groups from the same soil there was grimmer, more determined fighting than was seen at Verdun. The French civil population stood on the church-steps opposite the square and watched with amazement.

"Nom de Dieu! Are they crazy, then, these Americans, that they will kill each other!" (250)

Seen through the eyes of the French spectators, the prejudices of the white Americans become absurd and incomprehensible. Although much more violent in nature, these events parallel the Opera scene in *The Autobiography* in pointing to the fact that the move to a different, less prejudiced locale, i.e. Europe, provides no real relief from American racial discrimination. Both the scene in *There Is Confusion* and the one described by Johnson seem to indicate that as long as conditions are not altered in their home country, any experience of freedom for African Americans in Europe can at best be tenuous and temporary. The decision of all three authors discussed so far to have their characters return to America in the end appears to be related to this insight. The eventual move back to the American continent can perhaps best be understood in the light of contemporary developments in the U.S., that is, the cultural flourishing of the Harlem Renaissance, which engendered a new sense of possibilities for social change and racial equality.

In Paul Gilroy's study of the black Atlantic a central symbol is the ship, which functions as a vehicle for the cultural exchanges that take place across the continents. Not only Fauset but in fact all three authors make use of the "chronotope" of the ship. On the boat going to the battlefields in France, Peter is brought together with the white Meriwether Bye. This meeting with the erudite and open-minded Meriwether, which involves a lengthy discussion on racial issues in the US, has a profound impact on Peter. The two men will soon find out that they are related: the intermingling of the European settlers and their African slaves has given rise to a black and a white "branch" of the Bye family. The two offshoots of the family tree live completely separate lives, the black family of course barred from the family fortune and estate. In response to Peter's angry accusations Meriwether acknowledges his family's guilt in denying recognition to their colored kin. This is the first time in Peter's life that he has met with sympathy and understanding from a white man. He is impressed by Meriwether's opinion on the failure of America to live up to the country's founding principles: "Here America was founded for the sake of liberty and the establishment of an asylum for all who were oppressed. And no land has more actively engaged in the suppression of liberty, or in keeping down those who were already oppressed" (245). Meriwether becomes his first white friend, and he resolves hereafter to "be more generous in his thoughts of white men"

(249). Once on the battlefield in France, Meriwether is hit by a grenade and dies in Peter's arms:

> When the stretcher-bearers found them, Meriwether was lying across Peter's knees, his face turned childwise toward Peter's breast. The colored man's head had dropped low over the fair one and his black curly hair fell forward straight and stringy, caked in the blood which lay in a well above Meriwether's heart. "Cripes!" said one of the rescue men, "I've seen many a sight in this war, but none ever give me the turn I got seein' that smoke's hair dabblin' in the other fellow's blood." (253)

This scene, in which white Meriwether is locked in black Peter's arms, symbolizes the interlocked destinies of black and white Americans. The intertwined familial background of the two men is suggestive of that of many other families like them. Indeed, Fauset here seems to propose that the American family is ultimately of a mixed, hybrid nature. Peter's and Meriwether's final embrace thus represents the reconciliation between black and white Americans, which amounts to a prerequisite of their common future. Through the recognition of his mixed heritage, Peter is offered an opportunity to come to terms with his past and achieves a new sense of freedom to go on with his future life (294-97).

In this passage the French battlefield, somewhat paradoxically, figures as a place of imaginary enactment of inter-racial solidarity. The ambivalent position of the black soldiers in the war is once more highlighted by the reaction of the American medics who find the two Byes. Fauset's staging of this encounter between Peter and Meriwether Bye echoes that of a one-act play by Joseph Seamon Cotter, "On the Fields of France," which was published in the June issue of *The Crisis*, 1920. In the play, a black and a white American soldier die hand in hand while wondering why they had not lived that way at home. Fabre refers to this piece of fiction as an example of how participation in the war was imagined by black Americans. The reality turned out to be different, though. Although the French welcomed the black soldiers, they were discriminated against by their white fellow soldiers (Fabre 49). Fauset's depictions of the war scenes in *There Is Confusion* reflect her awareness of this issue.

Johnson's *The Autobiography* provides an interesting parallel to the Atlantic crossing in *There Is Confusion*. Whereas the trip to Europe is fairly quickly dealt with, the narrator's trip back from Liverpool to Boston is depicted in some detail. Like Fauset, Johnson lets the maritime journey be the site of discussions on American racial prejudice. Here, the narrator enters into conversation with "the broadest-minded colored man [he has] ever talked with on the Negro question" (476). Both Fauset and Johnson choose to let their focal characters meet with an impressive person who, in terms of reason and justice, condemns American racism.

In *Quicksand*, Larsen's depiction of Helga Crane's passage between the American and the European continent entails no encounters of this kind. Instead, the boat trip to Denmark functions as a locus of transition, where Helga is able to accommodate herself to life after arrival. Her long-forgotten knowledge of the Danish language comes back to her, for example. In addition, the purser recognizes her from when she made the same journey together with her mother as a child and makes her feel important by letting her sit at his table. This hint at Helga's conspicuousness and exclusive treatment will be developed into the major motif of her stay in Denmark.

In the works of Johnson and Fauset particularly, the voyage thus functions as a liminal space where the rules and boundaries pertaining on land no longer apply: arguably, a conversation as charged as that between the black and the white Byes on equal terms needs an extraordinary setting to become credible. Not only does the maritime journey make possible—and credible—an encounter, which would have been difficult to stage per se, but it also allows for the ferocity of the condemnation of American racist practices. Fauset's scene involves a complex nexus of repentance and redemption, where the white man is actually willing to give his life in recognition of the black lives sacrificed under slavery.

Paul Gilroy's theory of the black Atlantic is helpful in analyzing Fauset's writings about Europe (both in *There Is Confusion* and in her articles). Mary Jane Schenck argues for a couple of important links between Gilroy's version of modernity and the literary characters Jessie Fauset creates. Fundamental to Gilroy's analysis is the notion that the whole project of modernity rests on an "equivocation", namely that the ideas of enlightenment, human rights, and progress are parallel with, indeed dependent on, the subjugation of a large group of people through racial slavery. Fauset's characters, as indeed the characters depicted by Larsen and Johnson, serve as an indictment of this ideology of progress, with reference to their role in making this prosperity and progress possible while still being denied basic civil rights. Schenck finds that Fauset's characters are "illustrations of a particularly modern fusion or hybridity" (106).

This means that they cannot easily be pinned down to the reductive polarities of "white" or "black" but occupy an uncertain position of newness in-between the two categories. National borders do not suffice, nor do narrow ethnic definitions – the very definition of the black Atlantic is fluidity and openness. In terms of identity, this perspective offers a way of understanding the type of characters that Fauset depicted and that did not fit in with the expectations of what either white or black people should be.

One important part of the "New Negro" ideology that Fauset represented was, however, the nationalist focus: they were striving to change the idea of what 'American' (black or white) meant. At the time, this seemed to be an enabling strategy because of its link to the claim for full citizenship. Gilroy's concept of the black Atlantic, however, expands the idea of national identity without replacing it or rendering it defunct. With Gilroy's perspective we need not juxtapose "African (-American)" and "European" culture and see the two as essentially different. He deconstructs this dichotomy as a basis for understanding the experiences of black slaves and their descendants in the West, proposing instead that they cannot be separated, and that they have continued to influence and shape each other. The opposition is rather between "white" and "black" within and across cultures. Gilroy emphasizes the significance of historically shared cultural forms within the "black Atlantic" figuration, that is, Britain, Africa, America, and the Caribbean. The common experience of powerlessness and subjugation—which has taken place in the name of race—functions as a unifying experience for black people in the various parts of this formation. Gilroy replaces biological essentialism (common in the 1920s) with an "anti-anti-essentialism" based on experience. It is a kind of socially-induced essentialism that leaves more room for local, individual variation being played out against a common backdrop.

The eventual return to America (and the implicit deracination of those of Fauset's characters who stay on in Europe) indicates Fauset's loyalty to the cause of the "New Negro" artists. The battle for racial equality may be inspired by European experiences, but it should be fought at home. A propos of Joanna's struggle against discrimination of the American stage, Schenck finds another point of correspondence between Fauset's novel and Gilroy's idea of the black Atlantic, claiming that "*There Is Confusion* is a good example of what Gilroy calls 'the politics of fulfillment,' the black artist's desire for a realization of promised Enlightenment goals" (Schenck 107). Not only the figure of the artist, I would argue, but the setting of Europe contributes to throw these Enlightenment ideals of equality and democracy into relief, indicating the failure of the Western society of which they are a part to recognize African Americans as citizens with equal rights. Schenck concludes: "It is in this respect, not in respect to form, that we can speak of the modernity of Jessie Fauset" (Schenck 108).

The Europe of *Quicksand*
– The quicksand of Europe

The first question we need to ask about the fictional trip to Europe in *Quicksand* concerns the motive for traveling: why does Helga Crane leave America, and what does she expect to find in Europe that she could not find at home? My suggestion in the following is that the motive for Helga's European journey is primarily the search for freedom from racial discrimination as well as for family and a sense of belonging; an attempt at coming to terms with the duality of "double consciousness." Being of mixed heritage, Helga Crane in *Quicksand* hopes to heal her constant sense of "a lack somewhere" by tracing her familial origins in Denmark. But her journey also relates to the themes of education and art. After the pattern of the Bildungsroman, Helga's traveling leads to increased self-understanding as well as cultural reflection.

Although intrapersonal in its effects, an interactive perspective on identity is inherent in the metaphor of "double consciousness." Thus, a fruitful framework for the analysis of the European episodes is what M. L. Pratt has called the "contact zone." This term alludes to the "social spaces where disparate cultures meet, clash and grapple with each other, often in highly asymmetrical relations of domination and subordination – like colonialism, slavery, or their aftermaths, as they are lived out across the globe today" (Pratt 4). In Pratt's study the "contact zones" are the non-European destinations of explorers, missionaries, and adventurers of the seventeenth through the nineteenth centuries. Instead, the novels of Johnson, Fauset, and Larsen find Europe to be the site of cultural negotiation. Another important dimension to Pratt's "'contact' perspective is the emphasis on how subjects are constituted in and by their relations to each other. It treats the relations among colonizers and colonized, or travellers and 'travelees,' not in terms of separateness or apartheid, but in terms of copresence, interaction, interlocking understandings and practices, often within radically asymmetrical relations of power" (6-7).

What is important about the 'contact' perspective is the focus it places on the interactivity between colonizer and colonized. Thus, it allows us to see that both parties of the colonial encounters had some measure of agency and influence on each other.[25] For Helga, the meeting with her Danish relatives provides a link to her lost mother, as well as economic opportunities she has not experienced before. For the Dahls, Helga's appearance offers the chance of social advancement and, through her relationship with the painter Axel Olsen, the link to the artistic circles they want to enter. Their decision to re-fashion Helga into a Danish version of Josephine Baker shows that they are up-to-date with modernist primitivist ideas, and Helga's presence offers them a chance to create an impression of themselves as modern individuals.

Another important reason for using Pratt's term is her attention to the dialectical process of subject formation and her concern for the asymmetrical power relation in the meetings that take place. Pratt's focus on travel narratives is linked to a concern with imperialism. When the travelers of Johnson's, Fauset's, and Larsen's works enter into the "contact zone" of Europe, they take their sense of Americanness with them. In these meetings staged in the "contact zone" of Europe, the similarity between travelers and 'travelees' is emphasized. In other words, the African-American travelers are depicted as being at home in European culture, and the claim can thus be made that they should be seen as an integral part of it. Interestingly, this is a fact that cannot be accepted by Helga Crane's Danish relatives in *Quicksand*, for example.

Quicksand is the novel that has the most sustained set of tropes connected with city topography and its symbolical meaning. The physical aspects of the city of Copenhagen are an important part of Helga's European experiences, giving emphasis to the theme of freedom, in relation to 'difference' and cultural belonging. Throughout *Quicksand*, the street functions as an open space where Helga seeks freedom from emotional pressure and room to breathe. But it is also a dangerous and threatening place, which serves as a background for Helga's emotional turmoil. Wandering the streets of Chicago in search of a job, Helga is more than once accosted by men who mistake her for a prostitute. The cities of Chicago and New York offer glimpses of modern life. They are

---

[25] In this context it can be noted that this type of interaction was a limited process and that large sections of the colonized people had little or no contact with their foreign oppressors (Loomba 69).

at the same time hostile and welcoming places, where money rules but where Helga Crane, at least initially, feels at home among the multitudes (30, 43). The relative openness of the street is continually contrasted with the closeness of several of the rooms Helga inhabits. For example, her room at Naxos, to which she withdraws at night, refusing to open the door to her colleagues, at first appears a haven of tranquility but soon enough turns out to be a suffocating place in a narrow-minded environment. Similarly, towards the end of the novel Helga enters a storefront church in Harlem, and under the combined pressure of the congregation and her own fatigue she undergoes a religious experience that is a kind of conversion. The seeming protection of the church, and of Rev. Green, turns out to lead to a cramped existence in a small rural community in Alabama and an asphyxiating marriage. Helga's movement in the novel consistently follows the pattern of flight and subsequent entrapment. As we will see, Denmark turns out to be another quicksand.

In the city of Copenhagen, Helga is at first uncomfortable with the stares of Danes unaccustomed to her dark presence. The seeming openness of the street is at first compromised and, in fact, her situation assumes a touch of the panoptic as her every step is being observed by those around her. Her dark skin marks her difference from the Danes and makes it impossible for her to escape notice. On her first day in the Danish capital, Helga is constantly gaped at, and it is with a sense of relief she reaches her relatives' home where she can hide from the indiscreet stares of curious Copenhagen denizens. Several of the amazed Danes label Helga in their bewildered whispers "in which Helga made out the frequently recurring word 'sorte,' which she recognized as the Danish word for black" (69). "Sorte" here functions as a performative statement, that is, by naming Helga as black they define her racialized presence. Helga's situation is similar to that of Frantz Fanon being sized up by the child's exclamation "Look a Negro!," whereby he was given a sense of his position in the white world. 'Sorte' is a racializing act of address that produces Helga as "black" in a very distinct way. Accordingly, Helga acts to fulfill their expectations. Although at first uncomfortable in her new extravagant dresses and excessive make-up, which she is induced to wear by the Dahls, she realizes that this is the part ascribed to her and that grants her a position, albeit a dubious one, in Danish society.

Gradually, she and the Danes get used to one another, and Helga frequently walks the streets of the old city on her own. Here, greater freedom of movement allows her to make increasing use of public space. On her frequent walks through the Danish capital, roaming from the fishmongers at Gammelstrand to the changing of the guards at Amalienborg Palace, Helga compares what she sees with the cities of Chicago and New York. The image of Copenhagen that emerges is that of a clean, well-organized, sophisticated but somewhat antiquated city. There is no poverty, and the quiet streets are safe and clean:

> The charm of the old city itself, with its odd architectural mixture of medievalism and modernity, and the general air of well-being which pervaded it, impressed her. Even in the so-called poor sections there was none of that untidiness and squalor which she remembered as the accompaniment of poverty in Chicago, New York and the Southern cities of America. Here the door-steps were always white from constant scrubbings, the women neat, and the children washed and provided with whole clothing. Here were no tatters and rags, no beggars. (75)

At first, these observations appeal to Helga and appear as favorable in contrast to the American life she is used to. In time, the same features will alienate Helga from her new surroundings. Although pleasant, Larsen's version of Copenhagen seems to be almost clinically clean. Here is neither the threat nor the allure of the modern, bustling, and busy American cities. Instead, what we see here is the principle of rationality, which informs the entire Copenhagen episode, applied to the city itself. The fight against poverty suggests the social engineering of a burgeoning Scandinavian welfare state, but in this speckless, gleaming white city all unwanted elements are to be kept out of the public sphere. Black Helga's observations of the white and healthy Danes evoke the sinister symbolism of blackness versus whiteness, filth versus purity. In the scrubbed and shining whiteness of Copenhagen, Helga's blackness is made even more conspicuous and strange. Helga's failure to fit in among her relatives is underlined as the very whiteness and cleanliness of the city set off her difference and emphasize her sense of alienation. Her appearance in icy, clean Copenhagen is a striking representation of the cultural signifiers of black and white. The color symbolism of this part of Larsen's novel is very illustrative and deserves further explication.

The in/visible power of whiteness

The journey to Europe in *Quicksand* is a move into the white world. It is, paradoxically, both a journey in search of increased freedom and a journey on which Helga, as a black woman, suffers from circumscription that is differently encoded than in America. The color symbolism in which white is constructed as the opposite of black, and which is part of Western civilization, is important for understanding the use of color in the novel. In *White* (1997), Richard Dyer discusses the meaning of color in a visual culture such as that of our contemporary Western world. Sight is here the privileged sense of knowledge: to "read" or interpret our visual perceptions is the most important activity by which to gain a sense of ourselves and others in the world. This means that social groups need to be visibly distinguishable and recognizable in order for power and control to be maintained. Color is one important marker in this respect.

In a culture that is structured around visibility, there is power in remaining invisible—a watcher. The invisible watcher has the power to describe what s/he sees without being the subject of a similar scrutiny. Dyer argues that this kind of invisibility pertains to whiteness: "Whites must be seen to be white, yet whiteness as race resides in invisible properties and whiteness as power is maintained by being unseen" (Dyer 45). Whiteness has come to be the norm, the invisible center in relation to which other people are defined. Race has then come to be constructed as belonging to non-white people, while the racialization of whites often remains unrecognized. Whiteness has also been conceptualized as absence of color in Western culture, which has made possible the idea that white people could remain outside of the color-dependent racial scheme (Dyer 45).

Along the same lines, bell hooks discusses how in the American white supremacist society white people have been "accorded the right to control the black gaze" (168). For example, forcing black slaves to keep their eyes lowered was one way of denying them the subjecthood that is affirmed when squarely meeting someone's gaze. Instead, black people were often given the role of the invisible servant, seen only in "a pair of hands offering drinks on a silver tray."[26] In the eyes of white people, hooks contends, blacks are still largely "invisible," that is to say, so different that they need not be considered as equal to white people. Whiteness thus functions as an invisible—that is, ubiquitous yet often unacknowledged—norm. By contrast, blackness signifies a high degree of visibility, in its deviance from this norm, which in turn leads to *in*visibility in terms of the denial of black subjectivity on which white supremacy rests. And there are further intricacies involved in this complex matter.

---

[26] This striking description, found in bell hooks's *Black Looks* (168), is, however, not hooks's own but taken from Sallie Bingham's autobiography *Passion and Prejudice: A Family Memoir* (1991).

The power of the invisible watcher has been described most forcefully by Michel Foucault in his analysis of the development of the penal system from the eighteenth century onwards. Previous displays of public punishments to deter others from crime, as well as the—sometimes protective—darkness of dungeons where criminals were hidden from the world, were at this time replaced by a transparent system of surveillance. Jeremy Bentham's "Panopticon," in which every part of the prison cell came into the light, is the image of power exercised through visibility. About this construction Foucault writes:

> There is no need for arms, physical violence, material constraints. Just a gaze. An inspecting gaze, a gaze which each individual under its weight will end by interiorising to the point that he is his own overseer, each individual thus exercising this surveillance over, and against, himself. A superb formula: power exercised continuously and for what turns out to be a minimal cost. (Gordon 155)

Foucault makes clear that seeing is a way of knowing. It is evident that looking is never an innocent practice. Any act of looking demands a subject, who does the actual looking and is in control of the interpretation of what s/he has seen. This is the eye/I through which the object is registered. Then there is the object that is being watched and who may have more or less control over what s/he displays. In a crucial move, Foucault describes what happens to the object as s/he is aware of being under constant surveillance. The gaze of the overseer is internalized so that the person being watched objectifies himself and becomes watchful of his every move. In similar fashion, Frantz Fanon has described how the black man becomes the prisoner of the gaze of the white man. Knowing that he is constantly being watched by the white man, Fanon describes how he internalizes the inspecting gaze to the extent that it leads to self-contempt (Fanon, *Black Skin* 116). In an important scene described in *Black Skin, White Masks* Fanon meets the eye of the white person, a child who calls out to his mother that he is frightened at the sight of a black man. Fanon's response to the child's exclamation is to feel

> responsible at the same time for my body, for my race, for my ancestors. I subjected myself to an objective examination, I discovered my blackness, my ethnic characteristics; and I was battered down by tom-toms, cannibalism, intellectual deficiency, fetishism [sic], racial defects, slave-ships, and above all else, above all: "Sho' good eatin'." On that day, completely dislocated, unable

to be abroad with the other, the white man, who unmercifully imprisoned me, I took myself far off from my own presence, far indeed, and made myself an object. What else could it be for me but an amputation, an excision, a hemorrhage that spattered my whole body with black blood? [...] My body was given back to me sprawled out, distorted, recolored, clad in mourning in that white winter day. (112-13)

It is the power of the gaze of the white man that objectifies Fanon and stops him from being a man among men. Instead, the gaze of the white man dissects him, and the pieces of himself that are reflected back to him through the gaze of the other do not make up a coherent whole. (I will return to the theory of fragmentation and its relationship to the black body of Helga Crane further on.) In Fanon's account, the power of the gaze is crucially linked to the perception of his body. In a visual culture, the body acquires a special status as a source of knowledge. Nothing can be hidden on the human body, and therefore the ultimate truth can be found in its signs of difference. The notion of corporeal truth, for example, governed the categorizations of the human according to different races or types that acquired scientific status during the Enlightenment. But this thinking was guided by a belief that it was possible to separate the domains of corporeal materiality and the historical context in which the body exists. According to this line of reasoning there is an essence, or truth, resident in the body, unmarked by the imprints of its historical and cultural context. The literature of Johnson, Fauset, and Larsen all address this idea of how bodies can be read as markers of difference. Applying the notion of performance to their novels is a way of interrogating the power dynamics of the vision – visibility relationship that rests on a notion of an essence (of racial characteristics) locked to the body.

Richard Dyer divides his analysis of whiteness as color into three parts: white as hue, white as skin and white as symbol (45). About whiteness as hue he notes that there is a slippage between white as color and white as colorlessness, which forms part of "a system of thought and affect whereby white people are both particular and nothing in particular, are both something and non-existent" (47). This slippage can then be worked to advantage either through the claim of particularity or through non-existence, that is, whiteness interpreted as generality. Furthermore, white is the only color to have an opposite – black. This is true of no other colors; green is not thought of as the opposite of red. White, however, is hard to conceive of except in opposition to black (51). White as skin color is a categorization characterized by internal variability. Its boundaries are fluid and whiteness finally becomes "a matter of ascription – white people are who white people say are white. This has a profoundly controlling effect" (48). Arguably, the ascription of skin color rests partly on the opposition between black and white as hue. As a result of unequal power relations, white people not only say who is white but who is black, that is they use their opposite, black, to define themselves. Finally, the color symbolism of white and black attains a certain status in the Christian, European worldview, where whiteness is associated with purity, virginity, virtue, beauty, beneficence, and God. By contrast, blackness is associated with filth, sin, baseness, ugliness, evil, and the devil. There is thus a basic moral opposition of white as good and black as bad in European history.

While warning us against too easy a conflation of the three aspects of whiteness, Dyer argues that the slippage between them is pervasive and seems to be at work in all representations of white people (63). More than Johnson's or Fauset's Europe, Larsen's Denmark is the pre-eminent example of the white world, and an awareness of the interpretations of whiteness is crucial to understanding the symbolic geography drawn in the novel. Larsen's descriptions of the contrasting effects of white and black as they pertain both to the city of Copenhagen and its inhabitants are strikingly visual.

To begin with, the identity that is ascribed to Helga by the Danes is new and surprising to her. By decking her out as "a veritable savage" (69), they assist her in constructing an identity founded on essentialist notions of the black woman as a "jungle woman" (Ginsberg 81). To these white Europeans, the essential black woman is a naive, sensuous being who loves bright colors and beautiful clothes. It is clear that in her relatives' eyes the most important aspect of Helga's identity is her difference from them. Gradually, Helga is drawn into this game of identity construction: "after a little while she gave herself up wholly to the fascinating business of being seen, gaped at, desired. Against the solid background of Herr Dahl's wealth and generosity she submitted to her aunt's arrangement of her life to one end, the amusing one of being noticed and flattered" (74). Helga learns to see herself through the eyes of the Danes, and plays along in the game. With the help of the Dahls and their artist friend Axel Olsen, her histrionic and exhibitionist inclinations are given free play. The example of Josephine Baker, the best-known black artist in Europe at the time, provides an illuminating parallel to the issues of primitivism and female sexuality depicted in *Quicksand*. Indeed, Helga adopts a kind of stage persona for Danish social circles much as Josephine Baker does in her Parisian revues.

Helga's decision to emphasize her difference also involves a criticism of the hypocrisy of her Harlem friends who proclaim the importance of race pride while striving to imitate white American lifestyles. She finds the strong group identity and "racial uplift" ideology of the Harlemites limiting to her possibilities for individual expression. On the other hand, her difference from her Danish relatives isolates her, and the physical freedom Helga gradually comes to experience in Copenhagen cannot replace the spiritual freedom inherent in ethnic belonging. Helga's reflection "I'm homesick, not for America, but for Negroes" is simultaneously an expression of discontent with her home country and of the importance of racial identity typical of the Harlem Renaissance.

Helga's performance of "blackness" affects and is affected by the "whiteness" of the Danes. It is clear that her relatives can only accept her as different from them, and they go to great lengths to preserve this difference. Indeed, the Danes' construction of Helga in line with their perception of "blackness personified" seems to be a way of ascertaining the stability of their own whiteness. In the orderly white world of Copenhagen, there is no room for racial ambiguity. But there is a scene in which the carefully structured universe of bipolarity that is Larsen's Copenhagen threatens to break down, and the rigid divisions between black and white can no longer be maintained. On one of Helga's walks through the Danish capital, an interesting encounter takes place:

> an old countrywoman asked her to what manner of mankind she belonged and at Helga's replying: 'I'm a Negro,' [she] had become indignant, retorting angrily that, just because she was old and a countrywoman she could not be so easily fooled, for she knew as well as everyone else that Negroes were black and had woolly hair. (76)

The countrywoman's reaction complicates the signification of "blackness" as her response suggests that she has no way of conceiving of Helga's mixed-race appearance. The denial of recognition of her New World Africanity involves a denial of the historicity of Helga's person. Rather than seeing her as the product of the particular history of slavery in the New World, and of centuries of miscegenation, it seems the Danish countrywoman can only conceive of "blackness" as a fixed, ahistorical essence. Furthermore, her refutation of Helga's declared identity shows the anger and fear she feels at the uncertainty of her ability to name or know what she sees. It is as if she fears that there can be a "stranger in their midst" that she wouldn't recognize. In a discussion of how passing affects the relationship between knowability and visibility, Samira Kawash points out that "the possibility of a breakdown between the visible and its internal meaning occasions the threat of the collapse of whiteness itself" (132). Helga must retain her total "otherness," otherwise her presence threatens to destabilize the order of whiteness. And indeed it is as if the entire Copenhagen episode starts to "break down" after this disturbing note is added. Helga gradually realizes how untenable her situation has become, and begins to form the decision to return to America.

The passage about the Danish countrywoman is interesting because it suggests the difficulty of defining what a "Negro" (as contemporary idiom had it) actually means. Clearly, physical characteristics are not enough, since Helga's skin and hair do not accord with this Dane's idea of blackness. Author Richard Wright saw the Negro as "America's metaphor," by which he meant a historical and social construction which was intimately related to the institution of racial slavery and which corresponded to no fixed cultural or biological attributes common to blacks. Instead, Wright said, "the word Negro in America [is] something purely social, something made in the United States" (Gilroy 149). The Danish countrywoman's reaction illustrates Nella Larsen's view of race as fundamentally unstable. In pointing to the insufficiency of defining a person according to physical attributes, Larsen questions the whole notion of race as a classification of human beings and, together with it, the so-called "color-line" which underpinned American segregationist legislation. As the protagonists perform race and/or culture, the fictitious boundaries of these constructs are interrogated.

Whiteness in question

It is noticeable that Larsen's descriptions of Helga's encounters with Copenhagen and the Danes are permeated by the dichotomous thinking that is at the heart of cultural stereotyping. A conflict between emotion and reason is part of the complex of tropes surrounding *Quicksand*'s Harlem – Scandinavia axis. For example, descriptions of the city serve to offset Helga's emotions after a disturbing conversation with her aunt about marriage and miscegenation. Helga is in a state of emotional turmoil and her feelings of distance and estrangement from her Danish family are underlined when she looks out the window and is struck by "the amazing orderliness of the street" (79). Here, the external environment works as a contrast, augmenting her anxiety. Previously, in the American cities of New York and Chicago, the street worked in concordance with Helga's experiences, rather like a mirror. In contrast to cold, clean Scandinavia and its cold, superficial inhabitants, Helga remembers Harlem as a city with "dirty streets" filled with "dark, gay humanity" (92). Above all, on returning to Harlem "[t]he easement which its heedless abandon brought to her was a real, a very definite thing" (96). Life and society in cleanly Copenhagen with its "toy-like streets" (66) are frequently described in tropes of artificiality. There is also an air of artificiality, and superficiality, about the social life of the Dahls which revolves around theater and opera performances, teas and dinners.

The whole Copenhagen episode is structured in the same manner. Larsen's Denmark is a strictly categorized black and white world, without grey zones. In this part of the book, Larsen consistently negates traditionally valorized European ideals: reason and rationality are, for example, linked to being emotionally frozen. Other characteristics of the Danes are security, balance, control, and organization, which are all indicative of a lack of spontaneity, vitality, and passion. Depicting the positive traits stereotypically associated with whiteness as negative, and suggestive of lack of life, is an effective strategy for showing how absurd such reduced images of people are.

The icy coldness of Larsen's Copenhagen points to an interesting facet of the color representation that Richard Dyer analyzes. Dyer devotes an entire chapter of his book-length study *White* to "White death." He finds that the connection between whiteness and death is an ancient one; the classic marble sculptures were valued precisely for the stillness, lack of action or sign of life. He also notes that the lack of color in a person suggests precisely the absence of life. But, says Dyer, whites do not only embody death, they often bring it. As examples, he mentions the white-clad horse-men of the Ku Klux Klan, figured in the 1915 film by D. W. Griffiths, *The Birth of a Nation*, or the horror of vampirism (Dyer 209-10). A very well-known literary example of the linking of whiteness and terror is of course Herman Melville's *Moby Dick* (1851). Additionally, bell hooks analyzes how whiteness in the black imagination often equals terror. This perception of whiteness as terrorizing, says hooks, should not simply be understood as a reaction to stereotypes by inverting them so that white is made synonymous with "evil" and black with "goodness." Instead, she suggests that we can understand the link between whiteness as terror as "a response to the traumatic pain and anguish that remains a consequence of white racist domination, a psychic state that informs and shapes the way black folks 'see' whiteness" (hooks 169).

While the white Danes in *Quicksand's* Copenhagen primarily lack warmth and passion, white people have a terrifying aspect in some of the encounters in Johnson's *The Autobiography*. The narrator's millionaire friend often forces him to play the piano for him during long hours at night. At times like these, the narrator's impression of his patron and traveling companion reflects the slave-master nature of their relationship: "During such moments this man sitting there so mysteriously silent, almost hid in a cloud of heavy-scented smoke, filled me with a sort of unearthly terror. He seemed to be some grim, mute, but relentless tyrant, possessing over me a supernatural power which he used to drive me on mercilessly to exhaustion" (88). However, the fact that the Millionaire pays so generously for the services he demands makes up for the hardships he puts the narrator through. The connection to money is significant here, too. The millionaire, like the father who gave him a piano and the gold-piece to hang around his neck when he was a boy, represents material wealth and prosperity, which the narrator is tempted by. At the end of the novel his work in the white world of real-estate business has given him money—at the price of his blackness. Johnson, then, constructs and criticizes materialism as a feature typically associated with white life. And for all his money, allowing him to roam the world in search of happiness, the millionaire is consistently depicted as rather listless, detached from the people he entertains, and soon to be blasé even at the sights of Paris. A couple of years after the narrator leaves his traveling companion in Paris, we learn that he has ended his life.

White characters, when they do appear in *There Is Confusion*, are distinguished by similar references to lack of life. Fauset does not use white as a symbol in such a consistent manner as Larsen. It is clear, however, that both authors use color symbolism to imply a connection between colors—other than white—and life, passion, and diversity. At times, Fauset is being very explicit about the horror that white people represent. Toward the end of the novel, Joanna runs into her old friend Vera Manning. Vera is white enough to pass, and has made use of this possibility to work for civil rights in the South. Here, she has been able to gain insight into the lives and attitudes of several white people. Her experiences of mob violence and lynching in the South have, on the whole been frightful and her conclusion is: "Oh, Joanna, I'm glad I'm colored—there's something terrible, terrible about white people" (270). Jane Kuenz observes that in *There Is Confusion*, "[w]hite people, particularly white women, are repeatedly described as passive, listless, washed out, or 'freakish'" (Kuenz 100). By contrast, Joanna is described in terms such as "splendid, glowing, symbolic" (269), or as "a rosy brown vision" (131) when she appears on the stage. Even as a young girl, Joanna possesses "a certain grave beauty" (131). She wants to wear colorful clothes not only to underline the colorfulness of her skin but also because it will match her personality. This link between interior and exterior explains Joanna's sister Sylvia's ambition to become a dressmaker and teach colored people how to dress: "We will not wear these conventional colors—grays, taupe, beige [...] They're all right for these pale-faces. But colored people need color, life, vividness" (132).

If the white characters are portrayed as lackluster and wishy-washy, the black characters are given the opposite traits. Even as a child, Joanna was "a memorable type." Fauset describes her as having a "peculiar luminosity of appearance" which she shares with Sylvia. This is combined with a "mop of thick black hair" (20). Moreover, Joanna wants to keep her black appearance: "Joanna knew next to nothing at this time of those first aids to colored people in this country in the matter of conforming to average appearance...No hair straighteners, nor even curling kids for her" (20). Fauset explains that this has to do with Joanna's "variety of honesty," which demands of her that she does not to do anything that could be considered artificial. It also signals her refusal to conform to a white ideal of beauty that prescribed straight hair rather than afros. (Dyer notes hair and facial features, such as the nose, as "racial" in addition to skin, and the notion of hair as a sign of racial identity was echoed, for example, in the Black Power movement of the 1960s, when acquiring an "afro" haircut was seen as a gesture of pride in one's black heritage.) Similarly, the love of colors that is expressed by Joanna and Sylvia in *There Is Confusion* as well as by Helga in *Quicksand* translates into a desire for the recognition of the beauty of color as it applies not only to clothes but to people. The imagery of clothing underscores the importance of the recognition of nuances, of more colors than simply black and white.

Miss Sharples, who has come to see Joanna about the job as Ms. America at the District Line Theatre, causes comments from Sylvia concerning her dress and appearance: "'My Heavens, where do you suppose she finds her clothes? She hasn't a bit of color in her face and there she's wearing a stone gray suit and a gray hat with a brown, a brown scarf around it. Her hair is as straight as a poker and she wears it bobbed'" (225). Sylvia's assessment of Miss Sharples's appearance is reinforced by Joanna's impressions: "[S]he looked at Vera Sharples sitting insignificantly and drably in an armchair, her graying bobbed hair straggling a bit over her mannish tweed coat, her feet encased in solid tan boots. Only her eyes, looking straightforwardly and appraisingly from under the unbecoming hat, kept her from being dubbed a 'freak'" (225).

The straight bobbed hair, together with the fact that she sits smoking during her meeting with Joanna, suggests that Miss Sharples is a "New Woman," independent and professional. Although Miss Sharples helps Joanna to a job, there is no sense of community between the two. After her show has been a Broadway success, Joanna finds herself among a mixed group of professional people, who—like her—had "made it," but with a crucial difference: "These women had not been compelled to endure her long struggle against color" (235). Fauset focuses on Joanna's feelings of estrangement from the group, and the scene begs the question of whether this should be taken as conservatism on Fauset's part (the implication is that Joanna chooses domestic life over a continued career), or rather as an indication of the lack of corresponding needs as well as lack of contact, between white and black women. The scene is an example of how the race struggle takes precedence over the struggle against sexism, as Joanna identifies with the "New Negro" instead of the "New Woman."

DuCille observes that the texts of Fauset and Larsen are "characterized by the gradual resexualization of black womanhood" (10). One indicator of this concern is the great attention Larsen gives to clothes and color in *Quicksand* and "the extent to which these elements serve in the text as signifiers of both simmering sexuality and genteel femininity" (15). The analysis of the imagery of clothing, which both Larsen and Fauset attend to in great detail, will be continued in the next chapter. Here, clothes are found to present exterior markers of interior qualities, and are accordingly analyzed as a part of a performance of a certain identity.

Chapter 3

Black performance/Performances of blackness

> Acting black: a whole social world of irony, violence, negotiation, and learning is contained in that phrase.
>
> *Eric Lott*

> Looking and being looked at reproduce racial power relations.
>
> *Richard Dyer*

This chapter returns to the minstrel performer in an attempt to connect performance to racial identity. The issues of identity as performance or role-playing, authenticity and masking that are crucial to my analysis of Johnson's, Fauset's, and Larsen's novels all relate to the minstrel performance. Although music and jokes were an important part of minstrelsy, the whole performance rested on the perception of the actors as black. It was a spectacle dependent on the visual means of "blacking-up," mimicry and the clothes worn by the performers. The "blacking-up" typical of both white and black minstrel actors directly calls into question the meaning of "blackness." Minstrelsy has often been conceived of as an art form that makes use of racist stereotypes, but Eric Lott and Jennifer DeVere Brody, among others, have shown that it is a type of performance that is characterized by a play with racial images, drawing attention to the fluidity of racial categories. They suggest that while the denigrating images of blacks of the minstrel performance served to maintain American racial hierarchies and keep the black subject in an inferior social position, the ambivalence of the racial images in minstrelsy actually undermines the certainty of racial categories. In the minstrel show, white men assumed the markers of "blackness," which apart from the blackening of the face included facial mimicry and bodily gestures, (such as we will see described by Larsen in *Quicksand*) in an act designed to convey racial "authenticity." This assumed authenticity serves to question what "blackness" really is.

Adding further complexity to this tangled issue, Lott goes on to describe how white actors were actually considered the best performers of blackness. Although the whiteness of the performers showed in their faces, the audience accepted their appearance as an "authentic" representation of blackness. This willingness to be deceived suggests a racial anxiety induced by the mixed presence of the performers. The relationship between the performers and their audience reveals a complex relationship of expectations, power, and control. Any stage performance must be based on a consideration of what the audience wants to see or can accept. One of several meanings of the word "performance" is "to accomplish (any action involving skill or ability), as before an audience." Thus, to be perceived by another is a constitutive element of performance. In this sense, an actor needs a form of "double consciousness" (similar to that which DuBois identified as the gift and the burden of the African American).

Eric Lott suggests that early blackface performance is "one of the very first constitutive discourses of the body in American culture" (117). Observing that an exploitative organization of labor structures the economies of capitalist societies, he goes on to argue that the body is here "a potentially subversive site" (117). That is, by its mere visibility, the black body destabilizes the ideal order of a democratic, equal American society. The black bodies of the minstrel performance could, on the one hand, be perceived as representing the pre-industrial joys of the plantation days. On the other hand, they functioned as guilt-inducing reminders of human slavery. During slavery, black bodies had been exploited for purposes of labor and sex, to the extent that by the nineteenth century the black body had become a "cultural sign" of slavery and sexuality. To deal with such painful recognitions, Lott suggests that we devise certain cultural strategies, such as reducing the body merely to sexuality, or "colonizing" it with medical discourse that figures the body as discrete parts or organs. Another important strategy for dealing with the crucial role of the body in the economy is to tie the body to a discourse of racial biology. I will return to these strategies, and to the linking of sexuality, scientific discourse, and visibility in the discussion of stereotypes below.

Performance in *The Autobiography of an Ex-Colored Man*

Johnson's nameless narrator is not a minstrel performer, but he moves within the complex grid of performance, masking, and the dialectic of group and individual that was delineated by Douglas in the Introduction. The notion of performance works on several levels in *The Autobiography*, as regards both form and content. Indeed, I would argue that the book hinges on the tropes of performance and masking, which relate to the role of the author/narrator, to the rhetoric of irony, to "passing," to music and the narrator's work as a rag-time pianist.

The voice of the author/narrator

The Autobiography is framed as a confession: the book opens with the narrator comparing himself to "the un-found-out criminal," who needs to relieve himself of the "great secret" of his life, the "practical joke" he has played on society (1) – which, as we learn at the end, is his "passing" for white. The "secret" is never fully revealed, however, as the "autobiography" remains unsigned. The issue of names was especially pertinent in 1912 when the author's name also remained unknown due to the anonymous publication of the book. *The Autobiography* was, however, published in Johnson's name in 1927, and a couple of years later, Johnson published his own autobiography *Along This Way* (1933). In *The Autobiography*, we never get to know the narrator's name, and other characters are known merely as "mother," "father," "Red Head," or "Shiny." [27]

We can thus say that *The Autobiography* wears a generic mask; presenting itself as an autobiography, it is no more "biographical" than any novel. It is a book that plays with notions of genre and the boundary between fact and fiction. The notion of masking applies to several other aspects of *The Autobiography* as well. For example, masking is significantly related to the narrator's position vis-à-vis the story he is telling. As any life story, this "autobiography" is told from a first-person perspective, by an older man who looks back and comments on the experiences of his younger and more naïve self. However, this older man is not only more cynical, he has undergone a more radical change: he has in

---

[27] The only person who is actually named in the story is the former valet of the narrator's millionaire employer. Interestingly Walter, as he was called, never appears in the story and his name is mentioned only in passing.

effect acquired a new "racial" identity. He grows up thinking of himself as a white boy, but after an incident in school, he learns that he is to be counted among the colored children and so he turns to living life as a black person. At the end of the novel, however, he lives again as a white man. By letting the narrator assume several masks during the course of the story, Johnson toys with the idea of the in/visibility of blackness and the body as a source of "racial" knowledge. Benjamin Sherwood Lawson observes that it is not only these different masks that the protagonist wears that "[blur] the image of the central character." Johnson's narrative technique also makes it difficult for the reader to get a clear picture of the narrator, "since the book is a first person discourse which presents a rather naïve young man and a more cynical older man, one with a different name/identity, who comments upon his earlier self" (Lawson 95). The indefiniteness of the central character is emblematic of this text that deals vitally with the destabilization of certainties.

Robert Bone's argument that James Weldon Johnson let protest stand back in favor of artistry can be modified by the suggestion that Johnson was able to *mix* artistry with protest by the force of his rhetoric. In the next section, I will discuss how his irony can be interpreted as a device for voicing social critique while still reaching a mixed audience of white and black American readers. Irony was not the only means to create a text that could satisfy this "double audience," however. Another way that Johnson handled this difficult situation was by employing subtle shifts of narrative voice. In a 1997 article entitled "The Narrator's Editorialist Voice in *The Autobiography of An Ex-Colored Man*," F. Patton Walker observes that these shifts occur when Johnson wants to comment on social inequities, such as the effects of class structure on the black culture; on black contributions to the arts; and on the life and customs of the American South (78). In these instances, the story shifts from the first-person perspective and the individual level to the third-person point-of-view, whereby events at hand are interpreted and reflected on in a larger social perspective. Walker calls this particular third-person voice "the editorialist voice," suggesting that it should not be confused with that of a third-person omniscient narrator (91). Rather, it is a passive voice, which comments on events beyond those of the actual story. Walker sees this invention as Johnson's ingenious solution to the dilemma of facing a double audience. The editorialist voice, Walker claims, made it possible for Johnson to address and critique current social issues like those mentioned above, while still reaching a sizeable reading audience. The presence of this voice indicates that we should not conflate the narrator of the story with its author, Johnson, although the label "autobiography" invites such a conflation.

The type of masking achieved by the "editorialist voice," which enabled Johnson to explore taboo topics, was not unique to Johnson. Walker traces a tradition of masking to the nineteenth-century slave narratives (this is a point also made by MacKethan):

> Johnson was extending the artistry of masking, unique to the slave narrative. The slave perfected masking as a means of communicating intimate feelings to other slaves within an exclusive circle. Johnson's editorialist voice extended this exclusive, oral, slave community to encompass a broader, racially mixed audience receptive enough to comprehend his message. (Walker 73)

Another example of linguistic masking is irony, which Johnson made good use of in *The Autobiography*. The slave narratives also function as sounding-boards for the irony of Johnson's text.

Passing and textual appearances

One of the most fruitful ways of understanding *The Autobiography*, as well as an interesting way of probing the relationship between author and narrator, is to look deeper into the rhetoric of irony in the novel. Roxanna Pisiak links the irony in *The Autobiography* to subversion that has an effect far beyond the text: "By its very existence, this text demonstrates that the constructs upon which its story is based – the most important being the split between 'white' and 'black' in America – are themselves 'unreliable'" (85). Since the narrator's blackness can be genealogically traced to his mother but remains invisible in the son, his identity is impossible to pin down to an inherent essence. In Kathleen Pfeiffer's words, he "embodies the paradox of race and colour because he is both legally black and visibly white" (405). Both the blackness and the whiteness he assumes are, in effect, masks in that they are designations of identity that he can learn to perform. The irony of the book is largely directed at social structures, outside of the text. Thus, the artistry of the ironic language makes the book's note of protest more subtle. Indeed, if Johnson had confronted the problems that his narrator is faced with in a more straightforward language, it is possible that the novel would not have been published at all. Through the linguistic masking of irony, which is characterized by instability of signification, Johnson was able to find an audience for the story of his unnamed narrator. As previously discussed,

Johnson was well aware of the problem that the African-American author had of writing for both white and black Americans, each audience with its own restrictive demands. Being a double-edged mode of discourse that can be read on different levels, the irony that Johnson employs in *The Autobiography* was one way to attain the goal of fusing the black and the white audiences into one.

A significant part of Johnson's irony is, as suggested in the above quotation from Pisiak, related to the narrator's passing. He calls it "a practical joke" on society that he manages to live as a white man although he should be categorized as black according to contemporary legislation, but in the end he suspects that the joke is played on him. He seems to have lost too much by giving up his "true" identity and declining to identify with the oppressed black people. Indeed the novel ends with the narrator's bitter realization of having "sold [his] birthright for a mess of pottage" (154). Some critics of Johnson's novel, such as Marvin Garrett, discuss the "dishonesty" of the narrator and talk about his hypocrisy and cowardice, referring particularly to his ability to move back and forth across the color-line and his unwillingness (or inability) to fully identify himself as "black." The outcome of the novel has been the subject of much debate, particularly concerning the extent to which his final decision was limited by circumstances or followed from a free choice. Like the performance of gender identity described by Butler, the performance of a racial identity is determined by a reiteration of social norms. "White" and "black" are imagined and performed differently in accordance with discursive regulations, just like "man" and "woman." The body of the passer has the same ontological status as the transvestite—that is, s/he occupies the space in-between categories such as black/white, man/woman.

This space Marjorie Garber calls "a space of possibility structuring and confounding culture: the disruptive element that intervenes, not just a category crisis of male and female, but the crisis of category itself" (Garber 17). The narrator's "practical joke" reflects the paradoxical organization of society that depends on categories which demand that we separate "black" from "white." The joke is finally directed back at the reading public, who try to label the narrator throughout. Without recourse to the categories that force him into an untenable situation, we cannot make sense of his activities. (In this way the reader is subtly made a coadjutor in his deceit.) Outside of these organizing categories, there is nothing "dishonest" about his story. Instead, we can see it as a succession of performances made on the basis of social norms. His identity correlates with his musical development, which is vitally affected by his visit to

Europe, and is evidenced by his return and the subsequent attempt at immersion in black culture. The irony here is intertextual and relates to the structure of the narrative.

In Johnson's *The Autobiography*, the imitation of the white is near complete, including as it does even skin color. In this case, the inability to separate the passing black person from the white person, to separate copy and original, leads to a rearticulation of what it means to be white. If we cannot tell the copy from the original, the status of the original is called into question, and the anxious guarding of the original becomes pointless. The question concerning whether to read Johnson's text literally or figuratively also refers to one of the main groups of themes that have been identified in the preceding chapter as crucially related to African-American fiction about Europe, namely that of education and/or literacy. The irony of the text, the fact that the words of the text do not mean what they appear to mean and can be misread, has a parallel in the interpretation of the cultural signification of black and white bodies in the societal context. Ultimately, *The Autobiography* is about the possibility of reading bodies as "black" or "white," and of deciphering the cultural codes that go with these categories. In this sense, the book is fundamentally about literacy. Robert B. Stepto, who has written about this aspect of *The Autobiography*, finds that the ex-colored man "seems incapable of interpreting and 'reading' the significance of most events in his life. His circumstance obviously confirms the theory that one kind of illiteracy breeds another" (109). In other words, the narrator's fundamental inability, or unwillingness, to identify himself as "black" leads to other momentous misreadings as well.

The first example of such a misreading comes already on the second page of *The Autobiography*. The narrator reminisces about his childhood home in Georgia and proceeds to tell of his fascination with "a hedge of vari-colored glass bottles stuck in the ground neck down" (2) that could be found in the front yard. Curious about the nature of this "hedge," he decides to unearth the bottles—an act for which he receives a terrible spanking from his mother. Stepto identifies this hedge of bottles as an instance of African cultural retention, calling it "a spatial expression of community into which he is born" (100). Thus, Stepto sees a pattern being established in which the narrator fails to recognize and honor his African heritage:

> When the Ex-Colored Man digs up the bottles—ironically, in
> order to "know whether or not the bottles grew as the flowers
> did"—he performs an innocent yet devastating act of assault

upon a considerable portion of his heritage. That act prefigures his misdirected attempts to approach, let alone embrace, black American culture, including most obviously his desire to render the "old Southern songs" in "classical form." (Stepto 101)

The "old Southern songs" referred to here are the songs that he learns from his mother and that become the central image of his African heritage as they are juxtaposed with European classical music. The parallel drawn between the narrator's unearthing of the bottles and his subsequent attempt at musical fusion in the above example suggests that this latter act is also a "devastating assault," that the Southern songs are mistreated in the process. This sense of trespassing relates to a disrespect for his past, evidenced by the fact that he decides to do it for commercial purposes, and because his life has been lived in milieus that are not typical of the majority of African Americans. Therefore, with Stepto's line of reasoning, there is something cynical or at least inauthentic about his handling of the Southern songs.

Ragging the classics: music and passing

The narrator is an accomplished performer of ragtime music, and his experiences as a musician reflect the development of this type of popular music, which was reaching an increasing audience at the beginning of the twentieth century. Music in the novel, in fact, functions as a metaphor for cultural identity, and more specifically, "a metaphor for the consciousness of the mulatto" (Washington 239). His moving between the white and the black worlds can be read as reflections of his involvement with music of African-American origin and European origin respectively. Spatial movement accompanies his movement between musical styles: moving north to New York he starts playing as a professional entertainer, moving east across the Atlantic he starts to incorporate Western classical music into his repertoire of ragtime songs. Finally, he moves back to the US and the American South to immerse himself in African-American culture, aiming to develop ragtime (a choice partly motivated by financial considerations).

The narrator is, as it were, "whitened" as he passes for white in Europe and so is his music, which is a blend between ragtime and classical music. But to realize his musical plans of making ragtime classic he has to go to the American south to collect old slave songs and modern ragtime music. That is, he is not already familiar with this cultural tradition, but goes in search of it much like an ethnographer. In fact, Johnson's narrator here appears in a position similar to that of the white minstrel performer. Like the minstrel, the narrator copies the requisites of blackness; in this case, the knowledge of a musical idiom characterized by its attention to rhythms and cadences, and its popular appeal. Of course, the question remains to be asked how representative, or "authentic," the narrator is as a black musician, or the "black" music he creates. In this instance, it is as if Johnson, by the evocation of the commodified blackness of the minstrel performer, is telling us, tongue-in-cheek, that authentic blackness is a construct. The narrator's act of immersing himself in black culture instead points us to the relevance of the concept of performativity in this context. There are material reasons that govern his choice, such as the fact that he would have a greater chance of success as a "black" musician. This is partly due to the burgeoning contemporary interest in African influences on Western culture, and partly to the fact that his chosen repertoire is one of entertainment, that he in fact aims to popularize classical Western music and, given the connection to the popular roots of ragtime, his choice really appears logical.

Like the music he aims to create, which is characterized as a blend between classical European art music and his mother's Southern songs, the narrator himself is a blend of characteristics associated with the European (his white appearance and knowledge of European music and languages) and with the African-American (his upbringing as black and his musicality and sense of rhythm). He is a hybrid character who is not socially acceptable. As the millionaire points out: "What kind of a Negro would you make now, especially in the South" (106). The millionaire's question suggests that his move to Europe is a move to whiteness, culture and sophistication (a social space quite different from that of the South where he aims to go). The journey east has meant staying away from the South—the place of blackness, where African-American music styles originated—and it turns out that this journey cannot be reversed.

His return to the black world does not last long. In the South, the narrator encounters black working-class and rural people, from whom he seeks to distinguish himself. These people, whom he describes as "the desperate class—the men who work in the lumber and turpentine camps, the ex-convicts, the barroom loafers," have a very hostile relationship to white people and constitute a potential source of danger to society. He goes on: "I am sure there is no more urgent work before the white South, not only for its present happiness, but for its future safety, than the decreasing of this class of blacks" (56). Yet, it is this class of people that has created the ragtime music that he wants to make classic. Seen against this background, blending their music with Western classical music is by implication to assimilate the people it is associated with into white society. There is thus a parallelism between the musical harmonies that he aims for and a vision of social harmony. On the one hand, the people ought to become more refined, but on the other they should be credited as the artists they really are.

Alessandro Portelli, who makes this point in "The Tragedy and the Joke: the Autobiography of an Ex-Colored Man" (2001), goes on to connect the narrator's relationship to African-American music to his passing. His journey into the white world means that he, like the expatriate, has to leave certain parts of his past behind. The "fast yellowing manuscripts" of his mother's songs, which he keeps locked up in a box, symbolize his emotional exile from the black community:

> [I]n this case, what the narrator cannot bring with him across the racial boundary is the music. There is no reason, technically, why he could not work at making ragtime classic while passing as a white man in Germany. Rather, the reason is anthropological. Folk music, and black folk music especially, is not just a formal structure of sounds and words; it is the expression of an experience, one that includes also the pain and fear and shame instilled by white violence, as well as the memory and pride of resistance. This music of historic struggle cannot be turned into harmless and fashionable sounds of uplift. Precisely because he has been so keenly aware of the social context of the music and the poetry, he finds it impossible to reproduce them once he has run away from that environment and cut off his connections to it. (Portelli 156)

The music is thus a metaphor for his cultural identity. Cristina L. Ruotolo, in "James Weldon Johnson and the Autobiography of an Ex-Colored Musician" (2000), deals with the narrator's musical performances as inherently linked to his performances as white or black. She observes: "Comfortable and capable in both European and African American music, the narrator's musical performances function, more than once, as agents in his 'passing' as either 'white' or 'black'; indeed, his convincing performance of Frédéric Chopin ultimately convinces a 'lily white woman' to marry him, while his masterful performances of ragtime make audible a blackness invisible to the eye" (248). In fact, the narrator's exploration of the "audible colorline" between ragtime and Western classical music is an additional way of questioning the visible colorline. His attempt to rag the classics (which was actually quite common in the early decades of the twentieth century) would destabilize the audible colorline between different musical traditions—in which Western music figures as the notated, textually transmitted music and African-American music as oral and improvisatory. But his attempt fails; after leaving the black community he can no longer play the music associated with it. As Portelli points out, there is a world of feeling and experience that is coupled to the music and without which the music can in fact not be. So, while the ex-colored man's physical movement between the black and the white world exposes race as a construct along with the permeability of the colorline, his musical experiences provide another angle. The music has an ineffable, black quality that he cannot reproduce because he is too far removed from its sources. As a white man, his performance of ragtime risks becoming a blackface performance like that of the minstrel.

In the light of this outcome of *The Autobiography*, we understand the irony of the advice the narrator got from his millionaire friend, who tried to dissuade him from becoming a "black musician" by claiming that "[m]usic is a universal art; anybody's music belongs to everybody; you can't limit it to race or country" (105). This statement rather reinforces the selfishness and materialism that the white millionaire represents. Music is too closely linked to the narrator's sense of self to be so lightly dealt with.

An ironic inversion

Irony is a textual strategy that seems well suited for a text embodying double consciousness—a mode of perception of the world which emphasizes a dual perspective seems congenial with a textual rhetoric that permits interpretations from the various viewpoints of the reader. The frame of the story of *The Autobiography* is ironic in itself. The narrator starts out by telling the reader of the motivation for recounting his story in the following terms: "I think I find a sort of savage and diabolical desire to gather up all the little tragedies of my life, and turn them into a practical joke on society" (1). However, the ending shows that the joke may really be played on the narrator, as he thinks of himself as "a coward, a deserter, and I am possessed by a strange longing for my mother's people" (153). So, the joke that he considers himself playing on white society as a transgressor of the color-line turns out to be a very dubious one; it has made him an expatriate from the black world, alienated from his past and from his people. And concomitantly, a joke finally depends on the audience "getting it," that is, understanding that they have been fooled. While the telling of his tale is his way of letting the audience in on the joke and getting the point across, this point is dulled by the fact that he remains unrecognizable to the audience in his namelessness.

Like the kind of linguistic masking expressed through the subtle shifts of voice in the narrative, the irony that is embedded in the structure of Johnson's narrative can be traced to the accounts of former slaves. In fact, there are many ways in which *The Autobiography* inverts the typical structure of the slave narratives. For example, the trip from South to North, which was previously discussed as an important symbolic journey to freedom and a central motif in African-American literature, here takes the narrator into the slave-like relationship between himself and the white millionaire. As we have seen, this man, whom he meets in New York, employs him as a private pianist and eventually takes him to Europe.

Another example of such an inversion is the ten-dollar coin that the narrator's white father gives to him after drilling a hole through it. As it is thus rendered valueless it comes to symbolize a price put upon him by the white man and becomes an object rife with connotations of enslavement. In addition, his father draws a string through the coin and ties it around the son's neck in a reversal of the symbolic unfastening of the noose around the slave's neck. It is a somber reminder of the many blacks that were threatened with lynching in early twentieth-century America. According to Lucinda MacKethan, this scene is particularly important in showing the text's irony at the expense of the narrator. She writes: "[I]ts irony is so obvious, and yet the narrator himself not only avoids showing that he understands the irony but also makes a statement that reveals his inability to 'read' himself in his presentation of his past" (MacKethan 140). The irony of the coin scene has a parallel in the final scene of the book. Here, the narrator ponders on his life fearing that in his choice to refrain from living as a black man, he has sold his birthright for a mess of pottage. In MacKethan's view, this image is the "last image of a self enslaved by its own blindness to the joke that white society has played on it" (140-141).

Performance in *There Is Confusion*

The idea that cultural performances could have political effects was prevalent during the Harlem Renaissance, and seems to guide all the authors I study. For example, Johnson's narrator wants to elevate African American folk music to the same status as Western classical music through his own blend of musical styles. This cultural act is intended to have political effects: increased social equality as a result of artistic distinction and the elevation of a cultural tradition. Joanna Marshall in Fauset's *There Is Confusion* is barred from the ballet scene because of the political import of a black dancer performing a western, "high" cultural art form. The implication of such a performance, if it were to take place, would be equalization between black and white, and the story of Joanna's life turns on the exclusion from the classical ballet scene. The passage featuring the "Dance of the Nations" is an example of how charged these questions were. Here, Joanna has finally got a job as a dancer at the District Line Theater in New York. In the "Dance of the Nations," America is to be represented by three dances, "one for the white element, one for the black and one for the red" (226). Since the white lead dancer who performs Ms America, Ms Ashby, simply cannot dance the way colored people do, help is sought from Joanna. As it turns out, Ms Ashby after a time moves on to a new engagement, and the choice reluctantly falls on Joanna to replace her. Since Joanna is too dark to pass for white, the solution is for her to wear a mask on stage. But an old habitué in the audience senses that there is something strange about this arrangement and starts calling for Joanna to reveal her face. Finally, Joanna has to comply with the audience's demand and lifts the mask from her face with the following words: "I hardly need to tell you that there is no one in the audience more American than I am. My great-grandfather fought in the Civil War and my brother is 'over there' now" (232). After a moment's suspense, the audience shows their acceptance of Joanna's appearance and the show is a success.

In this incident, which constitutes the apex of her artistic ambitions, Joanna uses the stage to claim her Americanness. That she should do so wearing a mask not only evokes the tradition of blackface-masking in minstrelsy but the whole existence of the black population of America (put into words by Paul Laurence Dunbar in the poem "We Wear the Mask"). Joanna has to explain and give legitimization to her claim to being an American—a legitimization which she finds in generations of male ancestors. The assumption is that behind her mask she is white, that Americanness equals whiteness. The charged atmosphere surrounding the removal of the mask indicates that the matter of skin color goes to the heart of the nation, that is, it is a matter of national identity. There are two significant interpretations of this masked, presumably white, Ms

America (Kuenz 99). First, her appearance indicates that whiteness is a mask, to be put on and performed in accordance with the audience's expectations. Thus, it is a construction similar to that of blackness. The second implication is that African-Americans are actually at the center of American culture, and that behind the mask of Americanness is actually blackness. Together these gestures indicate that a resignification of "Americanness" is at stake in Joanna's performance.

The appearance of Joanna's masked black body on the stage echoes the minstrel performer, with similar guilt-inducing connotations of slavery and sexual exploitation. The audience's appreciation of the minstrel character—and Joanna in this case—is dependent on their recognition of their own suprem-acy, which is paired uneasily with the realization of the violence it is deeply connected to. The import of this charged scene is emphasized by the narrator's concluding comment: "Perhaps it would not have succeeded anywhere else but in New York, and perhaps not even there but in Greenwich Village" (232). Here is a recognition of the role place has in how race is perceived. It is only within a very limited area that Joanna is likely to enjoy success with this kind of performance, and her stage performance cannot break these (social and physical) boundaries.

As it turns out, her success does not translate into the social sphere in the way that she had hoped for. Although the production is moved to Broadway the following week and Joanna becomes a celebrated star, her joy at her success soon turns into disappointment. This accomplishment does not have the more far-reaching social effects that she hoped it would have: "She realized for the first time how completely colored Americans were mere on-lookers at the pos-sibilities of life"(235). Her frustration with what her achievement has brought leads to her decision to give up her stage career altogether in favor of making a home and a family with Peter Bye. The abrupt change in Joanna Marshall's priorities from solely thinking of her own career as a singer and dancer to becoming the adoring wife and perfect mother who gladly gives up her own ambitions for those of her husband and children has often been brought up, particularly by feminist critics, as an indication of Fauset's conservatism and support of a patriarchal ideology. However, a focus on performance in *There Is Confusion* may actually lead to a revaluation of Jessie Fauset's aesthetics. Jane Kuenz, for example, provides a fruitful alternative reading of Fauset's strategy here:

> Rather than read the moments of forced resolution in Fauset's novels as signs of her personal failure as a writer or thinker – as I believe most of her feminist readers still do – I would suggest instead that they mark the point at which the texts' internal contradictions overlap with and threaten to give voice to those contradictions general in the culture and, in this instance, in New Negro gender and racial ideology in particular. (Kuenz 95)

The contradictions inherent in the "New Negro" ideology, such as the conflict between individual and collective goals, or the celebration of racial difference vis-à-vis the struggle for equality, in the novel are played out through the trope of performance.

The reason why Joanna decides to give up her stage career is not lack of success, for this she finally achieves, but disappointment at the effect of her success. It turned to be a limited ego-boost, lacking the sought-for correspondence between artistic success and social equality. In this respect, Fauset actually seems to be seriously questioning the very foundation of the "New Negro" project, namely, that the individual work of art could contribute to the larger goal of social change (McCoy 103). Furthermore, Joanna's predicament indicates the effect of gender on the difficult balance between individual and collective goals that the "New Negro" artists had to negotiate.

While depicting strong women with ambitions regarding career and class mobility, *There Is Confusion* is not an edifying story of one woman's ascent. Fauset displays a keen awareness of how the pressures of gender compound those of race, in a manner related to the recurrent issue of individualism versus collectivism. At this time, African-American advocates of women's rights pragmatically stated that the battle against racism would have to take precedence over that of sexism. Isolated from white feminists, African American women would find (throughout the twentieth century) that the struggle for civil rights thus came to be fought mainly in terms of men's rights.

The implications of the seemingly forced resolution of *There Is Confusion*—in which Joanna hastily gives up her own ambitions concerning a stage career in order to devote herself to husband and children—does not necessarily imply that Fauset conceived of this as a "happy" ending. Instead, the rather far-reaching conclusion is that this ending points to flaws in the "New Negro" ideology that Fauset herself was promoting. The good interest of the race demanded that collective goals be put before individual ones. Owing to the hierarchical, patriarchal structure of society—black as well as white—this in actuality came to mean that, in the struggle for racial equality, it was more efficient to let men take precedence over women. Jane Kuenz explains this relationship in the following manner:

> Most obviously, the tension in New Negro ideology between individual and collective goals, the intertwining of those goals and the insistence that they are in the end the same thing, is structured differently for women than it is for men in the ideological rhetoric of the period. For women, the conjoining of the projects of advancing the self and advancing the race often becomes simply the one project of advancing the race alone. (Kuenz 96)

While Fauset's novel registers this dilemma on the part of African-American women, it offers no true way out of the situation. Instead, as an alternative to the coveted public life that Joanna cannot turn to the benefit of the collective, Fauset proposes the "safe spaces" of the home and the extended family. The concept of "safe spaces" comes from Patricia Hill Collins, who defines a safe space as "a prime location for resisting objectification as the Other" (Hill Collins 95). She suggests that extended families, churches and African-American community organizations are examples of "safe spaces." In Fauset's works, the idea of home is often featured as this kind of safe space. A parallel is offered by Elizabeth Ammons, who talks of the "life-giving vision of life" that Fauset presents, which "is based on the corporate values of community action and rootedness, female friendship, solidarity with men in the race struggle, membership in a church, and commitment to the bonds of family" (215). Important to Fauset's vision, then, is that the "New Negroes," for all their eagerness to start anew, should not forget to take sustenance in those aspects of the past that were positive and could continue to be of use. Referring back to Ann Douglas, I read Fauset's valuation of African-American life as a reflection of her sense of the New Negroes as a generation found. However, although Fauset creates strong female characters in both Joanna and Maggie, this approach is problematic as regards the struggle against sexism. The struggle against racism is given priority and, as Ammons suggests, the black woman is given the rather passive part of loyal helpmate to her man in this struggle.

Larsen, however, complicates the meaning of all these spaces in her emphasis on Helga's essential homelessness. The homes Helga manages to create for herself—with her relatives in Copenhagen and through marriage to the Southern preacher Rev. Green—are complex spheres which end up being so limited as to be suffocating. In the final analysis, Helga is trapped within herself, within her mind and body which are equally circumscribed by conventions:

> Fauset and Larsen, however, are concerned with the colonized mind—with female sexual subjectivity—as well as with the objectified body. Accordingly, their texts implicitly explore the ways in which social forces and patriarchal ideology inspire, if not demand, the participation of black women in their own objectification and domination. Characters such as Joanna Marshall in There Is Confusion and Helga Crane in Quicksand ultimately discover that acceptance as a woman and as an artist means defining themselves by someone else's terms and objectifying themselves for someone else's gaze. (duCille 94)

Du Cille here suggests that while Joanna and Helga voluntarily take part in their own objectification, in fact their choices or possibilities of resistance to the dominant forces are few. Importantly, du Cille's analysis takes note of the combined pressures of race and gender in this process of objectification and colonization. For Helga and Joanna, Fanon's internalized gaze is refracted through the two polarities of lady-like race woman and mother on the one hand and the sexually uninhibited exotic on the other. In their performances of racial and sexual identity, clothes have an important role to play. This will be analyzed below.

Performance in *Quicksand*

Lott's ideas concerning the social meaning attributed to the black bodies of the nineteenth-century minstrel performers form the basis for my analysis of how this meaning has been carried over into the twentieth-century representations of blackness by Johnson, Fauset, and Larsen. In Larsen's *Quicksand*, Helga Crane visits a vaudeville show, which appears to be an actual minstrel performance, at the Copenhagen Circus. The Danish audience loves the performance but Helga cannot laugh where the Danish audience laughs; instead she feels hatred and shame. Larsen focuses on Helga's troubled reactions to the performance as well as to the howling and shouting audience's response:

> Helga Crane was not amused. Instead she was filled with a fierce hatred for the cavorting Negroes on the stage. She felt shamed, betrayed, as if these pale pink and white people among whom she

> had lived had suddenly been invited to look upon something in
> her which she had hidden away and wanted to forget. And she was
> shocked at the avidity at which Olsen beside her drank it in. (83)

Helga is shocked by the artists' portrayal of simple stereotypes of "black" behavior. But she is likewise shocked by the audience who seem to believe in what
they see, since the performance corresponds to their expectations of what they
would see black people doing.

The performance gives Helga the sense that the audience sees something in
the performers that extends to her as well. Her shame at the 'cavorting Negroes'
on the stage echoes the feelings of the ex-colored man before the—rather more
brutal—scene of lynching that precedes his decision to pass. In these instances,
the ex-colored man and Helga both experience a form of self-hatred resulting
from the internalization of the white man's gaze that Fanon discussed. While
they appreciate what they see and shout for more, Helga is affected by the unequal relationship between audience and performers. This is a spectacle that
the white Danes are free to laugh at, knowing that it does not challenge their
social position. Rather, the respective positions of a white audience in possession of a controlling gaze and black performers forced to demeaning behavior
in adaptation to the taste of the white spectators are confirmed. The fact that
this performance takes place in a Danish context does not mean that it is free
from the contradictions suggested by Lott, which relate primarily to American
slavery. Denmark also has a colonial history involving African slavery, there
being Danish colonies in the West Indies (St Croix) where slaves were set to
work on sugar cane plantations.

The performance, in the novel accompanied by a nursery rhyme, suggests
a regression of the characters: "[H]ow the singers danced, pounding their
thighs, slapping their hands together, twisting their legs, waving their abnor-
mally long arms, throwing their bodies about with a loose ease! And how the
enchanted spectators clapped and howled and shouted for more!" [28] (83) These
playful bodily movements are thoroughly enjoyed by the white audience. This
is an image of "the Negro" that they can recognize and accept. The fact that
the music that accompanies the performance is a nursery rhyme strengthens

---

[28] Nella Larsen's account of the minstrel performers echoes the Knickerbocker review of a performance
by T. D. Rice, who was considered the "originator" of blackface performance (Lott 18): "Such a
natural gait"! – such a laugh! – and such a twitching-up of the arm and shoulder! It was THE Negro,
par excellence. Long live JAMES CROW, Esquire!" (quoted in Lott 142).

the notion of the childishness of the performers. Lott argues that the illusory presence of blackness in minstrelsy allowed the white spectators to pass it off as "naïve" black comedy, "the sort of comedy, according to Freud, in which spectators indulge in lost moments of childish pleasure evoked by the antics of children, or of 'inferior' people who resemble them" (143).

But there were other features of the minstrel show that served to keep the black people at a stage of infantilism. Lott sees a likeness between the minstrel show and the nursery not only in the music but also in the nonsense of the songs and puns and the "tirelessly absurd physical antics" of the performers. Another feature associating "black" people with children was the clothes typically worn by minstrel performers, such as oversized shoes and enormous shooting collars (143).

The nursery rhyme included in connection with the vaudeville incident in *Quicksand* undergirds Helga's reflections on black people in America. She finds that they are afraid of taking pride in their difference and are trying to be like everybody else, that is, imitate white people:

> They were all beggars like the motley crowd in the old nursery rhyme:
> Hark! Hark!
> The dogs do bark.
> The beggars are coming to town.
> Some in rags,
> Some in tags,
> And some in velvet gowns. (83)

In this passage, Helga designates to African Americans the demeaning role of dependent children. In fact, she even feels betrayed by the vaudeville performers and experiences an acute sense of discomfort, which seems to stem from her perception of the performative nature of the blackness on display in the scene. To "act black" was to be the subject of commodification, to be guided by a concern with what would bring an audience. Instead of challenging well-known cultural stereotypes of black people as happy, child-like, good dancers, the Circus performance reiterates these cultural expectations and thereby solidifies denigrating images of black people. Helga recognizes this and is disappointed with the fact that this cultural production does not make use of its ability to question present social mythologies and structures. Her frustration can be linked to her understanding of the performers' lack of recognition of the social and political import of cultural production. By drawing our attention to the complex negotiations that often lay behind African-American stage performance in this way, Larsen complicates the celebration of African-American culture that was part of the Harlem Renaissance.

The performance at the Copenhagen Circus later prompts Helga to muse on "difference" and the Dahls' need to stress her difference from them. Dyer points out that the exaggerations of blackface (reiterated in black filmic stereotypes during the twentieth century) served precisely the purpose of underlining the difference between black and white (Dyer 51). In this context, we need to remember that minstrelsy started as a performance by white actors acting "black." This meant that white actors had determined what black performance was, and what kind of blackness could be represented. Black stage performance is, then, at root a negotiated form of representation. Black performers were taking over a cultural act whose parameters had been set by white performers, but where at least there was a possibility for them to participate. Being on stage could be an opportunity to gain recognition for talent and skill. It could also involve a chance to modify, within limits, representations of blackness. These complex relationships are all part of Helga's experiences in Denmark where she is gradually made to feel like a "stage Negro" herself.

However, Lott warns us against the simplification of seeing blackface performance as a mere confirmation of already existent racist thought. Instead, he suggests that the cultural field is a battleground for social feelings and relationships, a continuous reproduction and negotiation of ideas and ideals. This idea of an ongoing struggle is reflected in the fiction of Johnson, Fauset, and Larsen, and indicates that the study of the significance of performance must resist both the simplification of seeing only the liberating potential of performance (a direction in which Roach leans), and a narrow focus on the suppressing structures of performance (proposed by Butler). With Lott's view of the battleground of culture, we cannot separate cultural performance on the stage from social performance. Stage performances and social attitudes inform one another: what is staged are cultural feelings and ideas which are, in turn, affected by the stage performance. Minstrelsy and the performance of racial stereotypes is only one, conspicuous example of the complexity of this issue.

In its tangled representations of blackness, minstrelsy throws the belief in corporeal truth into doubt. What is actually represented by the minstrel show is an instance of bodies that are not read correctly. The seemingly black bodies on stage are in reality white – or seemingly blackened white bodies are actually black. What this play with skin color shows is how untenable racial categories based on visual impression of bodies are. Bodies can apparently "lie," or, conversely, the categories are not fitted to reality. Ultimately, minstrelsy is a performance that shows how arbitrary the borders are between white and black. While seemingly reinstating the distinction between the two polarities, minstrelsy (like passing) points to a conflation between black and white identities. The minstrel performer and the passing mulatto complicate the locking of truth to the body, often simultaneously with the ascription of complete corporeality to the African American, by which white people have been put in the position of interpreters of the truth about the other. There are a number of ways in which this power of making intelligible is exercised, and in the following the role of gender in this process will be analyzed.

The respective experiences of Fauset's and Larsen's female and Johnson's male protagonists suggest that the normative categories of race and gender here converge and help constitute one another. In Copenhagen, the gendered nature of Helga's racial performance is primarily brought out by the relationship with the Danish painter Axel Olsen, whose perception of Helga represents the common stereotypes of black women.

Reading the body often involves a reduction to Nature, which was common in colonial depictions of native peoples. A most blatant—and illustrative—example is that of the African woman Saartje Bartman, also known as the Hottentot Venus. She was brought to England from South Africa by a Boer farmer and a doctor in 1819 and was exhibited for her physiognomy in London and Paris during the following five years. The discourse surrounding Saartje Bartman is analyzed by Stuart Hall in *Representation: Cultural Representations and Signifying Practices* (1997), and it reveals two important strategies of interpretation that apply to Larsen's novel particularly. These are fragmentation and the previously mentioned reductionism to Nature and body, both of which are known from the representation of women's bodies in pornography. The woman is turned into an object and the viewer sees only a portion of her body instead of a whole, integrated subject (Hall 266).

As noted in connection with the vaudeville performance above, the white Danes' perception of Helga is characterized by an obsession with marking her difference from them. This marking is done in gendered terms. Words like "mysterious," "savage," "exotic," "impulsive" and "not sufficiently civilized" are used to describe the Danes' perception of her. She is reduced to Nature and body, as opposed to culture or civilization. The painter Axel Olsen's "reading" of Helga is, in its fragmentation of her body into separate parts, similar to the descriptions of the "Hottentot Venus" as presented by Hall (265-66). Olsen's survey of Helga's physical appearance results in the following appraisal: "Superb eyes ... color ... neck column ... yellow ... hair ... alive... wonderful..." (Larsen 71). Olsen never actually addresses Helga herself, not even to ask her permission to paint her portrait. Helga is, as it were, disassembled into discrete parts by Olsen's gaze, and to him she does not really seem to exist as a person. But Helga plays an active part in the construction of a persona in accordance with this objectified view of the black woman, agreeing to wear spectacular clothes and speak faltering Danish. At first she is surprised by the stereotypical notions of difference that the Danes ascribe to her, but she does not refute them. Instead, she finds positive values in the passion, laughter, love of color, and sensuality attributed to her, according to the dictates of the current primitivism.

What we see at work in this part of the novel can be compared to the practice of trans-coding, that is, taking an existing meaning and re-appropriating it for new meanings (Hall 270). One way of doing this is by reversing stereotypes, or to value positively what has previously been thought of as negative. Primitivism's redefinition of the lack of reason, childishness, and simplicity previously ascribed to black people as greater access to passion, joy, and laughter is one example of such a reversal. As Hall points out, however, this strategy is not free from "the contradictions of the binary structure of racial stereotyping" or "the complex dialectics of power and subordination" through which black identities have been constructed (272). Ultimately, then, this strategy is not liberating, since it is still locked in a binary mode of perception. At best, it works in *Quicksand* to suggest the absurdity of this limited (because rigidly defined) mode of existence.

Cheryl Wall observes that Larsen's vocabulary is to a great extent influenced by anthropology in the section dealing with Copenhagen (Wall 101). This particular part of the book is characterized by images connotative of an exhibition, with Helga as the object on display. Helga is dressed in feathers, furs and "barbaric bracelets," which make her feel like "a veritable savage," or "a new and strange species of pet dog being proudly exhibited." Axel Olsen is particularly involved in this process of objectification. With his attempts to control her appearance by deciding what she is to wear, and with his painting, Olsen functions as the prime agent in the construction of Helga as a primitive. The portrait he paints of Helga is important as a reflection of contemporary representation of blacks by whites. He represents the white fascination with the "exotic" and the "primitive," which was a central concern to the Harlem Renaissance artists (Carby 171-72). The only way this artist can portray an African-American woman is as a wholly sensuous, sexual being. There is also something about Axel Olsen's painting of Helga Crane and the fixity of the portrait on canvas that accords with the whole structure of the Copenhagen episode. It represents stability and order, or lack of fluidity and open-endedness, fixing Helga within frames as a rare specimen and quite literally pinning her to the wall. Helga herself is very disturbed by the portrait, which she feels bears no resemblance to her at all, finding in it instead "some disgusting sensual creature with her features" (89). However, the painting is considered a success by Danish collectors and critics.

As an artist Axel Olsen, more than any of the other figures, embodies the idea of Europe as origin of culture. Olsen's paintings are mainly portraits of and for the social elite, and he is at the center of the social circles to which aunt Katrina and uncle Poul aspire. The characterization of Olsen is dominated by coolness, in combination with artificiality. Axel and Helga are in many ways described as each other's opposites: where Axel is blond, emotionally controlled and in possession of the artist's defining gaze, Helga is dark, passionate, and the object that is being observed. Helga's first encounter with Olsen is described as follows: "An artist, Helga decided at once, taking in the broad streaming tie. But how affected! How theatrical!" (70). Further on, this young painter is described as "[b]rilliant, bored, elegant, urbane, cynical, worldly, he was a type entirely new to Helga Crane, familiar only, and that but little, with the restricted society of American Negroes" (77). When Olsen finally proposes to Helga, his lack of passion makes the scene almost ludicrous: "[H]e kissed the small ivory hand. Quite decorously, Helga thought, for one so maddened that he was driven, against his inclination, to offer her marriage" (86). Later on she reflects on the incident: "He took it awfully well though – for a tragedy" (89). In passages like this, Larsen reproduces the same kind of dichotomous thinking that structures the oppression of African-American life. However, she turns the gaze back on the European to show that both parts of binary oppositions become equally limited. In addition, as should be obvious in some of the above examples, the rigidity of this kind of thinking adds a pertinent note of irony to her narrative.

Helga's art of identity construction is another significant contrast between her and Axel Olsen. Olsen's representation of Helga is a painted portrait, such as he makes for select members of high society. Helga, on the other hand, uses her own body as means of representation, again suggesting her exclusion from "high" culture. In her art of self-fashioning she uses clothes, jewelry, perfume, as well as the manipulation of speech: "Intentionally she kept to the slow, faltering Danish" (74). Clothes, of course, function as markers of group belonging and class status, and can indicate the attitudes and beliefs of the wearer. The meaning of Larsen's detailed descriptions of clothes, which is paralleled by Jessie Fauset in *There Is Confusion*, is best understood as part of the notion of masking featured in their novels. Like a mask, clothes are part of the interface between the body and the world: they are a kind of "second skin." The attention to clothes in both *Quicksand* and *There Is Confusion* is germane to the concern for skin color. Both Fauset and Larsen are careful to represent the internal variations of "blackness." Characters—even minor ones—are described by reference to their hue; they are, for example, "cream-colored," "yellow," or have the color of "coffee." These references to the many variants of black translates symbolically into the need for a recognition of the benefits of the diversity of a "multi-colored" society that ought to take the place of the contemporary one, which is so rigidly structured by the color-line.

The play with identity that Helga Crane engages in in Denmark is a form of passing; a passing as black, which is dictated by her Danish audience's expectations of what blackness is. As was suggested at the beginning of the chapter passing— although usually occasioned by a sense of deprivation and circumscription—has a possibly positive aspect in making experimentation with identity possible. In Copenhagen, Helga Crane does participate in a game of identity construction which would appear to allow her a measure of creativity. The identity she constructs is a means of gaining recognition, but it also puts her in a social void. Hers is a severely restricted creativity, as she is dependent on the Danes' notion of her "blackness." Helga's own means of expression remain limited. She is, for example, dependent on her white family's money in order to pursue her "art" of identity construction. This particular relationship can be read as a reflection on Harlem Renaissance artists who were dependent on white patrons, such as Langston Hughes and "Godmother" Charlotte Osgood Mason.

Judith Butler's definition of performativity is helpful in analyzing Helga's performance of "blackness" in Copenhagen. To Butler, performativity is "a reiteration of a norm or set of norms, and to the extent that it acquires an act-like status in the present, it conceals or dissimulates the conventions of which it is a repetition" (Butler12). The norm or convention of "blackness" that Helga is made to reiterate forms a site where the matrices of gender and race converge. In accordance with this norm, it is the primitive "jungle woman" that spells "blackness" to the Dahls and so they deck out their niece in a leopard-skin coat, "strange jewelry [...] and nauseous Eastern perfumes", as Helga describes it. Helga lets herself be drawn into this construction of "blackness" since she enjoys the attention that emphasizing her difference gives her. Appreciation and visibility, even if on limited terms, is a welcome change to the social invisibility of America.

However, her happiness in Copenhagen comes to an end, partly because of Axel Olsen's response to Helga's appearance. He offers Helga marriage, but only after first trying to make her his mistress. In his awkward proposal he makes his opinion of her clear: " 'You have the warm impulsive nature of the women of Africa, but, my lovely, you have, I fear, the soul of a prostitute. You sell yourself to the highest buyer'" (87). Axel's interpretation of Helga's Copenhagen performance (as is also evidenced by his portrait of her, which inscribes her as an erotic icon) draws attention to the complex issue of resistance. Butler sees every performance as imperfect, in that every repetition is different, and locates a measure of resistance to the circumscriptive norms in this circumstance. This idea is problematic when it comes to understanding Helga's performance, however. Helga's exaggerated enactment of blackness echoes that of the minstrels. Like the minstrel show, Helga's performance, as well as that of the Circus vaudevillians, has traces of the masquerade. That is, it works through an excess of signification that ultimately throws signification itself into doubt. But a masquerade performance always runs the risk of reinscribing or reinforcing the structures that it aims to deconstruct (Carlson 176). Rather than offering the liberation Helga sought for, her performance feeds into existing stereotypes. Instead of providing a lasting re-enactment of her socially determined identity, the European interlude sets off the strength of the cultural script in which she is an actor.

The portrait Olsen paints of Helga also brings out the vexed issue of black female sexuality. Olsen's representation of Helga is a sign of the power of his defining gaze, and fixes his interpretation of her in a manner that reflects primitivist notions of uninhibited sexuality and passion. Although she is aware of these preconceived notions, marriage and respectability are not an appealing alternative to Helga. The novel brings up several examples of Larsen's ambiguous attitude to the black woman's role as mother and home-maker (that was part of the "New Negro" ideal). For example, shortly after her arrival in Denmark Helga makes the following reflections on motherhood: "How stupid she had been ever to have thought that she could marry and perhaps have children in a land where every dark child was handicapped at the start by the shroud of color! She saw, suddenly, the giving birth to little, helpless, unprotesting Negro children as a sin, an unforgivable outrage. More black bodies for mobs to lynch" (75). There is an ironic twist, then, in the ending where she has four children—with a fifth on the way—and where she herself is nearly dying of the strain of too-frequent childbirth. The strength of Larsen's novel comes to a great extent from this awareness of how race compounds a gendered situation, making up the quicksand in which Helga flounders.

Clothes and self-fashioning in There Is Confusion and Quicksand

Helga Crane's performance of the exotic primitive in Copenhagen is only the most striking example of how clothes can be used as signifiers of identification. Both Fauset and Larsen pay close attention to the clothing of their characters, not only in *There Is Confusion* and *Quicksand* but in their other novels as well. [29] In *There Is Confusion* Joanna's sister Sylvia takes up work as a dressmaker. This image of the professional woman would reappear in Fauset's fiction, in the characters of Laurentine Strange, the protagonist of *The Chinaberry Tree*, and Phebe in *Comedy: American Style*. (Sewing, quilting and dressmaking are an important part of African-American women's tradition and recur in fiction of the later twentieth century, for example Alice Walker's *The Color Purple*, where Celie gains independence by sewing pants.) Perhaps the most interesting example of how Fauset uses descriptions of clothes to accentuate the characteristics of their wearer is the contrast between the colorful clothing of Joanna and Sylvia and the drab colors that the white people in the book are dressed in.

Sylvia's remarks that they ought to go to Paris to set up business there if it were not for family obligations at home indicate that there would be a chance of success for them as professional women in Europe. With this aside, Fauset establishes dressmaking as a real possibility of livelihood for women, while at the same time glancing at the conflicting demands of professional and family life that women had to navigate. Clothes also signal class belonging, as when the middle-class sisters Joanna and Sylvia meet working-class Maggie at school. What the girls are wearing is a focal point of their first meeting: Maggie notes

---

[29] For an analysis of clothing in Fauset's *Plum Bun* and Larsen's *Passing*, see DuCille 100-109.

with envy the "well-being and self-assurance" of the Marshall children, which is accentuated by their clothes. Joanna is "charming in a soft red cashmere dress made with a wide pleated skirt. She had on little patent leather, buttoned shoes with cloth tops, and a big red bow perched butterfly fashion on her dark head" (63). Maggie, on the other hand, "looked fresh and neat in a dark blue serge dress trimmed with black braid, the gift of melancholy Mis' Sparrow who in turn had had it from young Mrs. Proctor. The dress was worn but it was whole, and Maggie had tacked a tiny turn-over of white lace in the high collar" (62). The addition of the little collar to the hand-me-down clothing suggests Maggie's holding out against the poverty and dirt of her surroundings. Her life will be a struggle for "decency," and Maggie sees her only option in marriage. Through the character of Maggie, Fauset critiques the institution of the marriage market as the (sole) means of social mobility for a woman. Maggie's precipitate marriage to Henderson Neal is a bitterly ironic depiction of marriage for the purpose of acquiring the "respectability" she so ardently desires. Neal, who turns out to be a gambler and who tries to kill Maggie when she decides to leave him, offers her anything but respectability. It is only after venturing out to Europe as nurse for the wounded black soldiers in France that Maggie gains the independence and self-reliance to actually renounce marriage. She decides to start a business, not in dress-making but in another area of feminine self-fashioning, namely, hair care.[30]

The opening scene of *Quicksand* sets the stage for the vital role that vision and visibility are to play in the novel. It delineates Helga's carefully fashioned persona and establishes the link between clothes and accessories, and a dangerous difference—a difference which we will soon learn can be interpreted in terms of sexuality. This scene is worth quoting at length as it provides us with indices of recurring concerns throughout the novel, namely those of the comfort Helga takes in material things, her taste for beauty and the importance of colors:

> Helga Crane sat alone in her room, which at that hour, eight
> in the evening, was in soft gloom. Only a single reading lamp,
> dimmed by a great black and red shade, made a pool of light on
> the blue Chinese carpet, on the bright covers of the books which

---

[30]Ann duCille notes that the Harkness Beauty Shop of which Maggie's business is part is modeled on that of the famous Madame C. J. Walker, who became the first black woman millionaire by selling hair-care products for black hair, skin, and scalp. In her will, Walker stipulated that her business should always be run by women (duCille 88).

she had taken down from their long shelves, on the white pages
of the opened one selected, on the shining brass bowl crowded
with many-colored nasturtiums beside her on the low table, and
on the oriental silk which covered the stool at her slim feet. It was
a comfortable room, furnished with rare and intensely personal
taste, flooded with Southern sun in the day, but shadowy then
with the drawn curtains and single shaded light. Large, too. So
large that the spot where Helga sat was a small oasis in a desert of
darkness. (1)

The lighting of this scene suggests the position Helga will assume during most
of the rest of the novel: she is under the spotlight, as it were, always to be
gazed at; and well aware of this, she pays close attention to details of dress and
styling. Larsen goes on to describe Helga herself in the following terms: "In
vivid green and gold negligee and glistening brocaded mules, deep sunk in the
high-backed chair, against whose tapestry her sharply cut face, with skin like
yellow satin, was distinctly outlined, she was—to use a hackneyed word—attractive" (2). The attention to the clothes and the furnishings of her room suggests Helga's role as a consumer, an important new role for black women in
the 1920s, as Kimberley Roberts notes. Roberts cites early-twentieth-century
sociologist Georg Simmel claiming that consumption could be seen as a kind
of "safety valve" for women denied rights in many other areas (Roberts 116).
With this view, consumption is a field of independence, providing a chance to
form a preferred image of oneself. However, as Larsen makes clear in her novel,
this was a strategy of dubious success. To a great extent, it is in the Copenhagen
episode that the limits of consumerism are probed. Here, Helga's power as a
consumer set on self-fashioning is indeed limited.

Naxos, the southern school where Helga teaches at the beginning of the
novel, and Copenhagen are settings that function as each other's opposites
in the novel. One aspect of this polarity is, for example, that Helga's role
as a consumer—which is brought out at Naxos—is reversed so that she, in
Copenhagen, becomes an object of consumption. What is noticeable about
Helga's life at Naxos is her failure to fit in, which is figured significantly in
terms of clothing. Clothes are a point of contention at Naxos and Helga notes
with abhorrence the gray and drab colors that the other teachers wear. They, on
the other hand, are disturbed by the striking colors in which she likes to dress.

Thinking of Naxos, Helga notes that there is no room for individuality,
enthusiasm, or spontaneity: "Life had died out of it" (4). Indeed, clothes figure

significantly as background for Helga's decision to quit her school-teaching position. Larsen writes: "Clothes had been one of her difficulties at Naxos. Helga Crane loved clothes, elaborate ones. Nevertheless, she had tried not to offend. But with small success, for although she had affected the deceptively simple variety, the hawk eyes of dean and matrons had detected the subtle difference from their own irreproachable conventional garments" (18). That Helga's difference in this respect should be reproachable and offending suggests that morals are involved in the charged field of clothing. In the eyes of the hawk-eyed matrons, Helga apparel is "queer," at times even perceived as "positively indecent" (18). As Roberts points out, this is language that suggests the linking of clothes and sexuality:

> [T]he language governing moral sexual behavior is displaced onto criticism of Helga's clothes, as if to say that her clothing is a text where her morality can be read, an external manifestation of her inner being. By using the iconography of clothing as a symbolic register, Larsen successfully taps into the arguments raging during her time about proper behavior for black women. (Roberts 113)

With its strict dress code, Naxos represents the lady-like model of black womanhood, characterized by modesty and subdued sexuality. This is not an environment congenial to Helga's sensitive and passionate nature and she decides to leave, following the trail of the Great Migration from the rural south to the urban north. Via Chicago and New York, she then embarks for Copenhagen where, as we have seen, she is faced with the opposite role available to black women at the time: that of the exotic primitive. Here, too, the symbolic register of clothing is sounded, as the connection between clothes and sexuality is revisited, with a reversal of the roles of observer and observed. It is still the spectators that set the limits of her performance, but here it is Helga's sense of decency and moderation which is challenged. Indeed, Helga's first encounter with her Danish relative involves the trimming of a dress to the point where she herself finds it "too *outré*" to wear for tea. Her aunt, however, proposes that this is precisely the point; in her opinion, Helga should emphasize her difference and set out to make an impression (68). And, as we have seen, this continues to the point where Helga becomes a Baker-like erotic icon.

There is notably no similar concern on Johnson's part in *The Autobiography of an Ex-Colored Man*. There are at times detailed descriptions of a character's skin color or phenotypical features, but clothing is usually left without comment. The only time a description of clothes is effective as a textual signifier is when the narrator meets the white woman who is later to be his wife. Meeting her for the first time at a concert he is struck by the whiteness of her skin, which is underlined/matched by her white dress. She was indeed "the most dazzlingly white thing" he had ever seen (144). The woman's appearance here clearly suggests the color symbolism in which white is figured as virtue, beauty, and purity. The ex-colored man claims that his love for her is a "love which melted away my cynicism and whitened my sullied soul and gave me back the wholesome dreams of my boyhood" (147). But it also returns us to Dyer's analysis of whiteness as death. The white woman's appearance foreshadows the outcome of the novel in which she is physically dead and the narrator is spiritually dead in having lost his nurturing contact with his black roots, symbolized by the yellowing papers—his mother's songs—that are kept locked up in a box.

Chapter 4

Forms of black culture: race and representation

The Autobiography of An Ex-Colored Man, There Is Confusion, and *Quicksand* all feature significant episodes turning on the performing arts in which music is an important component. In this chapter, I discuss a number of such episodes, but I also aim to deepen the discussion by interrogating the role of the artistic medium in the construction of the "New Negro." Valerie Smith clarifies why we should not only use textual analysis, without historical context, in order to interpret African-American fiction: "[T]o emphasize the textual dimension is to misrepresent the complex origins and affinities of the black work of literature. Afro-American writers draw on both an oral and a literate tradition; their debts to the one influence shape them and distance them from the other. To focus on the texts' literariness, then, is to oversimplify their lineage, and pay homage to the structures of discourse that so often contributed to the writers' oppression" (6). This chapter is an attempt to relate the works of Johnson, Fauset, and Larsen to both the literate and the oral elements of African-American cultural tradition. Hence, my focal point is the form (that is, literary genre and style) and subject matter of the art produced by the Harlem Renaissance writers.

In the preceding chapter, we have seen how the notion of an *authentic* black identity—usually constructed by recourse to biological terms—is questioned through the analysis of performance in relation to identity. I have also suggested that black art—as part of a cultural identity—involves significant questions concerning authenticity. In the following, I will address the respective social roles of literature and music so as to extend the investigation of the meaning of authenticity in relation to black art and culture. The concept of authenticity is, in fact, integral to African American literary production. It relates both to the identity of the author and to the text s/he produces. Constructing an authenticity of identity means to seek validity through bloodlines and visible physical features. This kind of authenticity thus involves issues of color gradation and class belonging: having only "a drop of black blood" meant being light enough to move in higher social circles or to pass into the white world. It interacts with an authenticity of experience articulated through the notion of a shared history of oppression and of a particular set of relations to the white world, which in their turn are expressed in certain art forms. As I will show, Europe figures significantly in this context in terms of the valuation of European-derived art forms and the division into "high" and "low" culture.

According to Genevieve Fabre and Michel Feith, editors of *Temples for Tomorrow: Looking Back at the Harlem Renaissance* (2001), African-American music is the key to understanding the interwar period. They claim that "music was sensed as a major idiom that became a central reference for all, including writers like Toomer or Hughes and visual artists like Aaron Douglas [...] One could argue that music provided the pattern, the pace, the mood of the Renaissance as a new poetics, with its major trope, syncopation" (17-18). In the anthology *The New Negro,* which characterizes the era, African-American music occupies an important part. In the book's first section, which is devoted to arts, it is presented along with fiction, poetry, drama, and folklore. In addition to poetry by Claude McKay, Langston Hughes, and Gwendolyn Bennett, the section "Music" in the anthology includes an essay by Alain Locke on "The Negro Spirituals" and another entitled "Jazz at Home," written by J. A. Rogers. Music is prominent in the novels of Johnson, Fauset, and Larsen as well, figuring as an important motif referring to a shared past and signaling simultaneously cultural retention and renewal. In my analysis of their texts, music functions as an index of cultural identity and as a means through which this identity could be re-imagined. My exploration of the textual motif of music includes a brief history of African-American music as well as a discussion of the flourishing jazz scene of the 1920s.

With its African roots and rhythms, the music that originated among the plantation slaves in the American South is a collective form of art with links to the oral tradition that served to channel shared feelings of despair as well as joy. Spirituals and blues are the earliest examples of the new music that was created when millions of Africans were brought to America. As they were kept from reading and writing during slavery, music came to be an important means of poetical expression to the uprooted and enslaved Africans. The oral and rhythmic poetry of the slaves could serve the purpose of African cultural retention as well as creating meaning and providing solace after the displacement onto the new continent. In the African-American cultural tradition, the written text has a meaning that is significantly different meaning from that of the oral expression. LeRoi Jones/Amiri Baraka traces the origins of early twentieth century jazz to the blues, which in turn grew out of the work songs and field hollers of the plantation slaves (17-18). By comparison, the written poetry of Phillis Wheatley's collection *Poems on Various Subjects, Religious and Moral,* which is the first instance of printed African-American poetry we know of, was published in 1773, almost a century after the first African slaves came to America.[31] At the time of the Harlem Renaissance, African-American authors were beginning to publish their works to a greater extent than ever before, and a contentious issue was what form their literature ought to take. Many of the artists felt that it was important to create a distinctively black written literature, and the inclusion of, or references to, vernacular art forms was one way to achieve this. African-American "vernacular" art is identified in the *Norton Anthology of African American Literature* as consisting of "forms sacred—songs, prayers, and sermons—as well as secular—work songs, secular rhymes and songs, blues, jazz, and stories of many kinds. It also consists of dances, wordless musical performances, stage shows, and visual art forms of many sorts" (3). What these various art forms share is their "in-group" character, that is, the quality of being made by and for the black community. Thus, the vernacular art forms articulate a measure of resistance to the dominant values of the white society. As is stated in the *Norton Anthology,* "[r]efusing to subscribe wholly to the white Americans' ethos and worldview, African Americans expressed in these vernacular forms their own ways of seeing the world, its history, and its meanings" (2). In other words, these art forms—which do not include written literature— are aimed at the preservation of cultural distinction and are thus linked to the processes of retention and resistance.

The chapter centers on an interrogation of the complex issue of authenticity and how this relates to literature and music. This includes the analysis of the three authors' attitudes to the vernacular, as seen in their incorporation— or lack thereof—of spirituals, blues songs, or jazz. The import of African-American music, such as the blues and jazz of the 1920s, is considered both in relation to the role of music in the novels, and to the cultural significance of musical and literary forms of expression. The tensions between music and literature often surface in the texts as a conflict between "high" and "low" culture.

---

[31]Lucy Terry's poem *Bars Fight,* composed c. 1746, is the earliest known work of literature by an African American. It was, however, not published until 1855 (see the Norton Anthology of African-American Literature, 137).

Versions of authenticity

The first prose works by African Americans, the slave narratives, usually featured a preface by the (white) editor, who praised the merits of the author and guaranteed that it was a true story, written by the ex-slave her/himself. The same is true of the poetry of Phillis Wheatley.[32] This means that the focus was on the author as much as on the text. The text of the slave narrative was not treated as an entity in itself; instead it was always linked to the person behind it and valued according to its representation of "reality." The author, as ex-slave, was thus seen as a representative of the race, exemplifying a typical African-American experience of life in bondage and freedom. The expectation of, on the one hand, a correspondence between real-life and fictional events and, on the other, of the representation of an authentic, shared "black experience" forms a combination of aesthetic and political concerns that came to dominate the early African-American literary tradition of which Johnson, Fauset, and Larsen were a part. This critical complex can be seen as a debate about authenticity, which has continued to be of concern to African-American authors throughout the twentieth century, though in slightly different terms. The vernacular plays an important part in this debate since it is connected to an idea of art made for and consumed by the majority of African Americans. The fact that Johnson, Fauset, and Larsen produced art that was not, on the whole, informed by the vernacular tradition and that they presented middle-class characters, whose fictional lives seemed far removed from the daily toil of the urban black masses or of those in the segregated rural areas of the South raises the question of whether their works represented authentic black life. Additionally, the question of whether the concern with Europe makes the literature less authentic is valid in the case of Johnson, Fauset, and Larsen as well. The assumption would then be that a concern with European culture and mixed heritage set the writer off as part of an elite minority, since it would not be representative of a common experience.

Richard Wright provides a case in point for my concern about authenticity here. Leaving the US for Paris in 1947, Wright was soon accused of being deracinated, of having lost touch with the folk in his writings. Instead of merely relating to the vernacular, African-American tradition, Wright was influenced

---

[32]See the narratives of Frederick Douglass, Mary Prince et al. in Gates *The Classic Slave Narratives*. The prefaces to Wheatley's poems are found in Norton 167-168, and an extended account of Phillis Wheatley's trial before the publication of these poems is found in Gates, *Loose Canons*, 51-55.

by, for example, French existentialism. Rather than accepting the common view that Wright's work was thus "corrupted by his dabbling in philosophical modes of thought entirely alien to his African American history and vernacular style," Paul Gilroy suggests that we read the works of Wright and Sartre together, in dialogue with each other as part of the same tradition (156, 186). The example of Wright is important in that it draws attention to what was at stake for an African-American author who chose to remove himself, both physically and intellectually, from the African-American *milieu*. Wright was well established as a writer before he moved to France. For example, the novel *Native Son* (1940) was immediately picked up by the Book-of-the-Month Club and became the first African-American best seller. However, the books published after Wright's move to Europe have all been considered inferior to, and received less critical attention, than the first four works, which were published in the US. These issues are important to keep in mind when trying to assess both the authors' and the critics' relationship to literature dealing with Europe.

In the course of the twentieth century, the transatlantic exchanges are increasingly being recognized as integral to modern black experience. A vital point is the connection Ann Douglas makes between the 1920s and post-colonialism, referred to in the introduction of the present study. Not only does it provide support for my belief that the work of Edward Said, Homi Bhabha, and other post-colonial critics has shed new light on the authors I am studying and can continue to do so. Douglas's claim also supports my idea that the authors of this cultural moment actually inscribed themselves within some of the most influential literary traditions of the twentieth century, which is why their works so well sustain the critical interrogations connected primarily with post-colonialism and post-structuralism. The questions they raised concerning racial identity and cultural belonging have continued to be of importance throughout the century.

But how do we decide what can and cannot signify authenticity? Is not any determining practice of this kind in itself oppressive in the limitation of referring to a unified concept? In this case, does the authentic presuppose the repression of differences within the black community or the "black experience"? There is a complication inherent in the construction of the authentic, begging the question of who determines what authenticity is or what kind of authenticity is called for. Often demanding verification in "experience," "essence," or place, the sign of the "authentic" immediately gives rise to questions of inclusion and exclusion. Ideas of inclusion can, for example, be based in geo-politics;

in shared space and a shared political and historical experience of oppression. For instance, Gilroy's attempt to expand the terms of authenticity by proposing the concept of the black Atlantic embraces a new "anti-anti-essentialism" founded on experience. Another way to conceive of these issues is as a battle of representation, of giving meaning to a signifier such as "blackness." This means a focus on control over means of representation, including a concern with voice and perspective in cultural representations.

Within post-colonial studies, the analysis of authenticity shows how the formulation of the authentic—referring to a pre-colonial state of affairs—could become part of a strategy of resistance against a colonial policy of assimilation, which was aimed to suppress "difference" in colonized countries. On that account, national culture is often set against colonial culture. However, even if the concept of authenticity has been used to counter the discourse of an external colonial power, the formulation of what is authentic can become an equally hegemonic gesture. Against this Homi Bhabha, among others, has set the theorization of hybridity. The recognition of the essential hybridity of cultures makes it meaningless to talk of the authentic. There is no purity of origins to be found and set against the "tainted," only "two orders of the impure" (Tiffin and Lawson 83). The dichotomy of origin/purity on the one hand and difference/impurity on the other is thus rendered invalid.

Bhabha replaces "cultural diversity" with "cultural difference" (or culture's hybridity), which means that difference is to be found within culture rather than between cultures. His preference for "culture's hybridity" rather "the diversity of cultures" can be explicated in the following way. The latter concept, that of diversity, could be equated with a comfortable multi-culturalism in which various cultures are recognized but seen as existing separately, alongside each other, occupying quite distinct spheres. To talk of "culture's hybridity" would, on the other hand, according to Bhabha, take into account the inherent differentiation within one and the same culture. The theorization of culture's hybridity recognizes African-Americans as part of American culture (and black culture within Western culture to return to Gilroy's perspective) without negating African Americans' distinctiveness as a group.

Bhabha's distinction between the pedagogical and the performative nature of culture is also of relevance here. He writes that on the pedagogical level, the nation is projected in terms of unity, origin, and above all, a cohesive narrative. These narrative qualities are found, for example, in the way the nation is built on a sense of a shared past together with teleology and progress in which its subjects are part. The performative level, on the other hand, refers to the nation as a process, as something that is recreated every day and that is impossible to define in absolute terms or to express as a cohesive narrative. This means that in his understanding culture is not a fixed, homogeneous entity but something that takes place as it is formulated and enunciated. Consequently, he reads a measure of agency into the position of the colonial subject, exemplified by the interpretation and application of the colonial rules. The performative disrupts the linearity and homogeneity of the pedagogical as the daily acts performed by members of a specific culture (or nation) can be either in harmony or in discord with the pedagogical. An example is the polyphony created by immigrant groups recently arrived, who interrupt the homogeneity of the nation with their exile perspective. Bhabha significantly calls this aspect performative, emphasizing the way that all members of a nation/culture form it by a series of daily actions taking place in relation to the idea of the nation. In this way, the complete unity and authority of the nation is challenged by varying cultural interpretations and enactments. Here is a gap in which alternative narratives can be inscribed; a gap that the Harlem artists attempted to fill with their own narratives of their past and present.

While Bhabha's readings are often criticized for being overly abstract, and failing to recognize specific material historical conditions of space and time, his distinction between the two levels of culture easily translates into the context of early twentieth-century America. African Americans as a group highlight the rupture between the pedagogical and the performative, or the ideal and the real, in American culture. Their past constitutes a counter-narrative to the national projection of equal constitutional rights. Their presence as slaves and subsequent victims of segregationist policies continuously calls into question the spirit of the American Constitution. This theorization applies to Locke's recognition of "the great discrepancy between the American social creed and the American social practice" in *The New Negro*, but the questioning of America's failure to live up to its constitutional ideals is not new to the Harlem Renaissance (13). There are several nineteenth-century examples, of which Frederick Douglass' 1845 *Narrative* is one of the most memorable.

Applying the notion of the performative to culture draws attention to the significance of the daily enactments of the pedagogical (the narrative of the culture). It entails a privileging of practice rather than bloodlines in relation to the question of cultural belonging. w.e.b. DuBois was among those who at the time argued that, in this respect, "culture has no color," and that a cultural tradition "belongs" to those who use it rather than to those who were born in a certain geographic region or are part of a certain ethnic group (Posnock 10). The same idea is echoed by Jessie Fauset in her emphasis on Western literature in *There Is Confusion,* by Joanna Marshall's attempt at being accepted as a dancer of classical ballet, and by Johnson's ex-colored man in his attempt to blend classical music with ragtime.

The written text: a form of resistance?

In contrast to the early African-American music and oral poetry, the later written and formally more conventional literature has the ambiguous connotations of belonging to the culture of the white masters while also being closely linked to Emancipation. By mastering the language of their masters, the former slaves who were able to formulate their experiences in writing had a tremendous effect on anti-slavery opinion. Henry Louis Gates identifies the concept of literacy as fundamental to the slave narratives, in which it is also crucially linked to freedom.[33] For most of the former slaves, acquiring literacy was the first step on the way to breaking out of their bondage. For the Harlem Renaissance writers, the mastery of the novel genre and, perhaps more importantly, their formal experiments and variations within the genre became markers of the measure of freedom achieved since slavery. It was a way of showing intellectual and artistic capacity equal to that of the privileged white Americans, and it became a platform for demands for equal social rights. At the same time, they wanted to make something new, something distinctly different that deserved serious recognition. Additionally, certain class connotations pertained to the early African-American novel since its audience was necessarily limited by the fact that not all blacks could read. In this sense it was not a popular art form. In contrast to the vernacular art forms, its audience was from the start at least partly white.

Like the minstrel performer's stage art, African-American music, such as the blues and ragtime[34] that partly developed out of this tradition, was popular in that it came into existence by and for the "common people" and was not an art that required institutional sanctions. By contrast, written literature

---

[33]See the introduction to Gates, *The Classic Slave Narratives.*

[34]The spirituals occupy a kind of middle ground here, being "popular" songs with plantation origins. However, the content was serious and largely owing to the success of the Fisk Jubilee Singers (and various followers), the spirituals were established as part of the Christian tradition.

traced its origins to the European colonists and continued to look for inspiration from Europe. As Homi Bhabha argues in "Signs Taken for Wonders," the English book—that is, the Western text, be it the Bible that would convert the heathens or the treasures of English literature that would enlighten and bring culture to the uncultivated—is the sign of European hegemony and authority.[35] For the African Americans of the early decades of the twentieth century, to write a novel in the European tradition was to make a particular statement: to inscribe oneself within the tradition of Western civilization and education, and to establish one's predecessors as partly white and Euro-American. Accordingly some critics, such as Cheryl Wall and Angela Y. Davis speak of literature as an "alien" tradition to the African Americans and call for the recognition of the blues as a neglected art form.

Edward Said has discussed the connection between the novel and the study of "comparative literature" on the one hand and the period of European high imperialism on the other. Referring to the novel as "a cultural artefact of bourgeois society," he goes on to write: "Of all the major literary forms, the novel is the most recent, its emergence the most datable, its occurrence the most Western, its normative pattern of social authority the most structured; imperialism and the novel fortified each other to such a degree that it is impossible, I would argue, to read one without in some way dealing with the other" (Said, *Culture* 71). This passage begs the question of what it means for an African-American author, belonging to a group of people with partly non-Western origins victimized by imperialism, to use the novel genre. Part of an answer is that using a conventional form was a way of proving equal artistic capability and of reaching a larger readership.

But there are other factors that are important to consider as well. If we go on to consider imperialism as closely related to nationalism, the usefulness of the novel to these authors becomes more obvious. In the foreword to *The New Negro*, Alain Locke compares the work of the "New Negroes" with that of "those nascent movements of folk-expression and self-determination which are playing a creative part in the world today." As examples of international parallels, Locke mentions the "resurgence of a people" that could be observed in contemporary Egypt, Ireland, Russia, and Palestine (xxvii). At the historical moment of the Harlem Renaissance, African Americans were for the first time making a concerted effort to become narrators of their own history and

---

[35]This essay is included in Bhabha, *The Location of Culture* (1994).

identity. A range of art forms was used to express the past, the present and the future aspirations of the "New Negro" artists, who were aware of the significance of being the narrators of their own history. Again, I quote Said to clarify the relation between narration and power, especially power over the past:

> The power to narrate, or to block other narratives from forming and emerging, is very important to culture and imperialism, and constitutes one of the main connections between them. Most important, the grand narratives of emancipation and enlightenment mobilized people in the colonial world to rise up and throw off imperial subjection; in the process, many Europeans and Americans were also stirred by these stories and their protagonists, and they too fought for new narratives of equality and human community. (Culture xiii)

As we see here, narratives are important on a national level, bringing about a sense of a shared past and a measure of social cohesion. They can be both liberating and oppressive depending on who the narrator is. Narratives can help us create a "usable past" from which we can gain a sense of progress, teleology, and meaning. This is indeed what the authors of the Harlem Renaissance were doing: re-writing their past and interpreting it in their own, affirmative terms. By "digging up the past" and presenting it in their own particular way, the Harlem authors of the mid-1920s created a sense of their own modernity, at the same time as they asserted their belonging to a great historical, African and American, tradition.

Throughout the twentieth century, to re-write one's past as a way of reformulating one's identity has continued to be an important approach for various groups formed along lines of gender, ethnicity, and sexuality. As Michele Wallace puts it with regard to the history of black American women in the US, "the power to write one's own history is what making history is all about" (xxi). Though they were disempowered in many other respects, the force of writing was nevertheless an available tool to African Americans in the 1920s. The potency of the literary work resides in the notion that literary language is a performative practice, producing the things that are named. Writing about their past and their new identity, the Harlem Renaissance authors created both a history and the present. While other types of narrative are important in a process like this as well, the novel assumes particular significance in its links to the subject. In its emphasis on the individual, the rise of the novel is historically connected to the development of the concept of a subject (Watt 13-14; Taylor 287-88). The focus on individual consciousness and on everyday life that is characteristic of the novel made it a genre that was well fitted to the aim of establishing the character of the "New Negro."

In the articulation of alternative narratives of both past and present, in which the Harlem Renaissance authors were engaged, the notion of authenticity would surface: *who* was to represent *what* experience? Literary style was part of this debate: should literature be written in the vernacular and celebrate the "folk," making use of classic African-American settings, such as the rural south? Langston Hughes, for example, turns to ancient African history and myth as a source of pride in poems such as "The Negro Speaks of Rivers" (1921), or to modern African-American jazz and/or vernacular speech in "Jazz Band in a Parisian Cabaret" (1926) and other poems. The incorporation of folk speech and folk forms such as spirituals, gospels, and blues, as in Hughes's poetry, helped form a modern African-American poetic idiom. However, this meant emphasizing what was most different from white society and unavoidably came up against the problem of what "folk" actually meant and what could be considered an authentic African-American literary expression.

Very briefly, the other approach to literary subject matter and form can be described in terms of similarity or "universalism." In other words, the aim of the "New Negro" artists was to achieve equality by emulating the works of their Euro-American contemporaries. It is among this group that we find Johnson, Fauset, and Larsen.[36] Their choice of artistic medium (that is, novel writing) underlines their willingness to engage in an originally European tradition. The mastery of this literary form and the language in which it is articulated (in these works primarily Standard American English) indicates a formal linguistic and artistic ability equal to Euro-Americans—an ability that, one hoped, would yield acceptance in terms of citizenship. This stylistic choice begs the question of how to challenge the basic assumptions of a culture (in this case the Euro-American one) while employing the artistic forms through which that culture has been expressed.

---

[36] The kind of fiction they produced was representative of the art that was sought after by the engineers of the Harlem Renaissance, Charles S. Johnson and Alain Locke (Lewis 89-97). The poet and novelist Claude McKay, who set his novel *Banjo* (1928) among the sailors in Marseilles, France, does not belong to this school of fiction and thus falls outside of the scope of this study. McKay's novel is set among vagabonds and sailors in the rougher parts of Marseilles—a setting that is very different from that in the fiction of Johnson, Fauset, and Larsen. Thematically, his characters are not faced with the problem of addressing a dual heritage, and there is no connection to the search for a formulation of "the New Negro" similar to that in Johnson, Fauset, and Larsen.

Another way of formulating this predicament is to ask how "the folk" could be represented in a system built on Western tradition. Is it possible to see the authors' literary performances as acts of resistance to narrow definitions of blackness and black culture, exemplified by the authors' attitude to or incorporation of African-American folk culture? In my analyses of the fiction of Johnson, Larsen, and Fauset the use of dialect is considered in this context, as its occurrence and form reflect the authors' attitude to folk tradition. Another such index is the intertextual references that occur in their works.

Thus, it is worth reflecting on what literary predecessors Johnson, Fauset, and Larsen evoke in their texts. In Fauset's *There Is Confusion* there are allusions to Tennyson, Henri Bordeaux (his *La Peur de Vivre* is a sentimental novel built on the marriage plot, like Fauset's own novels) and Dante. In addition, Joanna quotes Goethe in her love-letter to Peter (166) and sings German *lieder*. Although the Harlem Renaissance had been preceded by a number of well-known African-American authors, such as Charles Chesnutt, Paul Laurence Dunbar and Pauline Hopkins to mention only a few, they are largely absent not only from Fauset's novel but also from the works of Johnson and Larsen. While both Fauset and Johnson are careful to insert into their novels the kind of historical facts that were omitted in American education, for example about great black leaders such as Toussaint l'Ouverture, W.E.B. DuBois, or Frederick Douglass, the literary references in their novels are usually to European and Euro-American works, which illustrates the authors' familiarity with and active engagement in this tradition. These references are indicative of the assertion of the interpenetration of white and black American culture, at the same time as they suggest the recognition of the fact that narratives structure our knowledge of the world. Examples of literary references that occur in the books under discussion include Johnson's mention of Harriet Beecher Stowe's *Uncle Tom's Cabin*. The retrospective narrator of *The Autobiography* observes: "I do not think it is claiming too much to say that *Uncle Tom's Cabin* was a fair and truthful panorama of slavery; however that may be, it opened my eyes as to who and what I was and what my country considered me; in fact, it gave me my bearing" (29). Stowe's *Uncle Tom* was the first book by a white American author to cast black characters in main roles, which were also sympathetic. However, as we have seen, the image of Tom soon got to be a negative stereotype of a submissive slave, partly through the minstrel shows and other stage performances. The narrator also hastens to make his position vis-à-vis this character clear: "For my part, I was never an admirer of Uncle Tom, nor of his type of goodness" (29). The passage amounts to a recognition of the constructed nature of knowledge and of the concept of blackness.

In *Quicksand*, Larsen stages a similar idea concerning the linguistic construction of blackness and personal identity. For example, the orientalist novel, Marmaduke Pickthall's *Said the Fisherman*, that Helga Crane is reading in the opening scene, as well as her clothes and the flowers, furnishing, and other decorations of her room, represent Helga's character. They are signs establishing her as a sophisticated woman with an interest in a world of adventure (and possible romance) outside of the closed domains of the school. Furthermore, as in the case of Johnson's narrator, a literary example serves to make Helga aware of how her racial identity is perceived in Europe. On her first day in the Dahls' household, Helga cannot help but notice the curious glances of the chambermaid: "Marie, she reflected, had probably never seen a Negro outside the pictured pages of her geography book" (68). As it turns out, the version of blackness that Helga is allowed to act out in the anthropologically informed descriptions of Copenhagen is a colonial fantasy. Helga's reflection on Marie's perception of herself suggests that literacy and the risk of misreadings are crucial to this episode from the outset. This incident anticipates what is to come in the meeting between Helga and the Danish painter Axel Olsen. In the end, it turns out that Marie is the only one who agrees with Helga that Olsen's portrait of her as an exotic temptress reflects the Danes' construction of her rather than her actual appearance (*Quicksand* 89).

The literary references in the novels are to works which are indirectly commented upon as the authors supply their own versions of similar subject matters. Said the Fisherman, with its orientalist bent, is thus set up as a precursor to the story of Helga's journey to the foreign continent of Europe. The representation of Uncle Tom is countered by the cosmopolitan, artistic and sophisticated mulatto in The Autobiography. Being the one who is more apt to see African-American past performances as a source of pride, Johnson also includes the example of the black preacher, John Brown, who moves his congregation with his magnificent powers of speech. Assisting the preacher at the "big meeting" is the one-eyed man known as "Singing Johnson." Johnson observes: "Both these types are now looked upon generally with condescension or contempt by the progressive element among the colored people; but it should never be forgotten that it was they who led the race from paganism and kept it steadfast to Christianity through all the long, dark years of slavery" (127-128). The passage suggests his recognition of the "New Negroes'" debt to their predecessors: how their performances in the present could only take place because of these past performances.

We have seen how Helga Crane in *Quicksand*'s Copenhagen continually negotiates her racial performance in relation to the Danes' ability to "read" the image of herself she presents them with. Literacy is a key word here, involving knowledge of cultural codes. As Helga learns to read the codes of the Danish society of the Dahls, she presents a public persona—a kind of colonial fantasy—constructed on the basis of her Danish audience's capabilities of interpretation. The battle over the means and meaning of racial performance runs through the whole Copenhagen episode. In the works of Johnson, Fauset, and Larsen the notion of literacy functions on several levels. It relates to the nineteenth-century theme of African-American travelers acquiring education in Europe, but the concept could also be extended to include a kind of cultural literacy. The protagonist/visitors to Europe learn to navigate a new cultural landscape and read its cultural codes, and through their increased literacy they gain a sense of their position in Western civilization. This is a process in which their double consciousness plays a significant role.

A related question is the meaning of literary style, that is, the discussion of the novels as African-American appropriations of the genre, and the establishing of in what ways they are "repetitions with a difference" of an originally European (and Euro-American) art form. The genre appropriation and the counter-narratives to the dominant racial ideology are the authors' ways of positioning themselves in relation to other performances, both literary and musical, and asserting their own modernity. One way to remold the established form for the benefit of their "double audience" was to combine African-American subject matter, such as passing, the experience of racism, and often an African-American setting, such as Harlem or the American South, with traditional European and Euro-American concepts of literary style and genre, as we see in the works of Fauset, Johnson, and Larsen. The conventional form thus becomes a vehicle for addressing unconventional topics. In her introduction to Fauset's second novel, *Plum Bun*, Deborah McDowell claims that "[a]s in so many novels written by women, blacks, and other members of 'literary subcultures,' indirect strategies and narrative disguise become necessary covers for rebellious and subversive concerns. Such writers often employ literary and social conventions that function as a mask behind which lie decidedly unconventional critiques" (xxi). This mask, McDowell rightly argues, has blinded readers to certain aspects of, for example, Fauset's texts.

Appropriating a literary tradition: repetitions with a difference

By employing one of the most important Euro-American art forms, the novel, the authors of *The Autobiography, There Is Confusion,* and *Quicksand* claimed their place in that European-derived tradition. This had consequences for their status within the African-American cultural tradition. The in-group character of the vernacular art forms offered the possibility of creating alternatives to the dominant, often denigrating representations of African Americans. Writing a novel, by contrast, meant turning to a white audience as well, and was felt to entail certain restrictions on the representation of black life. In the following, I will discuss how this meant risking the potential for authentic representation that the vernacular art forms offered. The discussion of what the *authentic black text* should include relates to the formal aspects of literary style and genre convention as well as to subject matter. Jessie Fauset's texts provide a case in point here. To Fauset, the modeling of her works on the Victorian novel, with a "marriage plot" at its center, was a way to gain an audience. Marion L. Starkey writes in her 1932 article about Fauset: "She confesses to studying whole issues of the *Saturday Evening Post* in a candid effort to analyze and isolate the germ of popular writing. In the meantime her own novels, though widely read, have never been best sellers. French classes, which pay better, must consume the better part of her energy" (217). The contemporary publishing market called for novels of a different kind than Fauset's: her novels were decidedly "anti-primitivist" and thus did not sell as readily as, for example, Claude McKay's *Home to Harlem* or Carl Van Vechten's *Nigger Heaven.* Fauset's novels belonged in the category of racial uplift, and were written to counter the dominant cultural narrative in which African-Americans were cast as intellectually and morally inferior to Americans of European descent. However, this choice involved avoiding certain aspects of black life.

The issue of authenticity is addressed by Ann duCille in her discussion of the critical evaluation of black women's texts. She examines why an author like Jessie Fauset has often been dismissed by contemporary black feminist criticism, and suggests that the reason for this is a critical misreading of her texts, particularly regarding her treatment of the "marriage plot," [37] known from European novels such as those of Jane Austen:

---

[37] DuCille uses the term "marriage plot" to "refer to a fictional formula that foregrounds romantic relationships, focuses on courtship (wanting, wooing, and winning, one might say) and generally culminates in marriage or at least betrothal. In perhaps the most traditional versions of the formula, white woman meets white man, sparks fly of one kind or another, and after several hundred pages of overcoming obstacles, hero and heroine marry and presumably live happily ever after" (duCille 13-14).

> African American literary history in general and black feminist
> criticism in particular have taken little note of the multiple,
> complex, and often contradictory currents of resistance that flow
> through black writers' appropriations of the 'white' marriage plot.
> This elision is due in part to the tendency to treat black literary texts
> not as fictive invention but as transparent historical documents,
> evaluated in terms of their fidelity to 'the black experience' and
> their attention to 'authentically black' subject matter (du Cille 6).

What duCille investigates is the notion that there are certain expectations that the critics have on the "black text," which include a reflection of lived experience in the social real. The life of the well-educated, well-to-do characters that Fauset depicts does not correspond to the experiences of the majority of working-class blacks. DuCille suggests that this is one reason why Fauset so often has been dismissed as echoing the values of white American society, and her art regarded as inauthentic, that is, not representative of the majority of black people's lives. Underlying this critique is, as duCille points out in the above quotation, the contested status of the African-American literary text. As we have seen in relation to the slave narratives, an important feature of African-American literature of the nineteenth century was its link to real-life experiences. DuCille suggests that this expectation of mimesis is still prevalent, as African-American literature is presumed to be reflective of objects and conditions in a world outside the text. But such a postulation fails to take note of the fact that while there is a sense in which the literary work is imitative of reality, it operates according to certain conventions (of genre and of style, for example) that have to be followed in order for the fiction to be recognized as such. As duCille reminds us: "Realism [...] is as much a code as romance" (72). The fictive status of the literary work comes into focus when we consider it in terms of performance. Vital to the notion of performance as I use it in this study is precisely its reiteration of conventions, the lack of a direct correspondence between the imitation and the object that is being imitated, and the "world-making" (rather than referential) qualities of language. Approaching Fauset's literature through the lens of the performative provides a possible alternative interpretation in answer to the criticism Fauset received from her contemporaries concerning her depiction of a world that was not true to life.

On the basis of the assumption that to employ a literary convention accommodating characters representative of merely a small section of black life are depicted is to retreat from the resistant potential embedded in the vernacular, critics have missed the finer points of Fauset's social critique. In this context, duCille draws attention to the importance of historicizing the fictional work, a critical act that, in this case, helps us see the unconventional way in which Fauset handles the "marriage plot." DuCille notes that for a generation of post-Emancipation slaves, whose love life and family relations had been the object of surveillance and circumscription, the concept of marriage meant something quite different than for the European middle or upper class women of Austen's novels. Rather than being an oppressive or self-limiting institution, to the recently freed slaves marriage signaled freedom and entitlement (duCille 14). The "marriage plot" structure is adapted by Fauset in order to probe the specific situation of the African-American woman in the 1920s. According to duCille, female African-American authors have used "coupling as a metaphor through which to examine and critique the color consciousness, class stratification, social conventions, and gender relations of their burgeoning black middle- and working-class communities" (67). Additionally, she asks:

> But just whose experience is being claimed as 'authentic' when a critic speaks of a distinctly African American or black female experience? Can a critical practice claim any black experience without privileging it as the black experience, without valorizing it as the master narrative of the race? Is it possible to theorize a critical practice that historicizes experience, acknowledging it as a social construction (rather than as objective reality), accessible only through symbolic systems? (6-7)

DuCille thus problematizes the notion of authenticity by referring to its basis in the necessary exclusion of certain experiences. The price to be paid for valorizing certain experiences and creating master narratives of the race, as duCille sees it, is the omission of "the fluidity, multivocality, and contradictory impulses" of African-American women's fiction (7). One such instance of omission duCille finds in the fiction of Jessie Fauset. The present moment, she argues, instead privileges the fiction of Zora Neale Hurston for dealing with "folk" material and depicting sexually independent women. She also observes that, as regards the historical moment of the Harlem Renaissance, blues artists like Gertrude "Ma" Rainey and Bessie Smith are generally credited with greater "authenticity" than the literary artists. By contrast, the fiction of Jessie Fauset describes the life of the well-educated middle class in the urban North. In this way, she is out of touch with the mass of working-class blacks, who were not a significant part of her audience. She presented a version of black life that was true to the experiences of a minor segment, and in doing so she provided an alternative to the dominant conception of black life. This alternative version arguably draws attention to the constructed nature of the concept of (authentic) blackness. It turns out to be a set of conventions according to which the enactment of a certain identity can take place.

The conventional form and the middle-class existence she portrays elicit comments on the similarities between the lives of Fauset's black characters and those of middle-class white people. Fauset's characters, who are well-educated, who strive for material success and recognition like Joanna Marshall, and who have no connection to African-American vernacular culture or speech, have been criticized for being too much like white people. By acquiring the education, speech and manners of her white counterparts, Joanna aims to transcend the color-line and be "somebody great." Practicing the art forms associated with European-based American cultural tradition, shown in her familiarity with Western literature, and her mastery of traditional European dance forms like classical ballet, or opera singing, Joanna makes a claim to "belong" to that tradition.

The notion of a mask put on before white society is a recurrent metaphor in African-American literature. (The double consciousness that DuBois theorized is part of this complex as well.) The mask put on even by the black minstrel performer likewise suggests that blackness is a mask put on for the white audience. The concept of an authentic blackness posits that there is something inauthentic about a large part of black peoples' acting in daily existence in white society. Certain kinds of behavior and attitudes that were displayed in the black community could not be shown in a context where white people were part of the audience. In this sense, then, there is an authenticity to the vernacular art that was produced for a black audience only. Gilbert and Gubar in *No Man's Land* (1994) observe that for many African-American thinkers "black impersonation begins as an enforced necessity, a punishment imposed by racist representations of African-Americans, a mode of survival in a hostile environment" (122). This is a very negative conception of impersonation; it is caused by dire circumstances and often also by a self-hatred engendered by the dominant modes of representation of black people. The idea of the mask is that it is a kind of protection, behind which one can keep an unsullied essence of blackness. This notion is challenged by Homi Bhabha in his discussion of mimicry.

Bhabha takes issue with the notion of authenticity in a way which provides an interesting perspective on Fauset's "imitation-white" characters. Mimicry is the term he uses to describe how the colonized acquire the cultural attributes, like the clothing, learning, or certain customs and manners, of the colonizer. This imitation or mime is never quite like the original it attempts to emulate, and it is precisely in this "failure" that Bhabha locates a possibility for transformation. Referring back to an assumed "original," the impersonation destabilizes the original—the repetition and imitation of an original is always something more and something different than the original it refers to. The replacement is thus simultaneously a reformulation of the performed identity.

Fauset's fiction addresses the ambivalence that is at the core of mimicry. Her presentation of characters that are similar to their Anglo-American counterparts in every respect except skin color, is not necessarily a way of endorsing white supremacy, but of calling this ideology into question. Rather than upholding a conservative attitude, then, her fiction can be seen as being engaged in the transformative potential of mimicry. Like Butler's concept of performativity, mimicry operates on the principle that the ambivalence of the performed identity disturbs the authority of the original. In this way, it has the (threatening) potential to destabilize the present social order. Bhabha emphasizes that mimicry is not to be understood as identification with the colonizer, and there is no presence, or unsullied "authentic" identity, behind the mask of mimicry: "The *menace* of mimicry is its *double* vision which in disclosing the ambivalence of colonial discourse also disrupts its authority" (Bhabha 88). Mimicry functions as a mask, through which the colonial subject can assume roles other than those that are socially prescribed.

Quicksand: a colonial travel narrative in reverse

We have seen how Johnson played with the notion of autobiography as less fictional than the novel, and that Jessie Fauset appropriated the "marriage plot" known from nineteenth-century European novels and created a modern black American romance. In this way, their works are "repetitions with a difference" of generic conventions, leaving their own imprint on them. In the following, I investigate how Larsen made "unconventional use of conventional literary forms" (duCille 3) by relating *Quicksand* to the colonial travel narrative. Larsen's depiction of Helga's sojourn in Copenhagen transforms the genre of travel writing in which the white male explorer sets out from the "center" to the colony in the "margin." In this narrative, it is the black woman who travels into the "heart of whiteness." Common to the eighteenth (and nineteenth) century travel narratives that Pratt analyzes, is what she calls the "seeing man," defined as "the European male subject of European landscape discourse—he whose imperial eyes passively look out and possess" (7). In Larsen's text the observer is a black woman, whose right to the possessive gaze is constantly called into question. Helga Crane is conspicuous and always aware of being the focus of the Danes' attention. In fact, it is Axel Olsen who is the owner of the imperial gaze, judging by the way he looks at Helga and shapes her appearance to fit his expectations. It should also be noted that while many critics have commented on the semi-autobiographical status of *Quicksand,* including Larsen's own disputed visit to Denmark,[38] the Copenhagen episode is here read primarily in terms of symbolic geography. This Nordic country is, as we have seen, a setting in which Larsen effectively managed to explore the symbolism of white and black.

John C. Gruesser points out that the genre of travel writing has an ambiguous position within the African-American literary tradition. The travel motif has imperialist connotations, in its links to colonial literature, and the limited and limiting descriptions of non-white people found there. In fact, as M. L. Pratt and others have observed, the narrative situation of travel writing, that is the relating of "them" to "us," in itself implies a colonialist situation, which is problematic in terms of the position of the narrating subject vis-à-vis the objects that he or she relates (735). The position of the subject—that is, Helga—is a contested one in *Quicksand.*

While Helga's journey to Denmark is motivated by a search for freedom and an escape from her constrained existence in racist America, the freedom she finds turns out to be compromised and she eventually decides to return to America. bell hooks claims in her discussion of journeying that "[f]rom certain standpoints, to travel is to encounter the terrorizing force of white supremacy" (hooks 174). From Helga's standpoint the encounter with white Copenhagen indeed turns out to be one in which white supremacy is confirmed. However, in narrative terms there is a way in which Helga retains a measure of control. Helga has a certain agency and potential which comes from being the focalizer, or narrative center, of *Quicksand.* She is the subject of this travel narrative, and the defining gaze at least partly belongs to her as she reflects on what she sees in this foreign world. But rather than functioning as a means of empower-

---

[38] See for example Thadious Davis' biography of Nella Larsen, and George Hutchinson in "Nella Larsen and the Veil of Race."

ment on the part of the African-American protagonist, this inversion of the convention of the colonial travel narrative importantly throws the limitations of certain narrative conventions into relief. For example, the dehumanizing imagery of blacks as brute beasts of burden, which was used as a part of the discourse of slavery and colonization, has certain analogies in the description of the Danes, who appear as almost completely devoid of human emotion. For example, aunt Katrina is characterized by coolness, security and balance (79). Animal imagery is used to characterize Axel Olsen, who is repeatedly compared to a lion, not only because of his coloring (he wags a "leonine head," for example) but because of his naturally assumed supremacy. Alternatively, he appears to Helga as being "affected," "theatrical," even "the most unreal figure in the world" (87). As these brief examples indicate, the Danes have no more complexity for Helga than she has for them. Larsen's descriptions of the Copenhageners and their city include an endorsement of the stereotypical image of the white European as too rational and frigid that was inherent in primitivism. In the end, the binary mode of thinking that underlies the stereotype gives rise to limitations in terms of identity and culture that turn out to be too constraining for Helga. There are no cracks to open, no space in-between the rigid categories that can sustain her mixed racial and cultural makeup. Her old restlessness awakens and she decides to return to America, well aware that things will be similar there. In the end, her only vision of life in that desirable space in-between comes from picturing herself "moving shuttle-like from continent to continent. From the prejudiced restrictions of the New World to the easy formality of the Old, from the pale calm of Copenhagen to the colorful lure of Harlem" (96).

Music and the making of modern Americans

Parallel to the literary outpouring of the Harlem Renaissance was the increased popularity of African-American music, which moved to the center of the American scene during the inter-war years. Jazz music is often used to characterize the era as one of joy, vitality and recuperation after the Great War.[39] Considering the fact that they both deal with the artistic scene, Fauset's and

---

[39] It should perhaps be clarified that "the term 'jazz' was used loosely in the 1920's to encompass everything from Tin Pan Alley pop to the music of Eubie Blake, Louis Armstrong, and Ellington, but it always meant a loosened beat and black sources, acknowledged or otherwise" (Haskell 186).

Larsen's reluctance to include jazz, either as subject matter or stylistically, is noticeable. We have seen that Johnson praised the accomplishments of black musicians, and in contrast to Fauset and Larsen, he "recognized the importance of the African American musical and performance tradition, and understood its major contribution to the transformation of American art from a mere imitation of older European models to a significant, world-class statement of artistic modernism in its own right" (Powell 31). Johnson was a musician himself, and in collaboration with his brother Rosamond Johnson, and Rob Cole he wrote several songs for Broadway musical shows. Among the trio's best known hits are "Under the Bamboo Tree" (1902) and "Congo Love Song" (1903). In *The Autobiography*, Johnson's promotion of African-American music was limited to the level of content. There is, for example, no formal fusion of music and literature as in DuBois' inclusion of bars of what he refers to as the Sorrow Songs at the beginning of every chapter of *The Souls*. However, Johnson does devote a fairly large section of *The Autobiography* (pages 126 to 133) to the sermon of John Brown and his leader of singing, Singing Johnson. In this context, he reproduces the lyrics of the songs "Swing Low..." and "Steal Away to Jesus," while carefully explaining the call-and-response pattern that the leader and the congregation are engaged in (130-31). As we have seen, music is intimately related to the narrator's identity, and the lack of further exploration of the form of African-American music is connected to his passing into the white world.

A couple of decades later, Ralph Ellison was to complicate the notion of African-American music as a signifier of the "authentic," by pointing out that "spirituals, the blues, and jazz have been recognized throughout much of the twentieth century as central to the mainstream of American music, even to constitute the nation's true 'classical' tradition." And, Eric Sundquist adds, "it was part of Du Bois's avowed purpose in *The Souls of Black Folk*, for example, to demonstrate that the black spirituals were integral to American culture, as much as slavery and the explosive issue of race itself" (4). The slippage between seeing black music as "national" culture and regarding it as an expression of the "folk" that Sundquist refers to recurs with regard to jazz in the 1920s:

> Once the new sound media made black music available, millions
> of people in America and Europe could discover for themselves
> that black music was not just an African American sound. As the
> black journalist J. A. Rogers put it in 1925, 'Jazz has absorbed the
> national spirit, the tremendous spirit of go and nervousness, lack
> of conventionality and boisterous good nature characteristic of the

American, white or black.' The music expressed, in James Weldon Johnson's words, 'not only the soul of [the black] race, but the soul of America.'" (Haskell 187)

The claim made here is that jazz is American music rather than an authentic African-American expression. In parallel, African-American musicians could be seen as American first of all. The music, dance and folktales of black America not only indicate the artistic capabilities of black Americans but they are, to Johnson, genuinely American art. And interestingly, in *The Autobiography*, the validation for the claim to greatness of these art forms comes by way of Europe. The narrator continues the musings referred to above:

> No one who has traveled can question the world-conquering influence of ragtime, and I do not think it would be an exaggeration to say that in Europe the United States is popularly known better by ragtime than by anything else it has produced in a generation. In Paris they call it American music. The newspapers have already told how the practice of intricate cake-walk steps has taken up the time of European royalty and nobility. These are lower forms of art, but they give evidence of a power that will some day be applied to the higher forms. (63)

Johnson here pinpoints the conflict that I brought up in relation to the meaning of the minstrel performer in the introduction: the conception of American cultural forms as generically popular and therefore "low" culture, and European art as "high" culture. Supporting his case by referring to the appreciation that popular cultural forms such as the cakewalk and ragtime had met with in Europe is an attempt to elevate their status by evoking associations with high culture, nobility and power. The popular aspect of African-American culture, which Robert C. Toll describes in relation to minstrelsy, was often valued as a positive contrast to the aristocratic, high-brow nature of European culture. However, Johnson's remarks reflect the fact that classifying African-American cultural forms as popular generates feelings of inferiority. A little further on in *The Autobiography,* the narrator observes:

> American musicians, instead of investigating ragtime, attempt to ignore it, or dismiss it with a contemptuous word. But that has always been the course of scholasticism in every branch of art. Whatever new thing the *people* like is pooh-poohed; whatever is

> *popular* is spoken of as not worth the while. The fact is, nothing
> great or enduring, especially in music, has ever sprung full-fledged
> and unprecedented from the brain of any master; the best that he
> gives to the world he gathers from the hearts of the people, and
> runs it through the alembic of his genius. (73)

This reflection obviously calls attention not only to the fact that great art has
popular roots, and answers to ideas and feelings found in the everyday life of
ordinary people. The statement also relates to the idea that African-American
culture is associated with the popular or "folk" within American culture and
to Johnson's notion that if African-American music (in this case ragtime) is
elevated to the level of national music, there is much to be gained by this. The
popularity of music with African-American origins could be used for political
purposes also. The use of art as a means of gaining full citizenship is, as we well
know, central to Alain Locke's *The New Negro*. The idea that artistic recognition could lead to social recognition is, in *The Autobiography* and the other
works studied here, rerouted by way of Europe to make the translation between
the cultural spheres easier. There were real-life examples of how recognition of
African-American artists by European audiences could affect attitudes in their
home country. When Duke Ellington made his first trip to Europe, he found
to his surprise that he was better known there than at home. Jazz music was
particularly important in this respect, and it came to challenge the notion of
Europe as originator of art and culture:

> The fact that jazz became popular in Europe increased its symbolic
> value in America. Furthermore, Americans eventually realized
> that by adapting this musical expression as "their" national tune,
> America had something to contribute to global culture. Exporting
> jazz, America, perhaps for the first time, made an impact on
> European culture. This process reversed centuries of transcultural
> relations. Jazz was a predecessor or vanguard for many other
> American cultural artifacts that would soon make a triumphant
> sweep through European popular culture. (Lemke 93)

In the light of this positive evaluation of jazz and given the authors' sensitivity
to Europe's role in African-American culture, it seems a little strange that they
did not employ more jazz elements. Critics have remarked upon the lack of appreciation of the jazz idiom in the literature of many of the Harlem Renaissance

authors and taken this as proof of their elitism. For example, Nathan Huggins observes that "Harlem intellectuals promoted Negro art, but one thing is very curious, except for Langston Hughes, none of them took jazz—the new music—seriously. Of course, they all mentioned it as background, as descriptive of Harlem life. All said it was important in the definition of the "New Negro." But none thought enough about it to try and figure out what was happening" (Huggins, *Harlem* 9-10). The reason why they did not consider the meaning of jazz more seriously was, according to Huggins, that they "were so fixed on a vision of *high* culture" (10). However, the reason why Fauset and Larsen refrained from deploying African-American music as a source of pride may have less to do with snobbishness than with the fact that jazz was connected to primitivism. As a form of primitivism, jazz had particular implications for black women. Primitivism was linked to a view of black, female sexuality that both Fauset and Larsen were reluctant to endorse. The example of Helga Crane's Baker-like transformation shows that jazz, understood in this sense, is a largely unsounded, but still audible, register of *Quicksand.*

Jazz music embodied what was at stake in the topical debate of gaining acceptance as Americans. While the music transcended its local, black roots and came to be seen as a form of music for all Americans, this recognition also entailed the absorption of black art into the commercial mainstream. Jazz music quickly came to be developed in co-operation with white musicians, and was thus the object of the kind of "adulteration" that Johnson describes with respect to the appropriation of ragtime music by white American musicians. However, the distinction of the music (and the reason for its great popularity) was largely based on its "difference" from contemporary European and Euro-American music. Picking up on Johnson's idea that the reception of African-American music in Europe had an impact on how it was evaluated at home, I will in the following concentrate mainly on the reception of jazz music in Europe, particularly in Scandinavia since this provides a framework for interpreting Helga Crane's experiences in Copenhagen.

The reception of jazz music can broadly be summarized as focusing on two different, but parallel, aspects. One is the dichotomy of civilization versus barbarism, including the praise or disapproval, depending on the reviewer, of primitivism. The other is the opposition between tradition (a kind of cultural conservatism) and modernity. This in turn includes the conflict between high culture and popular culture, and a generational conflict involving the formation of a youth culture. It was above all the rhythm of the jazz music that was found to give rise to wild and primitive instincts. There were those who conceived of this in positive terms, that is, that "primitive," "original" forms of expression would invigorate European art and music. But the effect of the music was frightening to more conservative reviewers. Their comments often involve the listeners as well, as the audience is often thought to over-react to the performance and show exaggerated enthusiasm. Some writers even associate the response with mass psychosis (Lyttkens 18). The negative comments concerning the audience's response can be linked to jazz as a youth culture phenomenon. This audience represented the "modern" people, who were also led astray and prey to baser instincts.

The Jazz Age is a transformative moment as regards the perception of African Americans by white Europeans, and Euro-Americans. Contemporary reviews reveal a tension between on the one hand a representation of the African-American performer as a pre-modern, or ahistorical, primitive "African." This type of representation was often based on confused or ill-informed notions of what "Africa" meant. Rather than being a place located in the particular historical and political moment of the 1920s, "Africa" remains a colonial fantasy. On the other hand, the African American was represented as an ultra-modern American bringing a renewed musical idiom to the jaded culture of Europe and giving expression to the pace and rhythm of modern, urban life. The primitivist critique that involved the ascription of a lesser degree of "civilization" to peoples of African descent could be answered in two ways. One response was the emphasis on black difference and on charging the qualities ascribed to blacks with positive connotations: for example, emotionality seen not as sentimentality or lack of reason but a healthy antidote to jaded, over-civilized rationality. Another way of relating to this was to ask for a different evaluation of existing cultures. In the journal *Forum*, a series of articles under the rubric "What is civilization?" was published in 1925.[40] W.E.B. DuBois wrote "Africa's Answer" listing three things that Africa has given the world: "Beginnings, the village unit, and Art in sculpture and music" (179). In his article, DuBois puts the present "modern civilization" into perspective by going to the beginnings of human culture and thereby finding Africa "the Father of Mankind." Again, the question of narrating the past surfaces as DuBois contradicts the notion that Africa was a continent without history. He praises the African village, which could socialize the individual without her/him losing individuality. However, what it gained

---

[40]Du Bois's article is found in *Forum* 73:2, Feb 1925.

in human terms, it lost in economic and military power and thereby became an easy prey for imperial powers. The price the Africans had to pay for the maintenance of this small-scale village structure, which DuBois calls a "perfect human thing," was in fact enslavement (*Forum* 182). Finally, DuBois credits Africa with the invention of primitive art, music and rhythm. He asks:

> [H]ave you heard a Negro orchestra playing Jazz? Your head may revolt, your ancient conventions scream in protest, but your heart and your body leap to rhythm. It is a new and mighty art which Africa gave America and America is giving the world. It has circled the world, it has set hundreds of millions of feet a-dancing, - it is a "new" and "American" art which has already influenced all music and is destined to do more. (*Forum* 186)

In one stroke, DuBois establishes the ancient heritage of the African Americans and acknowledges their role in the making of modern culture. What DuBois claims, then, is that African Americans are at the heart of American culture and contribute crucially to America's modernity. This belief is echoed by Johnson's rag-time player, by Helga Crane listening to the *New World Symphony* in Copenhagen, as well as by Joanna Marshall revealing herself as Miss America, the masked center of American culture.

As evidenced by a label such as "the Jazz Age," jazz music was intimately bound up with the times, that is, it was conceived as a modern phenomenon expressive of the spirit of the 1920s. Jazz is part of the development of an international popular culture with new art forms such as the moving pictures and new modes of distribution such as the radio and the gramophone, which made these forms of cultural expression popular in the sense of being fairly cheap and easily accessible. This music reached an audience outside of the elite circles that would have sought out and been able to pay for concert tickets. Thus it made for a measure of social leveling that seemed repellent to some elitist European critics.

The modernization of the 1920s was an international phenomenon. Increased globalization made possible, and demanded, increased flexibility, openness and mobility. An interest in other peoples and other cultures could be seen as part of this trend. For example, early jazz reviews show how the "modern" Swede, who wanted to appear open-minded, saw colored Americans as the artists of the future. It is perhaps in this light that we should read the reception of Helga by her Danish family. The game of identity construction that Helga and her family engage in of course affects both parties to the process. That is, the identity that the Dahls want Helga to assume is partly determined by the role they want to play themselves. Next to their niece's primitive Africanist persona, the Dahls can appear as more "modern," more in tune with the times. Their conscious social climbing, which Helga is thought to advance, suggests that they kept an ear to the ground as regards social mores. The following quotation from a review of the revue Black People in *Stockholms Tidningen*, 1926, shows that jazz was music by and for modern people:

> The rest of the show more or less fulfilled the expectations of the modern person, that is, the person who likes neon signs, noisy streets, cars, an accelerated pace of life and the Charleston. These modern people had a great time, applauded in the full glare of publicity, laughed and cheered. But the others, especially the distinguished older couples, wrung their hands and whispered: This is too much! I cannot take any more! [...] Are the Negroes the people of the future? No philosophies, but it is strange how well the Negroes suit our times. And how much they apparently have meant for the formation of these times. Yesterday it struck me that the modern revue is entirely the work of the Negroes. (Lyttkens 41, my translation) [41]

In this passage, jazz music symbolizes the clash between New World and Old World life styles. Another reviewer mentions a colleague, the Swedish journalist Torsten Tegnér in *Idrottsbladet*, who feels that Geo Jackson and the Chocolate Kiddies represent the essence of the twentieth century.[42] So, for some critics the rhythm of jazz music was associated with primordial instincts, while for others it was the essence of modernity. The syncopated, fast beat of the music was thought to reflect the new industrialized and urban lifestyle.

Against this was set the classical Western art music (the Danish composers Gade and Heise mentioned in *Quicksand*, for example), which in its for-

---

[41] "Fortsättning blev ungefär vad en modern människa väntat sig och hoppats på, d v s den människan som tycker om ljusreklamer, gatubuller, bilar, forcerad livstakt och charleston. Dessa moderna människor roade sig kungligt, applåderade för öppen ridå, skrattade och jublade. Med de övriga, främst de distinguerade äldre paren togo sig åt huvudet och viskade: - Det är för mycket! Nu orkar jag inte mera! [...] Äro negrerna framtidens folk? Inga filsofier, men underligt är vad negrerna passa bra in i vår tid. Och vad de tydligen betytt mycket för utformningen av denna tid. Man satt igår och gjorde den reflexionen, att hela den moderna revyn tydligen är negrernas verk.
[42] Incomplete reference in *Bonnier Veckotidning*; no date, no sign.

mal structure represented order where the intense rhythm and improvisation of jazz were perceived as chaotic, and therefore frightening. Many of the early Swedish and Danish reviews of jazz concerts concentrate on the artists and their performance on stage, rather than on the musical qualities of their work, which indicates that the appearances of the artists were as fascinating as the music they played. The conflict between "old culture" and "new culture" is substantiated in performances (fictional as well as real-life) where classical music is arranged as jazz. In their Stockholm performances, Sam Wooding and his Chocolate Kiddies, for example, played a Wagner medley which aroused vehement criticism in the Swedish press:

> There was no doubt a lot in these performances which could be labeled quite anti-musical and tasteless! It is an unseemly impudence that well-known Wagner melodies – in the overture – are travestied by being turned into Negro music. This widespread method of composition is more than anything else likely to be a discredit to jazz music with a cultivated audience [...] But on the other hand: one must admire these Negro musicians for their extraordinary sense of rhythm!   (Lyttkens 35, my translation from Swedish)[43]

Erik Wiedemann's study on jazz in Denmark, *Jazz i Danmark—i tyverne, trediverne og fyrrerne* (1982), contains similar examples from the contemporary Danish press. What is noticeable about the review quoted above is that it refers to a musical performance much like the one envisaged by Johnson's narrator, that is, a blending of European and African-American forms of music. The reviewer's comments indicate a conception of Negro music as "travesty," a label that suggests its status as "non-serious" music, as well as its imitative qualities. Their show is understood more as a spectacle than as a form of art. The irate reviewer suggests that the travesty mocks the original and that the Wagner melodies are defiled by the Negro musicians' rendition. The audible color-line between the Wagner melodies and the rhythms of jazz music is anxiously guarded, and this fear of the mixing of musical registers is often transposed onto the visual appearances of the performers. The frequent remarks on the physical appearance of the performers indicate that the visual color-line has to be emphasized more when the audible one is transgressed.

---

[43]Absolut otillständig är den fräckhet, med vilken allbekanta Wagner-melodier—såsom skedde i revyns "ouvertyr"—travesteras genom att omstöpas till negermusik. Denna för övrigt mycket utbredda kompositionsmetod är mer än något annat ägnad att misskreditera jazzmusiken hos en kultiverad publik (the article was originally published in *Scenen*, (15) 1925: 248).

Jazz figures very briefly in *Quicksand,* and in a way that reflects the ambivalence of what the music represented. A scene that takes place at a jazz club in Harlem relates to Helga's decision to leave America for Europe. To begin with, the jazz club appears to be a space with emancipatory connotations, a free zone for intermingling. Among the guests are both white and black people. The motley crew that frequents this place could not be seen in many other places at this time, and Larsen takes care to describe the gathering in detail:

> There was sooty black, shiny black, taupe, mahogany, bronze, copper, gold, orange, yellow, peach, ivory, pinky white, pastry white. There was yellow hair, brown hair, black hair; straight hair, straightened hair, curly hair, crinkly hair, woolly hair. She saw black eyes in white faces, brown eyes in yellow faces, gray eyes in brown faces, blue eyes in tan faces. Africa, Europe, perhaps with a pinch of Asia, in a fantastic motley of ugliness and beauty, semi-barbaric, sophisticated, exotic, were here. (59-60)

This scene, like the novel as a whole, contradicts the notion that blackness is an unequivocal bodily signifier. In *Quicksand's* Harlem Club, it is the music that provides the space where these many-shaded black people meet. The music they listen to is modern and so are they: they are the products of the New World, with its distinctive cultural hybridity, and far removed from the Africa they once came from. In a vital passage, Larsen focuses Helga's reaction to the music and the dancing:

> She was drugged, lifted, sustained, by the extraordinary music, blown out, ripped out, beaten out, by the joyous, wild, murky orchestra. The essence of life seemed bodily motion. And when suddenly the music died, she dragged herself back to the present with a conscious effort; and a shameful certainty that not only had she been in the jungle, but she had enjoyed it, began to taunt her. She hardened her determination to get away. She wasn't, she told herself, a jungle creature. (59)

In this scene, Helga's double consciousness is activated. Seeing herself with both African-American and Anglo-American eyes, Helga is torn between her enjoyment of the music and her will to abandon herself to it, and the realization that in doing so she fulfills the stereotype of the "jungle creature." The passage reiterates the conflict between civilization and primitivism. Her double perception of the event indicates that this polarity is both healthy and threatening: jazz symbolizes life and could function as a healthy antidote to a mechanized and industrialized world. It is also associated with lack of control, with instinct as opposed to reason—a situation that was both frightening and relieving. This jazz scene, which comes in the middle of the book, causes a turn of events. The experience of near-ecstatic abandonment to the music on the dance floor, together with her suppressed desire for Dr. Anderson, who is there in the company of another woman, contributes to a feeling of entrapment. The club suddenly turns into another cramped room reflecting the restricted conditions of existence for Helga in America. Fleeing the suffocating premises, she decides to leave America in the hope of finding greater freedom in Europe.

Jazz also figures as a reinforcement of Larsen's depiction of the clash between Old World and New World in Copenhagen. Over coffee and smørrebrod at a fashionable Copenhagen café, Fru Fischer, a friend of the Dahl's, comments that "she didn't—'begging your pardon, Helga'—like that hideous American music they were forever playing, even if it was considered very smart. 'Give me,' she said, 'the good old-fashioned Danish melodies of Gade and Heise'" (80). American music is here associated with modernity, while the Romantic musical preferences of the Dahl's and their high-society friends reinforces the notion that they are members of an old, and dying, European aristocracy with old-fashioned values and social mores. This is one way then, in which Nella Larsen, although always remaining ambivalent, refers to the infusion of African-American music into European culture. Again, there is the suggestion that the New World has something to offer the Old World in terms of culture, and that cultural hierarchies need to be reconsidered. Fru Fischer also comments on the clientele of the café, noticing that "the place was getting so common, always so many Bolsheviks and Japs and things" (80). Jazz is here associated with anything foreign and sets off the narrow-mindedness of the Danish woman. But most important of all is perhaps Fru Fischer's comment that this is "American" music, rather than African-American. Here, the role of jazz music as a world-wide phenomenon illustrates how the music was linked to goals similar to those of the "New Negro" artists, even though they did not always openly acknowledge it: "Where white musicians and audiences might have seen novelty and 'national' spirit, black musicians and audiences saw an opportunity to redefine the very idea of "American" as applied to music" (Ruotolo 254). This idea, that music is an index of cultural identity and a means through which this identity could be re-imagined, is found in, above all, Johnson but also Fauset and Larsen.

In Fauset's *There Is Confusion,* Joanna's projected means of gaining prominence is, in addition to dancing, through singing Tchaikovsky or German lieder. These musical references are significant when seen in the context of the
debate concerning African-American music and authenticity. An illuminating
example is to be gathered from Cheryl Wall whose comparison between the
Harlem Renaissance women authors and the contemporary blues women is relevant to the question of the artist's relation to her medium of expression. Wall
reminds us that contemporary with the genteel fiction of Harlem Renaissance
authors was the art of Bessie Smith, Ma Rainey, and other blues artists who also

> grappled with issues of identity, sought forms that could encompass
> the reality of their experience as black women, and struggled to
> control their own voices. Unlike the literary women, however, the
> blueswomen worked within an aesthetic tradition that recognized
> their right to speak. Free of the burdens of an alien tradition, a
> Bessie Smith could establish the standard of her art; in the process
> she would compose a more honest poetry than any of her literary
> sisters. (Wall 18)

In other words, Wall suggests that there is something fake or dishonest about the
literary works of Fauset, Larsen, and others. Blues is often thought of as the authentic signifier of African-American culture. As Evelyn Brooks Higginbotham
observes, "[i]mplicitly, if not explicitly, the blues is deemed the 'authentic' signifier of African-American culture. Blues culture, working-class culture, and
'blackness' become virtually synonymous" (157). The audience of this vernacular
art form is made into a model of black authenticity. There are ideological dimen-
sions of this comment in the idealization of the working class as the true representatives of the "people." This privileging of the experience of the working class
has affected the reception of a writer like Fauset, whose works deal primarily
with the middle classes.

In the story of Joanna Marshall, the would-be classical ballerina whose
dreams are thwarted by racism, Fauset clearly distances herself from blues as
well as working-class culture. Instead of describing characters who are rural,
Southern workers Fauset elects to depict well-educated, Northern urban artists, who have the mobility to go to Europe. This suggests Fauset's concern
with formulating an alternative conception to the blackness of the "folk."
However, Fauset does recognize vernacular culture through the incorporation
of the ring dance "Barn," which features colored children who are brought in

from the street to revitalize the show "Dance of the Nations." In fact, this part of the show is built around the game Joanna has played, and observed groups of African-American children play, in the street. Ten children are brought in from the neighborhood of the theater to accompany Joanna's dancing and acting of the game, singing "Sissy in the barn! Join in the weddin'!" (229). Here folk culture, through a traditional game played in the street, is elevated to represent black America in the "Dance of the Nations." The music has to have the right lilt, and the stage show is an interactive performance including the call-and-response procedure and polyphony of several voices that characterizes oral African-American tradition. The fact that children are thought to be adequate representatives of black America reflects the ambiguous contemporary perception of African Americans. The children embody the vivacity and joy that was to inject life into the jaded European cultural forms. But they are also indicative of the parts African Americans had to play on the American social scene at this time, being in effect treated as minors and denied full citizenship in America. The playful children of Fauset's barn dance game are to be understood in a manner parallel to that of the infantilized appearances of the vaudeville performers that Larsen describes. It is as children that African Americans can be received and appreciated on the American social and theater scene, since they do not present a challenge to the audience's sense of stability and control. Children also played a symbolic role in the primitivism of the era, as they (in a manner parallel to that of black people) represented innocence and were thought to be untarnished by civilization. The black children of Joanna's stage show thus reinforce the image of blackness as marked by naiveté.

Not only does the children's street dance function as a "counter-memory" (to the dominant white history) of the kind discussed by Roach when put on the stage to represent America. There is yet another interesting implication of this scene. The children of the street are the repositories of African-American culture that Joanna has to consult before she can give a credible performance of the colored part of Ms. America's dance act. Joanna's dependence on the children suggests her own removal from the sources of African-American culture/tradition. Her own sources of artistic inspiration are largely European-derived and so she has to learn how to perform the part of an "authentic" black American.[44] What Fauset describes here, then, is that the authentic is, in

---

[44] For a non-fiction exploration of similar ideas, see Fauset's article on the black minstrel performer Bert Williams, "The Symbolism of Bert Williams," *The Crisis*, May, 1922 (12-15).

fact, performative. The musical performances included in the novels studied also form a cultural critique as the complex relationship between traditional European and African-American forms of cultural expression is probed. A hierarchical sense of "culture" is involved here as European art music is associated with "high" culture while African-American music is associated with "low" or popular culture. Rather than seeing Joanna Marshall's struggles to enter the American stage as opera singer and ballet dancer as relating to the promulgation of imitation-white values of which Fauset has been accused, we can read it as an important comment on a very topical debate—indeed still topical when we consider that the highly successful South Bronx school KIPP (Knowledge Is Power Program) makes all its students play the violin as a way of disproving stereotypes about African Americans not being able to master the kind of string music that is associated with Western classical ideals (Klemming 13).

A contemporary example of an artist who did manage to enter into the closed spheres of high culture is singer Marian Anderson. She toured Europe in the early 1930's to great critical acclaim and public success. In 1934, she visited Copenhagen and the *Opportunity* reporter wrote: "And I may mention, for the encouragement of the dark folk of America, that after the concert I saw the American Ambassador seek her out amid mountains of flowers and ranks of people bending to do her homage, take her by the hand and say, 'We're proud of you, Miss Anderson. America will not forget you'" (deCoverley 271). The quotation referring to Anderson's Copenhagen concert suggests that the success of African-American artists in Europe could affect their reception in America: "The European belief that America's greatest contribution to the world's culture lay in its black popular music would open minds, and doors, at home" (Haskell 186). Taking their art to Europe has positive consequences for the return of the musicians, and in a parallel manner, Johnson and Fauset investigate the setting of Europe to reroute their claims for equal treatment back home.

Helga's decision to go back to America is crucially related to African-American music. Her initial shame and malaise at the Circus incident gradually give way to a burgeoning sense of the importance of recognizing her African-American heritage. This is one example of the novel's uneasy moves between cultural essentialism and hybridity. Soon after, Helga begins to form the decision to leave Copenhagen and go back home to Harlem. The final deciding point comes at a performance of Dvořák's "New World Symphony," a blend of spirituals and classical European music. This Dvořák symphony is a striking figure of the Old World—New World confrontation underlying the

Copenhagen episode of *Quicksand*. The symphony highlights the hierarchical relationship between the European art music of Dvořák and the African-American folk music. Helga is deeply affected not only by the underlying tones of the spiritual "Swing Low..." in the "New World Symphony:"

> Her definite decision to go was arrived at with almost bewildering suddenness. It was after a concert at which Dvořák's "New World Symphony" had been wonderfully rendered. Those wailing undertones of "Swing Low, Sweet Chariot" were too poignantly familiar. They struck into her longing heart and cut away her weakening defenses. She knew at least what it was that had lurked formless and undesignated these many weeks in the back of her troubled mind. Incompleteness. "I'm homesick, not for America, but for Negroes. That's the trouble." (92)

As in The Autobiography, music is here seen as intimately coupled to race: it is the company of Negroes Helga longs for, rather than America. Copenhagen is of course notably devoid of black people and offers only physical freedom, not the spiritual freedom that comes with being among her own people (96). Like Johnson's ex-colored man, Larsen's Helga has emotional ties to the music. It evokes in her memories of, and a yearning for, "the inexhaustible humor and the incessant hope [...] those things, not material, indigenous to all Negro environments" (92). Being removed from the sources of this music (the spirituals), Helga's feeling of alienation, lack of belonging and true self-consciousness are heightened.

In addition, what Larsen seems to suggest through the Dvořák symphony is a dismantling of the hierarchies inherent in the relations between white and black, and between Old World and New World. By bringing in traditional African-American music a new aesthetic idiom is created. Its modernity consists in its hybridity, its mixing of cultural forms. This is a good example of how Larsen suggests that African-American art forms make up a significant part of the concept of Western modernity. An important predecessor of Larsen in this respect is James Weldon Johnson's *The Autobiography*, where music also provides a key to insight concerning cultural identity. The stress on American culture in *The Autobiography*, and particularly the African American contributions to it, challenges the idea of Europe as originator of culture. The "ex-colored man's" vision of creating a blend between ragtime and classical music puts the two musical genres on a par with each other. The same idea is echoed in *Quicksand* by Larsen's inclusion of Dvořák's *New World Symphony*.

Apart from the inclusion of music as a signifier of the vernacular, there is another aspect of the three novels that is relevant to the discussion of how Johnson, Fauset and Larsen negotiated the two traditions (that is, the vernacular as opposed to the Euro-American, or Western, tradition). This is the use, or lack thereof, of dialect.

Through the mask of dialect

In the literature of, for example, Zora Neale Hurson, the use of dialect creates a certain notion of the black subject, and of black culture as connected to a rural, southern environment. In *Their Eyes Were Watching God,* Hurston sets up a narrative situation that is to give the impression of direct speech. Dialect is for Hurston a way to bridge the gap between the oral and the literary, of inserting a black voice within "an alien tradition." Interestingly, there is very little dialect speech in the novels of Johnson, Fauset and Larsen. It is known that, as an editor, Fauset had problems with the free verse form of Langston Hughes's poetry, in which he often aimed to incorporate vernacular musical or linguistic idioms, although she early recognized his poetic genius. Cheryl Wall calls Fauset "deaf to the poetry of the folk" (65), and even claims she has "a tin ear for black vernacular" (79).

To some Harlem authors who were seeking to represent the vernacular, the use of dialect had a bad ring as it was associated with stereotypes from plantation slavery.[45] In the preface to *The Book of American Negro Poetry,* James Weldon Johnson recognizes the benefits of writing in Negro dialect, but only if it can break free from the mould of convention in which it has been shaped in America. He remarks that several of the contemporary authors who are represented in the anthology have chosen to discard the kind of dialect that was

---

[45] Michael North's *The Dialect of Modernism: Race, Language and Twentieth Century Literature* (1994) deals with writing in dialect and suggests the different stakes involved for black and white modernist authors. To writers such as Gertrude Stein, T. S. Eliot and Ezra Pound the use of "black" dialect was a modernist strategy, but to black writers the use of dialect was a often a barrier to modernism. The African-American authors had to struggle to find alternatives to the conventional representations of black dialect, which were often linked to stereotypical characterization – the happy-go-lucky, banjo-playing darkie of the plantation – and associated with works of extreme sentimentalism or humor. To writers like Stein (in the short story "Melanctha") and Eliot (in "Sweeney Agonistes") on the other hand, the black voice had an insurrectionary function in that it deviates from the known and familiar in language. [In addition, the artist occupied "the role of racial outsider because he or she spoke a language opposed to the standard. Modernism, that is to say, mimicked the strategies of dialect and aspired to become a dialect itself." (North's preface, no page number).]

associated with a subject matter concentrated on plantation life, the dialect poetry having for its subject matter the plantation life of 'possums and watermelons. Instead, Johnson writes, the contemporary African-American poet needs to "find a form that will express the racial spirit by symbols from within rather than by symbols from without, such as the mere mutilation of English spelling and pronunciation. He needs a form that is freer and larger than dialect, but which will still hold the racial flavour" (43). These ideas are reflected in Johnson's own work, primarily in *God's Trombones: Seven Negro Sermons in Verse* (1927), and in the songs and poems in *Lift Every Voice and Sing* (1935). In the preface to *God's Trombones*, Johnson explicates his aim to reinstate an older form of Negro dialect that was used before the form for this dialect was conventionalized in the nineteenth century. This idiom of the early black American preachers, says Johnson, was "a fusion of Negro idioms with Bible English" (9). Basically, this dialect is sonorous, has a distinct rhythm, and uses Biblical metaphors and imagery. These observations made with regard to poetry do not translate into Johnson's prose work. There is not much dialogue at all in *The Autobiography* and the narrator is often like an observing sociologist commenting on the people and places he encounters. On a visit to Atlanta, he runs into some people of the "lower class," whom he finds very unattractive but for one thing—their dialect:

> I had read some Negro dialect and had heard snatches of it on my journey down from Washington; but here I heard it in all of its fullness and freedom. I was particularly struck by the way in which it was punctuated by such exclamatory phrases as "Lawd a mussy!" "G'wan, man!" "Bless my soul!" "Look heah, chile!" These people laughed and talked without restraint. In fact, they talked straight from their lungs and laughed from the pits of their stomachs [...] I have since learned that this ability to laugh heartily is, in part the salvation of the American Negro; it does much to keep him from going the way of the Indian. (40)

The perspective of the narrator is that of an outsider listening to the men talking and laughing. While he appreciates what he hears, linking their manner of conversation to a positive strategy of survival, he himself maintains his distance. There is a combination of repudiation and praise in his attitude to the speakers, whose dialect is a marker of their commonness at the same time as it creates a shared bond and source of strength that helps them survive as a group.

Fauset and Larsen did not employ the kind of developed dialect that Johnson called for and Toni Morrison, among others, later responded to. To them, dialect was to be avoided or, if used, it was to set off the urbanity of their main characters. Fauset's dialogue is generally rather stilted, so-called Standard American English dialogue, exemplified by such awkward exclamations as "Why, I love you, my dear" or "I should say so. Jolly little place you've got here" (136). The only black character with an unsophisticated dialect, which could be described as vernacular, is Maggie's mother's cousin, Mis' Sparrow, who is working as a cook in New York's infamous Tenderloin district. In "her own peculiar dialect," Mis' Sparrow is the one who suggests to Maggie that marriage provides a way for a woman to attain "decency": "H'm child, wouldn't you do anything to get away f'um hard work, an' ugly cloes and bills? Some w'ite folks has it most as bad as us poor colored people. On'y thing is they has more oppochunities" (56). Maggie is also a "true daughter of the Tenderloin district" and her uneducated speech at that time detracts considerably from her charm, Fauset tells us (58-59). The Tenderloin and its inhabitants represent everything that Maggie wants to escape from in her life: poverty, filth and lack of "decency." Thus, she takes the advice of Mis' Sparrow and marries to get away; a move that proves to be her greatest mistake in life. She does manage to lose her vulgar dialect, however. As in *The Autobiography*, dialect in *There Is Confusion* is thus used to signify class distinction.

Similarly, Larsen uses dialect to emphasize Helga's failure to adapt to married life. Instances of dialect speech occur in her depiction of the members of Reverend Green's congregation. These people appear in Helga's conversion experience in Harlem and in the rural Alabama community where Helga is about to meet her end. Issuing from the mouths of uneducated rural dwellers, among whom Helga does not feel at home and who talk about her as "dat uppity, meddlin' No'the'nah" (119), the black vernacular clearly has negative implications in Larsen's novel. Like the scorned Uncle Tom, these characters accept their incessant hardships by putting their faith in the Lord: "'Jes' remembah,' Sary went on, staring sternly into Helga's thin face, 'we all gits ouah res' by an' by. In de nex' worl' we's all recompense'. Jes' put yo' trus' in de Sabioah'" (125). Larsen here gives emphasis to Helga's feeling of being trapped by her marriage to the Reverend Green, and the passivity of the attitude expressed by his congregationists who wait for justice in the hereafter. By depictions such as this, Larsen eschews the "romantic evocation of the folk," as Carby put it, and points to the limited options of existence for an educated and urbane woman like Helga.

To Fauset and Larsen, then, the use of vernacular speech obviously had no positive connotations. Rather, it is associated with rural or working-class characters who are representative of conservative opinions on woman's role in society. Fauset's Mis' Sparrow affirms the possibility of marriage for purely financial purposes, while Larsen's rustics suggest that woman's mission is to bear children and put her trust in the father in heaven and the man at home. Critics often remark upon the fact that Larsen's *Quicksand* is one of the first secular novels written by an African-American woman. Helga's fate at the end of the novel involves a critique of black people who meekly give up trying to change things in this world in order to wait for better times in the next. Larsen writes: "How the white man's God must laugh at the great joke he had played on them!" (133). As Larsen shows, this joke was especially played on black women as they had even more limited opportunities than the men. The modern black subject of Johnson's, Fauset's and Larsen's novels still speaks with a voice coming out of the nineteenth-century novel. While their texts include variations on conventions of the structure of the novel, Fauset and Larsen were hesitant to include or refer to vernacular art. Rather, as the authors question the stability of what signified "blackness," they simultaneously question the notion of authenticity as applied to the black text. The fact that Johnson was more open to promoting what he thought of as "original" black American art suggests that the role of the male artist in the shaping of "new Negro" art was less complicated than that of women like Fauset and Larsen. The quicksand and confusion of the combined pressures of racism and sexism was felt not only in relation to Euro-American culture but on the precarious home ground of the black community as well.

Concluding remarks

In the present study, the relationship between the "New Negro moment" of the 1920s and the Old World of Europe has been explored. In an investigation of "the extraordinary perils, different from those of America but not less grave, which the American Negro encounters in the Old World," as James Baldwin phrased it, I have examined how Europe figures in James Weldon Johnson's *The Autobiography of an Ex-Colored Man*, Jessie Fauset's *There Is Confusion*, and Nella Larsen's *Quicksand*. The fact that James Baldwin, writing in the 1950s and 1960s, provides the opening of this study suggests that the questions approached by the Harlem Renaissance authors have continued to be of relevance long after they were written. Indeed, Baldwin's lucid depictions of the in-between status of African-Americans still form a good foundation for understanding many of the problems encountered by the black man entering the white world. His essays suggest how the colonial legacy still operates in structures of dominance in both American and Europe, in addition to illustrating how being an African American means living with the tension between being socially invisible and yet all too visible when it comes to group definitions that separate "white" from "black", "us" from "them." Finally, Baldwin shows how sojourns in Europe serve to strengthen the sense of his own Americanness. All of these parameters are part of my analysis of the authors whose texts, although they preceded Baldwin's by more than twenty years, deal with similar concerns.

In the 1990s, Paul Gilroy has shown that movement, forced as well as voluntary, east and west across the Atlantic is fundamental to Western modernity. Mobility and transformation are a vital part of Gilroy's concept *the black Atlantic*, which emphasizes interchanges of ideas and people across the Atlantic. In line with this reasoning, an internationalist perspective is vital to our understanding of the "New Negro." This is, in fact, what the texts of Johnson, Fauset, and Larsen indicate.

The protagonists of all the novels studied here are various kinds of artists. This is a narrative device that I interpret on the basis of Robert Powell's claim that many of the Harlem Renaissance writers would conceive of black artists as "cultural intermediaries," who articulated the desires and aspirations of the "New Negro." In the novels of Johnson, Fauset, and Larsen, this intermediary function is, I have suggested, directly related to the symbolic meaning of

Europe. Here, artists bridge the gap between African-American and European culture, national and folk culture, high and low culture. All of these factors are, for example, at work in the attempt of Johnson's narrator to fuse Western classical music with ragtime and his mother's "Southern songs."

A central purpose of this study has been to investigate how the representations of Europe relate to the concepts of "culture" and "race." To the African-American protagonists of the novels of Johnson, Fauset, and Larsen, Europe is a symbolic geography that has to be charted according to certain cultural codes. In nineteenth-century literature, Europe constitutes a geography with positive connotations, signifying not only physical freedom but also access to education and a chance of recognition for one's artistic work. In the early twentieth-century novels of Johnson, Fauset, and Larsen, these notions are questioned and problematized. In their works, Europe figures primarily as a symbolic geography with connotations of whiteness and civilization. Thus, its meaning is ambiguous to their protagonists. The physical freedom they find in Europe is compromised by the felt need for community and a sense of belonging that only black America can offer. This signals that the authors share the newfound sense of hopefulness and faith in the idea that conditions were actually going to change in America that characterized the Harlem Renaissance.

The European episodes in the novels of Johnson and Larsen are set in cosmopolitan milieus that are sophisticated but rather quaint. Important events take place in cultural venues, such as theaters and cafés. Being the site of war, Fauset's Europe deviates from this pattern. (However, in her 1933 novel *Comedy American Style*, Paris appears as a city of international affairs, but in the end the characters who stay in France—Olivia and Teresa—are lost and deracinated, staying there per force rather than of their free will.) Her descriptions of the muddy, chaotic European battle-fields also read like a critique of the state of contemporary European civilization. While important events that could not happen in America take place here, such as the reconciliation of the black and the white branches of the Bye family, it is clear that this is no permanent dwelling-place for the African-American characters.

The episodes set in Europe are a lens through which the role of the African American in Western civilization can be studied, and the complex symbolism of Europe includes issues of cultural belonging and representation. The concept of culture as it operates in the novels of Johnson, Fauset, and Larsen is best understood in its hierarchical sense. This allows us to see its relation to the notion of "civilization" in contrast to the common conception of African societies and people as "uncivilized" or "primitive." In *Quicksand*, for example, the Danes are depicted as members of an old, vanishing civilization. The wealthy Danish Dahls, whose home the impoverished Helga enters, have an old-fashioned, leisurely lifestyle. Helga is fascinated by their "pretentious stately life," and with the help of their money she becomes a spectacular social persona in Copenhagen (96). However, there is an element of critique of this civilization, which was considered the apex of human progress, in its misguided longing for an alternative lifestyle expressed in primitivism. Helga soon begins to feel uncomfortable as she is paraded like an exotic object for the Danes.

The idea that Europe and European art forms represent an old civilization and high culture resonates throughout all three novels. Whereas *There Is Confusion* describes a bleak, war-torn physical environment, the novel addresses most clearly the idea of European art forms as exclusive, high culture. Joanna Marshall faces discrimination in her attempt to enter the American stage. Fauset thereby suggests that in contemporary America certain art forms, such as opera or classical ballet, are best practiced by the descendants of Europeans—partly because of custom or tradition, and partly owing to the process of racialization. *Kultur* clearly coincides with race as exclusionary categories in Fauset's novel.

In all the novels, the racial category of *whiteness* is linked to the symbolism of civilization and high culture. Europe figures as a white world more accessible to the black American than the white world of her/his home country. The issue of "passing" does not apply in Europe, for example, and the ex-colored narrator of Johnson's novel simply accompanies his white Millionaire wherever he goes. For Helga Crane, on the other hand, residing in the white world of Copenhagen means having to emphasize and even exaggerate her blackness in order to gain a social position. The story of the black woman entering the white continent reads like an alternative version of a colonial travel narrative. Copenhagen is a "contact zone," in Mary Louise Pratt's terminology, where African-American and Danish cultures meet under the asymmetrical power relations that are the consequences of slavery and colonialism. The Copenhagen episode significantly includes a battle concerning definition and seeing: although Helga is the focalizer of the novel, she is still an object defined by the white gaze, and with the Dahls' money she is formed into a spectacular object of consumption. Again, Fauset's depiction is a little different in that a black regiment comes over and is welcomed by the French. American racism continues, however, and fighting between black and white American soldiers continues on European soil. The relocation of this interracial struggle to Europe, which means that it is taken it out of its usual context and thus "de-naturalized," strengthens Fauset's critique of American racism.

The relationship between place and performance is also probed. The notion of performance has a particular resonance in African-American history. Here, stage and social performances interact and overlap in a particular way. The parallels that can be drawn between the two types of performance concern the limitations and possibilities that surround them, relating primarily to audience and the discursive situation in which they are produced. In America, performance serves the purpose of cultural retention and renewal of cultural memory, restoring a sense of shared history and community. This is exemplified by the children's ring dancing in *There Is Confusion* and the ex-colored man's performance of his mother's Southern songs. Here, the music is a symbol of a certain experience, a common past, and he has to leave Europe in order to practice it. Europe, on the other hand, functions as a space where performances related to African-American culture and identity could be re-imagined and re-enacted. As we have seen, it is only by making the detour to Europe that the narrator of Johnson's text realizes what his musical project will be: the fusion of Western classical music and his mother's Southern songs. To Fauset's Maggie Ellersley, Europe is the place where she gains independence and begins to imagine a different role for herself in the future: that of a businesswoman and owner of a chain of beauty shops. Additionally, the brotherhood between black and white is forcefully staged here as white Meriwether Bye dies in black Peter Bye's arms. For Joanna Marshall, Europe appears on a figurative level, in terms of European cultural forms, such as opera and classical ballet, which indicate the complexities of cultural belonging. To Larsen's Helga Crane, her own social performance at first seems liberating, but it then turns out to be as oppressing as any of the roles offered the black woman in America. The revelation that her existence in Europe is in fact similar to that of a "stage Negro" comes through an American vaudeville performance at the Copenhagen Circus. Larsen thus presents the least promising vision in terms of the liberating potential inherent in the journey to Europe.

According to Judith Butler, performance is an inevitable element in the construction of personal identity. To Butler there can in fact be no subject without performance—a performance that is often rigidly defined by social norms and expectations of human behavior. While her examples concern gender, they can be applied to racial identity as well. The texts of Johnson, Fauset, and Larsen all include conflicts between the roles that their protagonists are expected to play and their actual performances. Helga Crane's forced performance of blackness in Copenhagen is the best illustration of Butler's ideas. In an attempt to flee her racialized existence in America (and a failed, possible love affair with Dr. Anderson) she departs for Denmark, where she attempts to redefine her self through clothes, behavior, and speech. For some time, she is happy there. Quite soon, however, it is obvious that her social performance is not the liberating pursuit it first seemed to be; and the norms and conventions that the Danes refer to in order to understand her, and that determine her actions, have become reductive and stifling. Reading Helga Crane's experiences through the grid of Butler's theories of gender identities, we see the various ways in which our social performance is always discursively embedded and restricted. Furthermore, Larsen's novel shows how conventions of race and gender intersect to complicate the situation of the African-American woman.

However, to interpret the process of identification from a performance perspective is not merely to see its limitations. It also offers a constructive possibility for unsettling fixed notions of stable—and often reductive—identification. This means that even if the performances of the protagonists appear to have "failed" in the sense that they have not led to a complete fulfillment of the original goal, they succeed in pointing to an underlying structure of categorization, which is not as stable or self-evident as it appears. In fact, on close examination we see that the texts reveal an inconsistency concerning racial classification. The fact that Johnson's narrator ends up living as an "ex-colored" man is a very concrete example of the absurd consequences this classification generates. The "problem of the color-line" is thus further complicated, as the boundary designating what is black and what is white turns out to be fundamentally indistinct. Reading performance as an approach to identification we can see it as a potentially empowering strategy, which calls attention to the untenability of reductive or essentialist notions of what it means to be black, or a woman. Both Helga's performance of blackness and the ex-colored man's performance of whiteness are "copies" that serve to blur the supposed "original." I have used the figure of the blackface minstrel performer to illustrate this displacement of blackness—and, consequently, whiteness.

The minstrel performer was also evoked to illustrate the complex idea of masking, which is used by all the authors. Metaphors of masking are common in early African-American literature, suggesting that some kind of role-playing in relation to white society is part of daily existence. The notion of masking operates on several levels in Johnson's *The Autobiography*, for example. This is evident already in the title, which indicates that Johnson's novel wears the mask of autobiography. In addition, the narrator is unreliable: not only does he remain unnamed, but the narrative voice and tone shifts in the text. Finally, there are the various roles of black, white, and finally ex-colored man that he plays. Jessie Fauset employs the idea of masking in the charged scene where Joanna performs her version of Ms America behind a mask intended to hide her blackness. This reads like a literal staging of the conditions of black existence in America. In Nella Larsen's Copenhagen, Helga's performed exotic persona is a mask that she puts on for the Danes—a mask which is very soon to become uncomfortable and stifling. The significance of masking has also been indicated by post-colonial critics, such as Homi Bhabha, who in his studies of mimicry questions whether the art of masking is necessarily tragic, hiding a true self that cannot be shown. Instead, he says, masking allows a double vision (not unlike DuBois' double consciousness) that could possibly destabilize the colonial social order. An application of Bhabha's approach would suggest that the "near-white" characters of Jessie Fauset are not necessarily to be understood as rootless and tragic. Instead, these hybrid characters constitute a challenge to the rigid separation and polarization of black and white that forms the basis of segregationist policies.

Turning on performers and performing arts, the books can be seen as performances in their own right. Considering the novels of Johnson, Fauset, and Larsen through the lens of performance has the advantage of recognizing the text's status as a cultural event, rather than as an objective reflector of the conditions of actual social life. At the same time the text's dependence on context is emphasized. The historical time of the production of these texts, and their interplay with the mixed white and black audience, are constitutive of these textual performances. This view of the text as an intervention into contemporary events is in line with the Harlem Renaissance connection between increased literary production and increased social rights. The textual performance is, however, circumscribed by discursive restrictions similar to those that relate to social and stage performances.

In sum, the trope of performance, based on the notion of double consciousness, is used to critique the notions of race and culture, whereby conceptions of racial essentialism and cultural authenticity are questioned. Johnson, Fauset, and Larsen seek to affirm a distinctive black identity and art, but aim to find new terms of formulation for this identity. They construct alternatives to the "Old Negro" stereotypes by presenting cosmopolitan characters with the financial means to go to Europe. Contributing to the Harlem Renaissance search for a modern black identity, these authors show that Europe ought to be considered as part of the African-American cultural heritage as well. Johnson, Fauset, and Larsen use the symbolic meaning of Europe as a sounding board in their construction of counter-narratives to the dominant racial ideology. In this sense, their novels function as performative acts that helped form the concept of a "New Negro" in the 1920s. In the process, formal variations of literary conventions, such as the autobiography and the romance, were of importance.

To appropriate a narrative convention such as the marriage plot and apply it to particularly African-American subject matters is a way of questioning the dominant ideology. Bringing up matters of race—segregation, race violence and sexual exploitation—in a well-known form such as the novel also ensures a mixed (or double) audience. To discuss, as I do in this context, the novel as a "European-derived" art form is a way of accounting for its very origin and its links to the values of bourgeois white society and to imperialism. It is not, of course, to deny that the American novel was a well-developed genre by the early twentieth century—even if authors like Hemingway and Fitzgerald were still aiming to write "the great American novel" in the 1920s. It is mainly to point to the fact that the early history of the novel shows that it was a European or Euro-American, rather than a black American, project. For African Americans, who had long been barred from reading and writing, oral poetry and music were the primary art forms. The authors of the Harlem Renaissance were only a few generations away from William Wells Brown, whose *Clotel, or The President's Daughter* (1853) is usually considered to be the first African-American novel. Subsequently, some Harlem Renaissance scholars, such as Cheryl Wall, have considered the form "alien" to African-American authors at this time. That is, the act of writing a novel rather than singing or playing the blues, for example, required a schooling and knowledge of a tradition, or art form, which had until the early twentieth century engaged mainly Europeans or Euro-Americans.

To approach the social meaning of these novels, they can be contrasted with vernacular African-American art forms, represented here by music, such as blues, ragtime and jazz. Music is of great significance in the texts of Johnson, Fauset, and Larsen, representing dreams of achievement while involving class mobility and the search for cultural identity. The novels suggest that music is connected to "race" in ways that had a particular meaning for African-American self-definition. The discussion of vernacular art forms is one in which the notion of authenticity surfaces, with regard to what constitutes a black identity and a "black text." I argue that music functions as an index of cultural identity and a motif through which this identity could be re-imagined. However, instead of offering simple affirmations of a shared black identity, the novels initiate discussions of what can and cannot signify blackness. The texts of Fauset and Larsen are particularly ambiguous in this respect, indicating the authors' sensitiveness to the combined limitations of race and gender.

A substantial part of the final chapter investigates the significance of jazz as music of African-American origin in relation to the white society of the early twentieth century. The music often brought about acceptance and increased interest in black culture, but it was also connected to primitivism. In contrast to Western classical music, jazz was a popular form of music which was connected to dancing and boisterous nightlife. Because it was perceived as sinful, and linked with uninhibited sexuality, it was problematic particularly for black women. Jessie Fauset avoided the inclusion of jazz in her depictions of respectable black middle-class life, and Nella Larsen approaches music in ambiguous terms. The Harlem jazz scene she describes activates Helga's double consciousness as she becomes aware of the negative connotations of the music. This prefigures her subsequent experiences in Denmark, where similar ambivalent feelings are evoked by the Danes' longing for the primitive. Johnson's male narrator, on the other hand, takes pride in the ragtime that was an early form of jazz and becomes an active performer of this music, thereby celebrating his musical predecessors and his own African-American heritage.

The discussion of jazz music fills two other important functions. One is to relate the novels to a wider cultural context, which also includes describing the minstrel performances and the pictures of the "Old Negro" that circulated in film, advertisements, and other media. Finally, the discussion of jazz serves the purpose of giving what we may call the other side of the picture. Through a survey of the reception of jazz musicians, and their predecessors on the European musical scene, we gain insight into how African Americans were known in Europe in the early twentieth century. The music of the Fisk Jubilee Singers, the musical clowns, and the post-World War I jazz bands helped create an image of the African American in the mind of the European. These musical performances often constituted the first European meetings with cultural manifestations of African-American origin and provide the background against which we must read the production of the texts of Johnson, Fauset, and Larsen. Some interesting aspects of contemporary European reviews of the performances are, for instance, the guarding of the "audible" color-line—that is, the dislike of mixing classical European music with music of African-American origin—and the reviewers' focus on stage performance rather than on musical qualities. These and other issues are addressed in the novels and indicate the compromised nature of African-American artistic production in a white-controlled cultural market.

This ambivalence is at the root of the problem of what is considered to be authentic art. To pursue any kind of art that is thought to be authentic may serve certain purposes, such as the creation of a common sense of identification. This approach was favored by some Harlem Renaissance authors, such as Langston Hughes and Zora Neale Hurston, who infused their texts with speech and manners thought typical of the (Southern, rural or working-class) life of the black majority. The writers selected for this study question the meaning of such a concept of authenticity. The characters and settings that they describe resist any simple, unitary definitions of what it means to be black. In this, they anticipate a debate that has gone on throughout the twentieth century. In the aftermath of colonialism, the notion of hybridity has surfaced to account for the mixed world that it left behind. Here, I analyze the performances in the novels as ways of questioning the concept of authenticity applied to cultural identity. Rather than interpreting the authors' concern with European culture as a form of elitism, we can see it as a claim to the necessary hybridity of culture—a hybridity that replaces the notion of authenticity with regard to African-American identity and cultural production. This modern hybridity extends to their texts as well. Instead of dismissing the texts (particularly those of Fauset and Larsen) as conventional, we need to look for resistance in new places. Not only do they resist, or construct alternative views of, American social life when it comes to the subjects that are dealt with. They also use form to articulate this resistance, which is seen in their variations on traditional genres—what I have discussed as "repetitions with a difference." For example, Johnson's anonymous novel destabilizes the very idea of the autobiographical subject along with the categories of white and black; Fauset's handling of the marriage plot questions the traditional idea of gender roles often found in earlier European novels; and Larsen's inversion of the colonial travel narrative interrogates the relationship between the seer and the seen, between subject and object, in a way that relates to the structures of domination in the post-colonial world.

In the narratives of Johnson, Fauset, and Larsen we find attempts to break out of a confining, racialized existence by means of a relocation from America to Europe. The hybrid—and often masked—characters that they present are situated between the white and the black worlds, between vernacular and Euro-American cultures. These texts question the founding mythology of America, which includes liberty, equality, and the pursuit of happiness for all its citizens. They point to the "equivocation" at the root of Western civilization—that is, that the progress and liberation of some is only made possible through the subjugation of others—discussed by Paul Gilroy in *The Black Atlantic*. This close and often uneasy coexistence between white and black, characterized by interdependence and unequal interaction, is typical of Western modernity.

No entirely happy endings are offered the reader of these novels. Europe could only be a temporary home to the traveling protagonists of Johnson's *The Autobiography of an Ex-Colored Man*, Fauset's *There Is Confusion*, and Larsen's *Quicksand*. The America they return to still offers scant opportunities for its black population. Although writing a couple of decades later, Baldwin suggests how one might interpret the return to the constricted conditions in America. Reflecting on how a stay in Europe affects the American writer, Baldwin observes that "if he has been preparing himself for anything in Europe, he has been preparing himself—for America. In short, the freedom that the American writer finds in Europe brings him, full circle, back to himself, with the responsibility for his development where it always was: in his own hands" (141). Significantly, the spatial relocation leads to a re-evaluation of the situation in his home country. In the end, the novels provide no simple solutions—but the journey epitomizes the African American's situation in-between geographical, racial, and cultural worlds. Traveling to Europe gives the protagonists a sense of what they could be, helping them see their own position in America more clearly. With compassion and wit, the authors indict America for failing to fulfill its constitutional ideals. The road to Europe was thus a road leading back, to the same place perhaps, but to a different conception of that place.

Works Cited

Primary material:

Fauset, Jessie Redmon. *There Is Confusion*. New York: Boni and Liveright, 1924.

Johnson, James Weldon. *The Autobiography of an Ex-Colored Man*. 1912. New York: Penguin, 1990.

Larsen, Nella. *Quicksand* and *Passing*. New Brunswick, New Jersey: Rutgers U P, 1986.

Secondary material:

Ammons, Elizabeth. "New Literary History: Edith Wharton and Jessie Redmon Fauset." *College Literature* 14.3 (1987): 207-218.

Anderson, Benedict. *Imagined Communities. Reflections on the Origin and Spread of Nationalism*. London and New York: Verso, 1991.

Anderson, Marian. *My Lord, What a Morning*. London: Cresset Press, 1957.

Andrews, William L., Frances Foster Smith and Trudier Harris. *The Oxford Companion to African American Literature*. New York and Oxford: Oxford U P, 1997.

Andrews, William L. and William S. McFeely. *Narrative of the Life of Frederick Douglass, an American Slave, Written by Himself*. New York and London: Norton, 1997.

Austin, John L. *How To Do Things with Words*. 1962. Cambridge, Mass.: Harvard U P, 1975.

Baker, Houston A. *Singers of Daybreak. Studies in Black American Literature*. Washington D. C.: Howard U P, 1974.

---. *Modernism and the Harlem Renaissance*. Chicago: University of Chicago Press, 1987.

Baldwin, James. *Collected Essays*. New York: The Library of America, 1998.

Barthes, Roland. *Mythologies*. 1957. New York: Noonday, 1992.

Bhabha, Homi. *The Location of Culture*. London and New York: Routledge, 1994.

Blackman, Lisa and Valerie Walkerdine. *Mass Hysteria. Critical Psychology and Media Studies*. Basingstoke: Palgrave, 2001.

Bogle, Donald. *Toms, Coons, Mulattoes, Mammies, and Bucks. An Interpretive History of Blacks in American Films.* New York: Viking Press, 1973.

Bontemps, Arna. *The Harlem Renaissance Remembered.* New York: Dodd, 1972.

Bone, Robert. *The Negro Novel in America.* New Haven and London: U P, 1965.

Braithwaite, William Stanley. "The Novels of Jessie Fauset." *Opportunity. Journal of Negro Life* 12.1 (1934): 24-28.

Brantlinger, Patrick. "Victorians and Africans: The Genealogy of the Myth of the Dark Continent." in Gates, Henry Louis, Jr. *"Race," Writing, and Difference.* Chicago and London: U of Chicago P, 1986: 185-222.

Brody, Jennifer DeVere. *Impossible Purities. Blackness, Femininity, and Victorian Culture.* Durham and London: Duke U P, 1998.

Brooks, Van Wyck. *America's Coming-of-Age.* New York: B W Huebsch, 1915.

Brooks Higginbotham, Evelyn, "Black Religion and Race Records in the 1920s and 1930s." Wahneema Lubiano, ed. *The House That Race Built,* New York: Vintage, 1998. 157-77.

Brown, William Wells. *Clotel, or the President's Daughter.* 1853. New York: University Books, 1995.

Judith Butler. *Gender Trouble: Feminism and the Subversion of Identity.* New York: Routledge, 1990.

---. *Bodies that Matter. On the Discursive Limits of "Sex."* New York and London: Routledge, 1993.

Carby, Hazel V. *Reconstructing Womanhood. The Emergence of the Afro-American Woman Novelist.* New York and Oxford: Oxford University Press, 1987.

Carlson, Marvin. *Performance: A Critical Introduction.* New York: Routledge, 1996.

Chabot, Barry C. *Writers for the Nation: American Literary Modernism.* Tuscaloosa and London: University of Alabama Press, 1987.

Champion, Laurie, ed. American Women Writers, 1900-1945. *A Bio-Bibliographical Critical Sourcebook.* Westport, Conn.: Greenwood Press, 2000.

Chatman, Seymour, ed. *Approaches to Poetics.* New York: Columbia U P, 1973.

Childs, Peter and Patrick Williams. *An Introduction to Post-Colonial Theory.* London etc: Prentice Hall, 1997.

Christian, Barbara. *Black Women Novelists: The Development of a Tradition 1892-1976.* Westport, Conn.: Greenwood Press, 1980.

Clarke, Cheryl. "Race, Homosocial Desire, and 'Mammon' in *Autobiography of an Ex-Colored Man*." *Professions of Desire: Lesbian and Gay Studies in Literature*. Eds. George E. Haggerty and Bonnie Zimmerman. New York: M. L. A., 1995. 84-97 .

Collier, Eugenia. "The Endless Journey of an Ex-Colored Man." *Phylon* 32 (1971): 365-73.

Condé, Mary. "Europe in the Novels of Jessie Redmon Fauset and Nella Larsen." *Difference in View: Women and Modernism*. Ed. Gabriele Griffin. London and Bristol, PA: Taylor and Francis, 1994 .

Cowley, Malcolm. *Exile's Return*. New York: Penguin, 1976.

Culler, Jonathan. *Literary Theory. A Very Short Introduction*. Oxford U P, 1997.

Davis, Thadious M. *Nella Larsen. Novelist of the Harlem Renaissance*. Baton Rouge and London: Louisiana State University Press, 1994.

DeCoverley, Roy. "Marian Anderson in Denmark: An Appreciation." *Opportunity* 12.9 (1934): 270-71.

Delanty, Gerard. *Inventing Europe: Idea, Identity, Reality*. Basingstoke: MacMillan, 1995.

Derrida, Jacques. *Limited Inc.* Evanston, Ill: Northwestern U P, 1988.

Diamond, Elin. *Performance and Cultural Politics*. London and New York: Routledge, 1996.

Douglas, Ann. *Terrible Honesty. Mongrel Manhattan in the 1920s*. 1995. London and Basingstoke: MacMillan Papermac, 1997.

DuBois, W E B. *Writings*. New York: The Library of America, 1986.

---. "The Black Man in the Revolution of 1914-1918." *The Crisis* (March 1919).

---. "The Colored American in France." *The Crisis* (Feb. 1919): 167-169.

---. "Criteria of Negro Art." *The Crisis* (Oct. 1926): 290-97.

---. "What Is Civilization? Africa's Answer." *The Forum* 73.2 (1925): 179-188.

DuCille, Ann. *The Coupling Convention. Sex, Text, and Tradition in Black Women's Fiction*. New York and Oxford: Oxford U P, 1993.

Dyer, Richard. *White*. London and New York: Routledge, 1997.

Ellison, Ralph. *Shadow and Act*. New York: Vintage, 1995.

Eze, Emmanuel Chukwudi, ed. *Race and the Enlightenment*. Malden, Mass. and Oxford: Blackwell; 1998 .

Fabre, Genevieve, and Michel Feith. Eds. *Temples for Tomorrow: Looking Back at the Harlem Renaissance*. Bloomington: Indiana U P: 2001.

Fabre, Michel. *From Harlem to Paris. Black American Writers in France 1840-1980.* Urbana: University of Illinois Press, 1991.

Fanon, Frantz. *The Wretched of the Earth.* New York: Grove, 1963.

---. *Black Skin, White Masks.* 1952. New York: Grove, 1967.

Fauset, Jessie Redmon. *Plum Bun. A Novel Without a Moral.* 1929. Boston: Beacon Press, 1990.

---. *The Chinaberry Tree. A Novel of American Life.* 1931. Boston: Northeastern U P, 1995.

---. *Comedy: American Style.* 1933. New York: G.K. Hall, 1995.

---. "Dark Algiers the White." *The Crisis* (April 1925): 16-20.

---."The Emancipator of Brazil." *The Crisis* (March 1921): 208-09.

---. "The Enigma of the Sorbonne." *The Crisis* (March 1925): 216-19.

---. "Impressions of the Second Pan-African Congress." *The Crisis* (Jan 1921): 12-18.

---. "The Negro in Art: How Shall He Be Portrayed?" *The Crisis* (June 1926): 71-73.

---. "Nostalgia." *The Crisis* (Aug. 1921): 154-58.

---. "Saint-George, Chevalier of France." *The Crisis* (May 1921): 9-12.

---. "Yarrow Revisited." *The Crisis* (Jan. 1925): 107-109.

---. "Looking Backward." *The Crisis* (Jan. 1922): 125-26.

---. Letter to Langston Hughes. 6 January 1925. James Weldon Johnson Collection. Yale University.

Fish, Stanley. *Is There a Text in This Class? The Authority of Interpretive Communities.* Cambridge, Mass.: Harvard U P, 1980.

Fleming, Robert E. "Contemporary Themes in Johnson's *Autobiography of an Ex-Colored Man.*" *Negro American Literature Forum* 4.4 (1970): 113-19.

---. "Irony as Key to Johnson's *The Autobiography of an Ex-Colored Man.*" *American Literature* 43.1 (1971): 83-96

Garber, Marjorie. *Vested Interests: Cross-Dressing and Cultural Anxiety.* New York: Routledge, 1992.

Garrett, Marvin P. "Early Recollections and Structural Irony in *The Autobiography of an Ex-Colored Man.*" *Critique: Studies in Modern Fiction* 13.3 (1971): 5-14.

Gates, Henry Louis Jr., ed. *The Classic Slave Narratives.* New York: Mentor, 1987.

---. *The Signifying Monkey. A Theory of Afro-American Literary Criticism.* New York: Oxford U P, 1988.

---. *Loose Canons. Notes on the Culture Wars.* New York and Oxford: Oxford U P, 1992.

Gates, Henry Louis, Jr., and Nellie McKay, ed. *The Norton Anthology of African American Literature.* New York and London: W. W. Norton & Co., 1997.

Gilbert, Sandra M. and Susan Gubar. *No Man's Land. The Place of the Woman Writer in Twentieth Century. Vol 3.* New Haven and London: Yale U P, 1994.

Gilroy, Paul. *The Black Atlantic. Modernity and Double Consciousness.* Cambridge, Mass.: Harvard U P, 1993.

Ginsberg, Elaine K., ed. *Passing and the Fictions of Identity.* Durham and London: Duke U P, 1996.

Gloster, Hugh. *Negro Voices in American Fiction.* Chapel Hill: U of North Carolina P, 1948.

Goellnicht, Donald C. "Passing as Autobiography: James Weldon Johnson's *The Autobiography of an Ex-Colored Man.*" *African American Review* 30:1, 1996. 17-33.

Goffman, Erving. *The Presentation of Self in Everyday Life.* 1959. Harmondsworth: Penguin, 1971.

Gordon, Colin, ed. *Power/Knowledge.* New York: Pantheon Books, 1980.

Gray, Jeffrey. "Essence and the Mulatto Traveler: Europe as Embodiment in Nella Larsen's *Quicksand.*" *Novel: A Forum on Fiction* 27.3 (1994): 257-270.

Griffin, Farah Jasmine. *"Who Set You Flowin'?" The African American Migration Narrative.* New York and Oxford: Oxford U P, 1995.

Griffin, Farah J. and Cheryl J. Fish. *A Stranger In the Village. Two Centuries of African American Travel Writing.* Boston: Beacon, 1998.

Gruesser, John C. "Travel writing." Gates, Henry Louis, Jr., and Nellie McKay. Eds. *The Norton Anthology of African American Literature.* New York and London: W. W. Norton & Co., 1997. 735-736.

Hall, Stuart, ed. *Representation. Cultural Representations and Signifying Systems.* London: Sage, 1997.

---. "Kulturell identitet och diaspora." *Globaliseringens kulturer. Den postkoloniala paradoxen, rasismen och det mångkulturella samhället.* Eds. Eriksson, Eriksson Baaz and Thörn. Nora: Nya Doxa, 1999. 231-243.

Haskell, Barbara. *The American Century. Art & Culture 1900-1950.* New York and London: Whitney Museum of American Art and W. W. Norton, 1999.

Hill Collins, Patricia. *Black Feminist Thought. Knowledge, Consciousness, and the Politics of Empowerment.* New York and London: Routledge, 1990.

hooks, bell. *Black Looks. Race and Representation.* Boston: South End Press, 1992.

Holstein, Casper. "The Virgin Islands." *Opportunity* 3.34 (1925): 304-306.

Hughes, Langston. *Collected Poems*. New York: Vintage Classics, 1994.

---. *The Big Sea*. 1940. New York: Hill and Wang, 1993.

Huggins, Nathan. *Harlem Renaissance*. New York: Oxford U P, 1971.

--- ed. *Voices From the Harlem Renaissance*. New York and Oxford: Oxford U P, 1995

Hutchinson, George. *The Harlem Renaissance in Black and White*. Cambridge, Mass. and London: Belknap Press of Harvard U P, 1995.

---. "Nella Larsen and the Veil of Race," *American Literary History* 9.2 (1997):329-49.

---. *In Search of Nella Larsen. A Biography of the Color Line*. Cambridge, Mass. and London: The Belknap Press of Harvard U P, 2006.

Japtok, Martin."Between 'Race' as 'Construct and 'Race' as Essence: *The Autobiography of an Ex-Colored Man" Southern Literary Journal* 28.2 (1996): 32-47.

Johnson, James Weldon. "Double Audience Makes Road Hard for Negro Authors." 1918. Wilson, Sondra Kathryn.*The Selected Writings of James Weldon Johnson. Vol 2*. Oxford and New York: Oxford U P, 1995. 408-12.

---. *The Book of American Negro Poetry*. 1922. San Diego, New York and London: Harcourt Brace & Co., 1969.

---. *God's Trombones. Seven Negro Sermons in Verse*. 1927. New York: Penguin, 1990.

---. *Black Manhattan*. 1930. New York: Atheneum, 1968.

---. *Along This Way*. New York: Viking, 1933.

---. *Lift Every Voice and Sing*. 1935. New York: Penguin, 2000.

Jones, LeRoi. *Blues People.The Negro Experience in White America and the Music that Developed from it*. New York: Morrow Quill Paperbacks, 1963.

Kawash, Samira. *Dislocating the Color Line. Identity, Hybridity, and Singularity in African-American Narrative*. Stanford, California: Stanford U P, 1997.

Klemming, Sofia. "Pluggskolan som blivit ett ideal." *Dagens Nyheter* 30 Oct. 2000: A13

Kroell, Sonja. "A Bitter Journey: The 'Passing' Mulatta as 'Expatriate' in Jessie Redmon Fauset's *Plum Bun*." *Prospero* 2 (1995): 35-45.

Kuenz, Jane. "The Face of America: Performing Race and Nation in Jessie Fauset's *There Is Confusion*." *The Yale Journal of Criticism* 12.1 (1999): 89-111.

Lawson, Benjamin Sherwood. "Odysseus's Revenge: The Name of the Title Page of *The Autobiography of an Ex-Coloured Man*." *Southern Literary Journal* 21.2 (1989): 92-99.

Lemke, Sieglinde. *Primitivist Modernism. Black Culture and the Origins of Transatlantic Modernism.* Oxford and New York: Oxford U P, 1998.

Levinson, Susan. "Performance and the 'Strange Place' of Jessie Fauset's *There Is Confusion.*" *Modern Fiction Studies* 46.4 (2000): 825-848.

Lewis, David Levering. *When Harlem Was In Vogue.* 1979. New York: Penguin, 1997.

Lindberg-Seyersted, Brita. *Black and Female. Essays on Writings by Black Women in the Diaspora.* Oslo-Copenhagen-Stockholm: Scandinavian U P, 1994.

Locke, Alain, ed. *The New Negro.* 1925. New York: Simon & Schuster, 1997.

Loomba, Ania. *Colonialism/Postcolonialism.* London and New York: Routledge, 1998.

Lott, Eric. *Love & Theft. Blackface Minstrelsy and the American Working Class.* Oxford, 1995.

Lotz, Rainer E. *Black People. Entertainers of African Descent in Europe, and Germany.* Bonn: Birgit Lotz Verlag, 1997.

Lupton, Mary Jane. "Clothes and Closure in Three Novels by Black Women." *Black American Literature Forum* 20: 4 (1986): 409-421.

Lyttkens, Bertil. *Svart och vitt. Utländska jazzbesök 1895-1939 speglade i svensk press.* Stockholm: Svenskt Visarkiv, 1998.

MacKethan, Lucinda. "*Black Boy* and *Ex-Colored Man:* Version and Inversion of the Slave Narrator's Quest for Voice." *College Language Association Journal.* 32.2 (1988): 123-147.

Malik, Kenan. "Race, Pluralism and the Meaning of Difference." *New Formations* 33 (1988) 125-135.

---. *The Meaning of Race. Race, History and Culture in Western Society.* Basingstoke and London: MacMillan, 1996.

Marks, Carole and Edkins, Diana. *The Power of Pride. Stylemakers and Rulebreakers of the Harlem Renaissance.* New York: Crown, 1999.

McCoy, Beth. " 'Is this really what you wanted me to be?': The Daughter's Disintegration in Jessie Redmon Fauset's *There Is Confusion.*" *Modern Fiction Studies.* 40.1 (1994): 101-117.

Martin, Charles. "Coloring Books: Black Writing on Europe." *Mosaic* 26.4 (1993): 53-67.

McLendon, Jacquelyn Y. *The Politics of Color in the Fiction of Jessie Fauset and Nella Larsen.* Charlottesville and London: U of Virginia P, 1995.

Miles, Robert. *Racism.* London and New York: Routledge, 1989.

Nelson, Emmanuel. *African American Authors, 1745-1945. A Bio-Bibliographical Critical Sourcebook*. Westport, Conn.: Greenwood Press, 2000.

North, Michael. *The Dialect of Modernism: Race, Language and Twentieth Century Literature*. New York: Oxford U P, 1994 .

Pfeiffer, Kathleen. "Individualism, Success, and American Identity in *The Autobiography of An Ex-Colored Man*" *African American Review*30: 3 (1996): 403-16.

Pisiak, Roxanna. "Irony and Subversion in James Weldon Johnson's *The Autobiography of an Ex-Colored Man*." *Studies in American Fiction* 21.1 (1993): 83-96.

Portelli, Alessandro. "The Tragedy and the Joke: James Weldon Johnson's *The Autobiography of an Ex-Colored Man*." *Temples for Tomorrow. Looking Back at the Harlem Renaissance*. Genevieve Fabre and Michael Feith. Eds. Bloomington and Indianapolis: Indiana U P, 2001. 143-158.

Posnock, Ross. *Color and Culture. Black Writers and the Making of the Modern Intellectual*. Cambridge, Mass. and London, England: Harvard U P, 1998.

Powell, Richard J. *Black Art and Culture in the 20ᵗʰ Century*. London: Thames and Hudson, 1997.

Pratt, Mary Louise. *Imperial Eyes: Travel Writing and Transculturation*. London and New York: Routledge, 1992.

Rahbek, Ulla. "Black British Travel Literature." *The European English Messenger* 10.2 (2002): 22-26.

Roach, Joseph. *Cities of the Dead. Circum-Atlantic Performance*. New York: Columbia U P, 1996.

Roberts, Kimberley. "The Clothes Make the Woman: The Symbolics of Prostitution in Nella Larsen's *Quicksand* and Claude McKay's *Home to Harlem*." *Tulsa Studies in Women's Literature* 16.1 (1997): 107-130.

Ross, Stephen M. "Audience and Irony in Johnson's *The Autobiography of an Ex-Colored Man*." *College Language Association Journal* 18.2 (1974): 198-210.

Ruotolo, Cristina L. "James Weldon Johnson and the Autobiography of an Ex-Colored Musician." *American Literature* 72.2 (2000): 249-274.

Said, Edward. *Orientalism*. 1978. London: Penguin, 1995.

---. *Culture and Imperialism*. New York: Vintage, 1993.

Schenck, Mary Jane. "Jessie Fauset: The Politics of Fulfillment vs. the Lost Generation." *South Atlantic Review* 6.1 (2001): 102-125.

Schultz, Jennifer L. "Restaging the Racial Contract: James Weldon Johnson's Signatory Strategies." *American Literature* 74.1 (2002): 31-58.

Searle, John R. *Speech Acts: An Essay in the Philosophy of Language.* Cambridge: Cambridge U P, 1969.

Simon, Zoltan. "From Lenox Avenue to the Charlottenborg Palace: the Construction of the Image of Europe by Harlem Renaissance Authors." *British and American Studies* 4.2 (1999): 105-12.

Singh, Amritjit. *The Novels of the Harlem Renaissance. Twelve Black Writers 1923 – 1933.* University Park and London: Pennsylvania State U P, 1976.

Singh, Amritjit, William S. Shiver and Stanley Brodwin. Eds. *The Harlem Renaissance: Revaluations.* New York and London: Garland, 1989.

Starkey, Marion. "Jessie Fauset." *The Southern Workman* 61.5 (1932): 216-220.

Stepto, Robert B. *From Behind the Veil. A Study of Afro-American Narrative.* Urbana, Chicago and London: U of Illinois P, 1979.

Stovall, Tyler. *Paris Noir. African Americans in the City of Light.* Boston and New York: Houghton, 1996.

Sundquist, Eric J. *To Wake the Nations. Race in the Making of American Literature.* Cambridge, Mass. and London: Belknap Harvard U P, 1993.

Sylvander, Carolyn Wedin. *Jessie Redmon Fauset, Black American Writer.* Troy, New York: Whitston, 1981.

Taylor, Charles. *Sources of the Self. The Making of the Modern Identity.* Cambridge, Mass.: Harvard U P, 1989.

Tiffin, Chris, and Alan Lawson. Eds. *De-Scribing Empire. Post-colonialism and Textuality.* London and New York: Routledge, 1994.

Toll, Robert C. *Blacking Up. The Minstrel Show in Nineteenth-Century America.* New York: Oxford U P, 1974.

Walker, F. Patton. "The Narrator's Editorialist Voice in *The Autobiography of an Ex-Colored Man*." *College Language Association Journal* 41.1 (1997): 70-92.

Wall, Cheryl A., "Passing for What? Aspects of Identity in Nella Larsen's Novels." *Black American Literature Forum,* 20:1-2 (1986): 97-111.

---. *Women of the Harlem Renaissance.* Bloomington and Indianapolis: Indiana U P, 1995.

Wallace, Michele. *Black Macho and the Myth of the Superwoman.* 1978. London and New York: Verso, 1990.

Washington, Salim. "Of Black Bards, Known and Unknown. Music as Racial Metaphor in James Weldon Johnson's *The Autobiography of an Ex-Colored Man*." *Callaloo* 25.1 (2002): 233-256 .

Watt, Ian. *The Rise of the Novel: Studies in Defoe, Richardson and Fielding.* 1957. London: Pimlico, 2000.

Wiedemann, Erik. *Jazz i Danmark—i tyverne, trediverne og fyrrerne. Vol.1.* Copenhagen: Gyldendal, 1982 .

Wilson, Kevin and Jan van der Dussen, eds. *The History of the Idea of Europe.* London and New York: Routledge, 1993.

Wilson, Sondra Kathryn. *The Selected Writings of James Weldon Johnson. 2 vols.* Oxford and New York: Oxford U P, 1995.

Wonham, Henry B. *Criticism and the Color Line. Desegregating American Literary Studies.* New Brunswick, N. J.: Rutgers U P, 1996.

LUND STUDIES IN ENGLISH

Founded by Eilert Ekwall.
Editors: Marianne Thormählen and Beatrice Warren

001 BERTIL WEMAN. 1933. Old English Semantic Analysis and Theory. With Special Reference to Verbs Denoting Locomotion. 187 pp.

002 HILDING BÄCK. 1934. The Synonyms for child, boy, girl in Old English. An Etymological-Semasiological Investigation. xvi + 273 pp.

003 GUSTAV FRANSSON. 1935. Middle English Surnames of Occupation. With an Excursus on Toponymical Surnames. 217 pp.

004 GUSTAV HOFSTRAND. 1936. The Seege of Troye. A Study in the Intertextual Relations of the Middle English Romance The Seege or Batayle of Troye. xv + 205 pp.

005 URBAN OHLANDER. 1936. Studies on Coordinate Expressions in Middle English. 213 pp.

006 VIKTOR ENGBLOM. 1938. On the Origin and Early Development of the Auxiliary Do. 169 pp.

007 IVAR DAHL. 1938. Substantival Inflexion in Early Old English. Vocalic Stems. xvi + 206 pp.

008 HILMER STRÖM. 1939. Old English Personal Names in Bede's History. An Etymological-Phonological Investigation. xliii + 180 pp.

009 UNO PHILIPSON. 1941. Political Slang 1759–1850. xvi + 314 pp.

010 ARTHUR H. KING. 1941. The Language of Satirized Characters in Poëtaster. A Socio-Stylistic Analysis 1579–1602. xxxiv + 258 pp.

011 MATTIAS T. LÖFVENBERG. 1942. Studies on Middle English Local Surnames. xlv + 225 pp.

012 JOHANNES HEDBERG. 1945. The Syncope of the Old English Present Endings. A Dialect Criterion. 310 pp.

013 ALARIK RYNELL. 1948. The Rivalry of Scandinavian and Native Synonyms in Middle English, especially taken and nimen. With an Excursus on nema and taka in Old Scandinavian. 431 pp.

014 HENNING HALLQVIST. 1948. Studies in Old English Fractured ea. 167 pp.

015 GÖSTA FORSSTRÖM. 1948. The Verb to be in Middle English. A Survey of the Forms. 236 pp.

016 BERTIL WIDÉN. 1949. Studies on the Dorset Dialect. 179 pp.

017 CLAES SCHAAR. 1949. Critical Studies in the Cynewulf Group. 337 pp.

018 BERTIL SUNDBY. 1950. The Dialect and Provenance of the Middle English Poem The Owl and the Nightingale. A Linguistic Study. 218 pp.

019 BERTIL THURESSON. 1950. Middle English Occupational Terms. 285 pp.

020 KARL-GUNNAR LINDKVIST. 1950. Studies on the Local Sense of the Prepositions in, at, on, and to, in Modern English. 429 pp.

021 SVEN RUBIN. 1951. The Phonology of the Middle English Dialect of Sussex. 235 pp.

022 BERTIL SUNDBY. 1953. Christopher Cooper's English Teacher (1687). cxvi + 10* + 123 pp.

023 BJÖRN WALLNER. 1954. An Exposition of Qui Habitat and Bonum Est in English. lxxi + 122 pp.

024 RUDOLF MAGNUSSON. 1954. Studies in the Theory of the Parts of Speech. viii + 120 pp.

025 CLAES SCHAAR. 1954. Some Types of Narrative in Chaucer's Poetry. 293 pp.

026 BÖRJE HOLMBERG. 1956. James Douglas on English Pronunciation c. 1740. 354 pp.

027 EILERT EKWALL. 1959. Etymological Notes on English Place-Names. 108 pp.

028 CLAES SCHAAR. 1960. An Elizabethan Sonnet Problem. Shakespeare ' s Sonnets, Daniel's Delia, and their Literary Background. 190 pp.

029 ELIS FRIDNER. 1961. An English Fourteenth Century Apocalypse Version with a Prose Commentary. Edited from MS Harley 874 and Ten Other MSS. lviii + 290 pp.

030 The Published Writings of Eilert Ekwall. A Bibliography Compiled by Olof von Feilitzen. 1961. 52 pp.

031 ULF JACOBSSON. 1962. Phonological Dialect Constituents in the Vocabulary of Standard English. 335 pp.

032 CLAES SCHAAR. 1962. Elizabethan Sonnet Themes and the Dating of Shakespeare's Sonnets. 200 pp.

033 EILERT EKWALL. 1963. Selected Papers. 172 pp.

034 ARNE ZETTERSTEN. 1965. Studies in the Dialect and Vocabulary of the Ancrene Riwle. 331 pp.

035 GILLIS KRISTENSSON. 1967. A Survey of Middle English Dialects 1290–1350. The Six Northern Counties and Lincolnshire. xxii + 299 pp.

036 OLOF ARNGART. 1968. The Middle English Genesis and Exodus. Re-edited from MS. C.C.C.C. 444 with Introduction, Notes and Glossary. 277 pp.

037 ARNE ZETTERSTEN. 1969. The English of Tristan da Cunha. 180 pp.

038 ELLEN ALWALL. 1970. The Religious Trend in Secular Scottish School-Books 1858–1861 and 1873–1882. With a Survey of the Debate on Education in Scotland in the Middle and Late 19th Century. 177 pp.

039 CLAES SCHAAR. 1971. Marino and Crashaw. Sospetto d'Hero d e. A Commentary. 300 pp.

040 SVEN BÄCKMAN. 1971. This Singular Tale. A Study of The Vicar of Wakefield and Its Literary Background. 281 pp.

041 CHRISTER PÅHLSSON. 1972. The Northumbrian Burr. A Sociolinguistic Study. 309 pp.

042 KARL-GUSTAV EK. 1972. The Development of OE y and eo in South-Eastern Middle English. 133 pp.

043 BO SELTÉN. 1972. The Anglo-Saxon Heritage in Middle English Personal Names. East Anglia 1100–1399. 187 pp.

044 KERSTIN ASSARSSON-RIZZI. 1972. Friar Bacon and Friar Bungay. A Structural and Thematic Analysis of Robert Greene's Play. 164 pp.

045 ARNE ZETTERSTEN. 1974. A Critical Facsimile Edition of Thomas Batchelor, An Orthoëpical Analysis of the English Language and An Orthoëpical Analysis of the Dialect of Bedfordshire (1809). Part I. 260 pp.

046 ERIK INGVAR THURIN. 1974. The Universal Autobiography of Ralph Waldo Emerson. xii + 288 pp.

047 HARRIET BJÖRK. 1974. The Language of Truth. Charlotte Brontë, the Woman Question, and the Novel. 152 pp.

048 ANDERS DALLBY. 1974. The Anatomy of Evil. A Study of John Webster's The White Devil. 236 pp.

049 GILLIS KRISTENSSON. 1974. John Mirk's Instructions for Parish Priests. Edited from MS Cotton Claudius A II and Six Other Manuscripts with Introduction, Notes and Glossary. 287 pp.

050 STIG JOHANSSON. 1975. Papers in Contrastive Linguistics and Language Testing. 179 pp.

051 BENGT ELLENBERGER. 1977. The Latin Element in the Vocabulary of the Earlier Makars Henryson and Dunbar. 163 pp.

052 MARIANNE THORMÄHLEN. 1978. The Waste Land. A Fragmentary Wholeness. 248 pp.

053 LARS HERMERÉN. 1978. On Modality in English. A Study of the Semantics of the Modals. 195 pp.

054 SVEN BÄCKMAN. 1979. Tradition Transformed. Studies in the Poetry of Wilfred Owen. 206 pp.

055 JAN JÖNSJÖ. 1979. Studies on Middle English Nicknames. I: Compounds. 227 pp.

056 JAN SVARTVIK & RANDOLPH QUIRK (eds). 1980. A Corpus of English Conversation. 893 pp.

057 LARS-HÅKAN SVENSSON. 1980. Silent Art. Rhetorical and Thematic Patterns in Samuel Daniel's Delia. 392 pp.

058 INGRID MÅRDH. 1980. Headlinese. On the Grammar of English Front Page Headlines. 200 pp.

059 STIG JOHANSSON. 1980. Plural Attributive Nouns in Present-Day English. x + 136 pp.

060 CLAES SCHAAR. 1982. The Full Voic'd Quire Below. Vertical Context Systems in Paradise Lost. 354 pp.

061 GUNILLA FLORBY. 1982. The Painful Passage to Virtue. A Study of George Chapman's The Tragedy of Bussy D'Ambois and The Revenge of Bussy D'Ambois. 266 pp.

062 BENGT ALTENBERG. 1982. The Genitive v. the of-Construction. A Study of Syntactic Variation in 17th Century English. 320 pp.

063 JAN SVARTVIK, MATS EEG-OLOFSSON, OSCAR FORSHEDEN, BENGT ORESTRÖM & CECILIA THAVENIUS. 1982. Survey of Spoken English. Report on Research 1975–81. 112 pp.

064 CECILIA THAVENIUS. 1983. Referential Pronouns in English Conversation. 194 pp.

065 NILS WRANDER. 1983. English Place-Names in the Dative Plural. 172 pp.

066 BENGT ORESTRÖM. 1983. Turn-Taking in English Conversation. 195 pp.

067 EVA JARRING CORONES. 1983. The Portrayal of Women in the Fiction of Henry Handel Richardson. 183 pp.

068 ANNA-BRITA STENSTRÖM. 1984. Questions and Responses in English Conversation. x + 296 pp.

069 KARIN HANSSON. 1984. The Warped Universe. A Study of Imagery and Structure in Seven Novels by Patrick White. 271 pp.

070 MARIANNE THORMÄHLEN. 1984. Eliot's Animals. 197 pp.

071 EVERT ANDERSSON. 1985. On Verb Complementation in Written English. 293 pp.

072 WIVECA SOTTO. 1985. The Rounded Rite. A Study of Wole Soyinka's Play The Bacchae of Euripides. 187 pp.

073 ULLA THAGG FISHER. 1985. The Sweet Sound of Concord. A Study of Swedish Learners' Concord Problems in English. xii + 212 pp.

074 MOIRA LINNARUD. 1986. Lexis in Composition. A Performance Analysis of Swedish Learners' Written English. x + 136 pp.

075 LARS WOLLIN & HANS LINDQUIST (eds). 1986. Translation Studies in Scandinavia. Proceedings from The Scandinavian Symposium on Translation Theory (SSOTT) II. 149 pp.

076 BENGT ALTENBERG. 1987. Prosodic Patterns in Spoken English. Studies in the C o r relation between Prosody and Grammar for Text-to-Speech Conversion. 229 pp.

077 ÖRJAN SVENSSON. 1987. Saxon Place-Names in East Cornwall. xii + 192 pp.

078 JØRN CARLSEN & BENGT STREIJFFERT (eds). 1988. Canada and the Nordic Countries. 416 pp.

079 STIG CARLSSON. 1989. Studies on Middle English Local Bynames in East Anglia. 193 pp.

080 HANS LINDQUIST. 1989. English Adverbials in Translation. A Corpus Study of Swedish Renderings. 184 pp.

081 ERIK INGVAR THURIN. 1990. The Humanization of Willa Cather. Classicism in an American Classic. 406 pp.

082 JAN SVARTVIK (ed). 1990. The London-Lund Corpus of Spoken English. Description and Research. 350 pp.

083 KARIN HANSSON. 1991. Sheer Edge. Aspects of Identity in David Malouf's Writing. 170 pp.

084 BIRGITTA BERGLUND. 1993. Woman's Whole Existence. The House as an Image in the Novels of Ann Radcliffe, Mary Wollstonecraft and Jane Austen. 244 pp.

085 NANCYD. HARGROVE. 1994. The Journey Toward Ariel. Sylvia Plath's Poems of 1956–1959. 293 pp.

086 MARIANNE THORMÄHLEN (ed). 1994. T. S. Eliot at the Turn of the Century. 244 pp.

087 KARIN HANSSON. 1996. The Unstable Manifold. Janet Frame's Challenge to Determinism. 149 pp.

088 KARIN AIJMER, BENGT ALTENBERG & MATS JOHANSSON (eds). 1996. Languages in Contrast. Papers from a Symposium on Text-based Cro s s - l i n g u i s t i c Studies Lund. 200 pp.

089 CECILIA BJÖRKÉN. 1996. Into the Isle of Self. Nietzschean Patterns and Contrasts in D. H. Lawrence's The Trespasser. 247 pp.

090 MARJA PALMER. 1996. Men and Women in T. S. Eliot's Early Poetry. 243 pp.

091 KEITH COMER. 1996. Strange Meetings. Walt Whitman, Wilfred Owen and Poetry of War. 205 pp.

092 CARITA PARADIS. 1997. Degree Modifiers of Adjectives in Spoken British English. 189 pp.

093 GUNILLA FLORBY. 1997. The Margin Speaks. A Study of Margaret Laurence and Robert Kroetsch from a Post-Colonial Point of View. 252 pp.

094 JEAN HUDSON. 1998. Perspectives on fixedness: applied and theoretical. 177 pp.

095 MARIE KÄLLKVIST. 1998. Form-Class and Ta s k - Type Effects in Learner English: A Study of Advanced Swedish Learners. xii + 226 pp.

096 AGNETA LINDGREN. 1999. The Fallen World in Coleridge's Poetry. 264 pp.

097 BJÖRN SUNDMARK. 1999. Alice in the Oral-Literary Continuum. 224 pp.

098 STAFFAN KLINTBORG. 1999. The Transience of American Swedish. 171 pp.

099 LARS HERMERÉN. 1999. English for Sale. A Study of the Language of Advertising. 201 pp. + 53 reproductions.

100 CECILIA WADSÖ LECAROS. 2001. The Victorian Governess Novel. 308 pp. Ill.

101 JANE MATTISSON. 2002. Knowledge and Survival in the Novels of Thomas Hardy. 423 pp.

102 ROWENA JANSSON. 2001. Getting It Together. Agenre analysis of the rhetorical structure of Open University television programmes in science and technology. 211 pp.

103 MAGNUS LEVIN. 2001. Agreement with Collective Nouns in English. 180 pp.

104 MONICA KARLSSON. 2002. Progression and Regression: Aspects of advanced Swedish students' competence in English grammar. 222 pp.

105 MARIA WIKTORSSON. 2003. Learning Idiomaticity. A corpus-based study of idiomatic expressions in learners' written production. viii + 182 pp.

106 LISBET KICKHAM. 2004. Protestant Women Novelists and Irish Society 1879–1922. 252 pp.

107 MATHILDA ADIE. 2004. Female Quest in Christina Stead's For Love Alone. 221 pp.

108 ANNIKA SYLÉN LAGERHOLM. 2005. Pearl and Contemplative Writing. 186 pp.

109 GUNILLA FLORBY. 2005. Echoing Texts: George Chapman's Conspiracy and Tragedy of Charles Duke of Byron. 181 pp.

110 GUNILLA LINDGREN. 2005. Higher Education for Girls in North American College Fiction 1886–1912. 296 pp.

111 LENA AHLIN. 2006. The "New Negro" in the Old World: Culture and Performance in James Weldon Johnson, Jessie Fauset, and Nella Larsen. 198 pp.